ROUTLEDGE LIE
ADULT EI

Volume 27

# ADULT EDUCATION AND SOCIALIST PEDAGOGY

# ADULT EDUCATION AND SOCIALIST PEDAGOGY

## FRANK YOUNGMAN

Routledge
Taylor & Francis Group

LONDON AND NEW YORK

First published in 1986 by Croom Helm Ltd

This edition first published in 2019
by Routledge
2 Park Square, Milton Park, Abingdon, Oxon OX14 4RN

and by Routledge
52 Vanderbilt Avenue, New York, NY 10017

*Routledge is an imprint of the Taylor & Francis Group, an informa business*

*British Library Cataloguing in Publication Data*
A catalogue record for this book is available from the British Library

ISBN: 978-1-138-32224-0 (Set)
ISBN: 978-0-429-43000-8 (Set) (ebk)
ISBN: 978-1-138-36078-5 (Volume 27) (hbk)
ISBN: 978-1-138-36087-7 (Volume 27) (pbk)
ISBN: 978-0-429-43292-7 (Volume 27) (ebk)

**Publisher's Note**
The publisher has gone to great lengths to ensure the quality of this reprint but points out that some imperfections in the original copies may be apparent.

**Disclaimer**
The publisher has made every effort to trace copyright holders and would welcome correspondence from those they have been unable to trace.

# Adult Education and Socialist Pedagogy

Frank Youngman

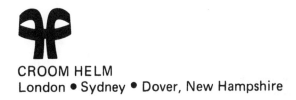

CROOM HELM
London • Sydney • Dover, New Hampshire

©1986 Frank Youngman
Croom Helm Ltd, Provident House, Burrell Row,
Beckenham, Kent BR3 1AT
Croom Helm Australia Pty Ltd, Suite 4, 6th Floor,
64-76 Kippax Street, Surry Hills, NSW 2010, Australia

British Library Cataloguing in Publication Data

Youngman, Frank
    Adult education and socialist pedagogy.
    1. Adult education   2. Communism and education
    I. Title
    374    LC5219
    ISBN 0-7099-2911-0


Croom Helm, 51 Washington Street, Dover,
New Hampshire 03820, USA

Library of Congress Cataloging in Publication Data

Youngman, Frank.
    Adult education and socialist pedagogy.
    (Radical forum on adult education series)
    Bibliography: p.
    Includes index.
    1. Adult education–political aspects–China–case
studies.  2. Adult education–Political aspects–
Portugal–case studies.  3. Adult education–Kenya–
political aspects–Kenya–case studies.  4. Socialism
and education–China–case studies.  5. Socialism and
education–Portugal–case studies.  6. Socialism and
education–Kenya–case studies.  I. Title.  II. Series.
LC5257, C6Y68    1986       374       85-30881
ISBN 0-7099-2911-0

Printed and bound in Great Britain by
Biddles Ltd, Guildford and King's Lynn

# CONTENTS

## ACKNOWLEDGEMENTS

It is a pleaure to thank publicly those who have
helped me in producing this book. In Southern
Africa I would like to thank those comrades who
participated in many discussions about its
theoretical foundations. Acknowledgement is due to
the University of Botswana for granting me the
sabbatical leave during which the bulk of the
writing was undertaken. I am grateful to Lauren
Vlotman for her work on the final manuscript.

In Britain, I wish to thank the following at
the University of Hull - Noreen Frankland for her
help in many ways, Barry Bright and Judi Irving for
their moral support, and Paul Armstrong, whose
erudition and encouragement I have especially
valued. Lionel Cliffe of the University of Leeds
made particularly helpful comments.

I also acknowledge gratefully the support of my
parents Frank and Kathleen Youngman, and the
solidarity and practical assistance of my wife Phora
Gaborone-Youngman.

Finally, while acknowledging my intellectual
debt to the many writers I have cited, I would like
to emphasise that the sexist language which appears
in quotations from other authors has been retained
only in the interests of veracity to the original.

Gaborone, Botswana

Chapter One

## ADULT EDUCATION FOR SOCIALISM

Adult education is no longer marginal. In the last two decades there has been a massive expansion of educational programmes for adults. This expansion has taken place throughout the world, in both the advanced industrialised countries and the underdeveloped countries. In the industrialised countries, economic restructuring, technological development and demographic changes are among the factors which have led to the greater involvement of adults in educational activities. Surveys in the USA in the 1970s suggested that one in three adults participated in some form of organised learning.[1] In the UK a 1980 survey showed that a total of 47% of the adult population had engaged in educational activity at some stage after their initial education.[2] In the underdeveloped countries, strategies for national development include a significant adult education component, for example in programmes to modernise agriculture, improve public health and raise levels of literacy. In Tanzania in 1975 two and a half million adults participated in a nutrition education campaign.[3] In Brazil the national literacy programme, MOBRAL, reached thirty million adults between 1970 and 1978.[4] Such examples illustrate the expansion that has taken place in adult education. This growth has occurred throughout the wide spectrum of fields that the concept of adult education encompasses, from basic education to professional training, from recreational activities to community development programmes.

The organisational structure of adult education remains very diverse in all countries. It stretches far beyond ministries of education to include other central government departments, local authorities, commerce and industry, trade unions, political parties, voluntary organisations and so forth. This organisational diversity makes it difficult to comprehend adult education as a whole. But grasping the essential unity of educational activities for adults is important because the recent rapid development of adult education has made it more integral to national systems of education. Indeed the expansion of educational opportunities beyond initial schooling for the young has contributed to education systems being conceived more and more as 'lifelong'systems which offer the possibility of 'recurrent' education at different points of the individual's life-span.

To see the unity of adult education and to locate it within a national system is to understand why adult education must be regarded sociologically and politically as part of the single social institution that is education. This is not to deny that there are important differences between the education of adults and the education of children. For example, the education of adults is seldom compulsory, usually part-time, and frequently occurs in contexts which respond to particular interests. Also the social position of adults is different, for instance in their personal autonomy and their experience of work. But these differences are subsumed within the wider social institution that also involves children and which has other age-related differentiations, such as kindergarten education. Consideration of adult education has to take into account that it is a part of the organised processes in society which systematically shape consciousness, develop knowledge, impart skills, and form attitudes.

It is within this context that the role of adult education in society needs to be analysed. The world-wide expansion of state-funded education for the young since 1945 has led to the great salience of questions about the political implications of education. For instance, the student movement of the 1960s which challenged the nature of university education in the advanced capitalist countries reverberated in wider questions about the nature and functions of education. Similar questions were vigorously addressed in China during the Cultural Revolution in the period from 1966 to 1976. The issues raised can perhaps be summarised in a single question: to what extent (and in what ways) is education a force for reproducing the status quo or a force for social change? Because of adult education's increased impact on social life, it is also faced more insistently by this question.

The political nature of adult education has received increasing attention since the early 1970s. The writings of Paulo Freire with their emphasis that no education is neutral have been particularly influential and some adult educators have begun to consider how adult education can contribute to social transformation. In doing so, as Hall has pointed out, they have started to recover a historical tradition in which adult education is linked to political action against capitalism.[5] This tradition indicates that adult education has often been seen by socialists as an important front in the struggle to change society. For example, the growth of the labour movement in the industrialising countries of the nineteenth century led to active independent adult education programmes for workers, such as the Chartist meeting halls in England in the 1830s and the evening schools in Russia in the 1890s. Historical study shows that in different periods socialists have regarded adult education as a source of support for the economic and political struggle to overthrow capitalism and construct a socialist society. The re-emergence of this tradition in the 1970s has led more adult educators to consider the political implications of their own work. As Hall put it:

> ...in adult education, we may now have to look much closer at the role we are playing...As long as the share of the world's wealth is so unevenly divided between those who rule and those who produce, there will be a struggle. We must know which side of the scale we are on.[6]

One result of this development has been a growing practical interest in the use of adult education as a means of advancing socialism in both the industrialised and underdeveloped countries. It is this interest which provides the rationale for this study.

A key problem facing socialist adult educators is how to achieve a unity of political theory and educational practice. In the burgeoning literature in English which considers adult education as a field of study, very few authors have taken an explicitly socialist perspective. The purpose of this book is therefore to contribute to the development within adult education of a socialist pedagogy, that is, an approach to teaching and learning which is based on principles consonant with socialist theory.[7] This approach must be characterised by a distinctive perspective on matters such as the process of knowledge acquisition, the role of language and literacy, the social relations of the educational situation, the methods of teaching, the mode of evaluating learning and teaching, and the relation of learning to production and political action. The concept of a socialist pedagogy provides a politically-informed stance towards both the content and processes of the adult education encounter. Consistency between content and processes is important because an adult educator's political position is not only expressed in the choice of subject matter and learning materials but it is also mediated by the methods used and social relationships established.

The need to unify content and processes has been discussed by Giroux in his chapter 'Beyond the limits of radical educational reform: towards a critical theory of education.'[8] Here he argues that on the educational left in North America 'two major positions stand out: these can be loosely represented, on the one hand, by the content-focussed radicals and, on the other, by the strategy-based radicals.'[9] He suggests that those who focus on content give priority to challenging the dominant ideology and developing critical ideas, while those who focus on strategy (i.e. processes) give priority to challenging the hierarchical social relations of the classroom and developing personal autonomy. He argues that it is incorrect to separate the two aspects of education, criticising the content-focussed group for failing to see the ideological dimensions of the learning experience itself, and the strategy-focussed group for failing to locate classroom social relations within a critical analysis of the wider society. He concludes that there is a need for an integrated approach which is underlain by a coherent political theory:

> ...any viable radical educational theory has got to point to the development of classroom interactions in which the pedagogical practices used are no less radical than the message transmitted through the specific content of the

course. In brief, the content of classroom instruction must be paralleled by a pedagogical style which is consistent with a radical political vision.[10]

This is a conclusion which I regard as being of great relevance to adult education because the problem of achieving an integrated approach arose for socialist adult educators in many different contexts during the 1970s. The relationship of content and form has been the subject of argument. For example, Yarnit has criticised much of the community-based adult education in England in the 1970s for 'an obsession with form at the expense of content' which he feels reveals a 'superficial radicalism'. He argues that socialist adult education must stress the content of what is taught:

> To put content before form is not to deny the importance of pedagogy or to equate content with a perpetual diet of politics. It is merely to affirm that in the end if education is to grow deep roots in the working class then they will be nourished more by what people learn than by how they learn.[11]

This example indicates that there is a tendency to dichotomise content and processes in socialist adult education which is similar to that identified by Giroux in radical school education. My aim in this book is to make a contribution to resolving this dichotomy.

This contribution consists of attempting to clarify the nature of a socialist pedagogy for adult education. Such a pedagogy seems to me to be less accessible to the adult educator at the moment than a socialist curriculum because most subject areas have their own body of socialist interpretation which can provide the basis for the selection and organisation of teaching content. My main concern is therefore with educational processes but this does not overlook the need to develop critical content. My focus is the analysis of learning theory in order to develop the principles of a socialist approach to adult education. However, before considering adult learning it is necessary to adopt a social theory which is fundamentally critical of capitalism and which can provide the broad theoretical framework within which to analyse educational issues.

5

## MARXISM AS A THEORETICAL FRAMEWORK

The theoretical position that I have adopted in seeking to develop a socialist approach to adult education is that of Marxism. Socialism as a concept is susceptible to different meanings although its common denominator, as Berki[12] has argued, is an opposition to capitalist society. A number of different socialist theories have arisen since the bourgeois economic and political revolutions of the seventeenth and eighteenth century established the capitalist epoch. The two main positions today are those of the social democrats and the Marxists. The social democrats envisage the possibility of a gradual reform of capitalism which will reduce its social injustice (for example, through the welfare state) while retaining its economic basis, namely private enterprise. The Marxists, on the other hand, see the necessity for a more fundamental transformation of society that will totally replace the capitalist mode of production by a new form of society, communism. This position is based on a well-developed theoretical tradition which provides both an overall explanation of society and the analytical principles for studying particular aspects of social existence. This seems to me to offer the most coherent and global account of capitalist society and how to change it, and in so doing it furnishes the conceptual tools for studying issues of education. It thus opens up the possibility of unifying theoretically a political goal for society at large with actual practices of adult education in specific social contexts. I have therefore adopted Marxism as the theoretical framework for this study, and I use the concept socialism to denote the revolutionary transformation of capitalist society as propounded by Marxism.

However, it is necessary to point out that Marxism is not a monolithic tradition. The writings of Marx and Engels between 1843 and 1895 were voluminous and the scope and time-scale of their work inevitably meant shifts in thinking, variations in analysis, and unfinished areas of investigation, despite the basic consistency of theoretical approach and political commitment. These ambiguities have been reflected in subsequent interpretations and applications, which exhibit many differences. The major figures of twentieth century

Marxism include people such as Lenin, Lukacs, Luxemburg, Trotsky, Gramsci, Mao, Sartre, Althusser and Habermas whose writings represent a great diversity of views. But it is also true to say that attempts have been made to canonise the work of Marx and Engels and produce a single 'correct' version of Marxism. In particular, the use of their work as a unifying ideology by political parties has led to simplifications and dogmatism, so that Marxism has often been equated with the offical positions of Communist Parties, especially that of the Soviet Union (because of its historical role as the first Marxist party to achieve state power). But such 'official' versions tend towards a closed system of thought and to absolute truths which are in contradistinction to Lenin's assertion of the open-ended quality of Marxism:

> We do not regard Marx's theory as something completed and inviolable; on the contrary, we are convinced that it has only laid the foundation stone of the science which socialists must develop in all directions if they wish to keep pace with life.[13]

The very fact that theory arises within the context of particular historical situations and contributes to changing them means that Marxism has inevitably developed as new problems have arisen for solution. Indeed, it is better to conceptualise Marxism as a theoretical framework which can provide a guide to action than as a static, unitary body of thought and practice.

Since the criticism of Stalin at the Twentieth Congress of the Communist Party of the Soviet Union in 1956, there has been a renaissance of Marxist theoretical debate and analysis. In the 1960s, economic events (such as the end of the post-war period of expansion by the end of the decade), political events (such as the Sino-Soviet split, the war of liberation in Vietnam, and the crisis in France in 1968), and intellectual events (such as new editions of Marx, Gramsci and Lukacs) all contributed to the renewal of the Marxist tradition. This renaissance took place not only in Europe and North America but also in the Third World. During the 1970s there was widespread political activity influenced by Marxism (in countries as diverse as Chile, Italy and Mozambique) and a creative application of Marxist analysis in many areas of study (ranging from feminism to aesthetics to development theory). The renewed Marxist scholarship has been vigorous, iconoclastic and polemical, reviving earlier debates that had been frozen during the twenty-five years of Stalinist theoretical dominance and analysing Stalinism itself. Its new vitality has opened up fruitful lines of research in a wide variety of fields. This has been especially noticeable in the English-speaking world, where Marxism has had a growing impact on intellectual life despite the traditional prejudice of Anglo-Saxon empiricism against general theory. Marxism today therefore appears as a complex and many-faceted intellectual and political tradition. My own position within it will emerge as I apply it to questions of teaching and learning in adult education.

In undertaking this application I am able to draw particularly on the body of Marxist analysis of education which has been produced in the last decade as part of the general development of Marxist perspectives. The main focus of these studies has been the nature of education in advanced capitalist society. They have approached this question at two levels. The first is that of the relationship between education and society, considered at the structural level. Here education has been analysed from a historical perspective which locates it within the wider social context of the structure of class and power. The work of the North American writers Carnoy, Bowles and Gintis has been important in developing this political economy of education. The second level is that of the educational institutions themselves, considered in terms of their organisation, social processes, curriculum content and teaching methods, that is, at the cultural level. Here studies have investigated exactly how educational practices serve to maintain and legitimate the capitalist social order and what forms of resistance occur. This level has been explored by British sociologists such as Whitty, Young and Willis, and by North American curriculum theorists like Apple and Giroux. To some extent these levels have been analysed separately but it is increasingly recognised that they must be unified in a theoretical totality, for example in Apple's recent collection entitled (significantly) <u>Cultural and Economic Reproduction in Education</u>.[14]

The need to relate theoretical analysis to actual educational activity has not gone unrecognised either:

> The importance of education for capitalism is
> clearly revealed by the state's action in taking
> control of educational institutions and
> expanding them; the question for Marxists is
> <u>why</u>. We can take it as given that education
> does fulfil a basic function for capitalism, the
> task is to understand this function.
>
> But there is a further task for Marxists: to
> relate this theoretical understanding to day-to-
> day educational practice.[15]

To a certain extent, recent Marxist writers have put
forward ideas for socialist educational practices
which embody Marxist theory, for example, the
contributors to <u>Studies in Socialist Pedagogy</u>.[16]
Thus I am able to refer to a small group of writers
who have applied a Marxist theoretical framework to
practical educational issues in capitalist society,
although most of this writing has been on school
education. In fact, despite the upsurge of Marxist
scholarship that has taken place, there has been
very little writing in English on the theory and
practice of adult education from a Marxist
perspective. This book attempts to go some way
towards filling that gap.

## THE POLITICAL ECONOMY OF ADULT EDUCATION

I have noted above the need for educational
studies to unite the structural level of analysis
with the cultural level (of intellectual processes
and social practices) in a theoretical totality.
This is not an entirely straightforward task as the
relationship between the two is one of the main
sources of contention within contemporary Marxism.
Kitching in his book <u>Rethinking Socialism</u> discusses
how many of the new Marxist writers of the last
twenty years have stressed humanist themes of
alienation, human agency, consciousness, ideological
oppression, personal liberation and so forth and
have under-emphasised economic analysis of the class
structure, material production, the dynamics of
capitalist accumulation and so on.[17] They have done
so in a conscious attempt to distance themselves
from the theories of economic determinism associated
with the Marxism of the Stalinist era and hence

from the political record of the USSR (particularly
the crimes committed in the name of Marxism in the
1930s). But Kitching argues that in so doing they
have adopted theoretical positions which are
seriously flawed because they neglect the economic
basis of society, which Marx regarded as fundamental
for explaining political and cultural phenomena. He
adds that 'A commitment to some of the central
concepts of Marx's political economy need not
necessarily lead to the adoption of elitist or
Stalinist political positions.'[18] However, it is
undeniable that achieving a comprehensive exposition
of the dialectical unity of the structural and the
cultural, the objective and the subjective, is a
long-standing problem within the Marxist tradition.
Nevertheless, it remains a central goal, whose
theoretical foundation was crystallised by Marx in a
famous passage in his <u>Preface to a Contribution
to the Critique of Political Economy</u>:

> In the social production of their life, people
> enter into definite relations that are
> indispensable and independent of their will,
> relations of production which correspond to a
> definite stage of development of their material
> production forces. The sum total of these
> relations of production constitutes the economic
> structure of society, the real basis, on which
> rises a legal and political superstructure and
> to which correspond definite forms of social
> consciousness. The mode of production of
> material life conditions the social, political
> and intellectual life process in general.[19]

This proposition that the economic structure
conditions social institutions and intellectual
processes is central to the Marxist study of
education. However, specifying the exact
relationship between the economy and the nature of
education has been as difficult and contentious as
in the analysis of other social institutions. This
is exemplified by the controversy among Marxist
educationists over the theory put forward by Bowles
and Gintis in <u>Schooling in Capitalist America</u>[20] on
the close correspondence between the social
relations of capitalist production and the social
relations of education.[21] The controversy centres
on the question of whether Bowles and Gintis have
overemphasised the determining role of the economy
to the neglect of the political and cultural realm.

The debate illustrates why it is important to seek the correct formulation of the relationship. Perhaps because education is one of society's social institutions, there has been a tendency for analysis to neglect its structural determinants. Because of this I feel it is vital for me to establish at the beginning of this study the structural context of adult education practices. I conceptualise this context as the political economy of adult education, by which I mean that the nature of adult education is shaped by the distribution of political power in society, which is in turn a reflection of the economic structure. This is not to say that all aspects of adult education are in some way directly determined by economic factors but simply to assert that adult education is not an autonomous institution which generates all of its own characteristics. Its nature has its own logic but this is embedded in the larger logic of the economic structure. The analysis of the political economy of adult education rests on certain key concepts of Marxist social theory which need to be introduced at this point.

Marx and Engels developed a theory for the analysis of society as a totality which they called 'the materialist conception of history'. They derived it from a synthesis of three currents of European thought of the early nineteenth century - German philosophy, French socialist politics, and English economics. The theory was first formulated in The German Ideology and it provided the basis of their subsequent work. Engels summarised it in this way:

> ...that view of the course of history which seeks the ultimate cause and the great moving power of all important historic events in the economic development of society, in the changes in the mode of production and exchange, in the consequent division of society into classes, and in the struggle of these classes against one another.[23]

Marx and Engels viewed any given society as a historical product undergoing a process of change. They identified the ultimate source of social change in changes in the economic structure and political conflicts between classes. A fundamental category in their social theory is the mode of production.

11

The concept of the mode of production is used to differentiate periods of history according to the nature of the economy. Considered abstractly, a mode of production is a combination of the forces of production and the social relations of production. The forces of production include the means of production (such as land, raw materials, tools, machinery) and human labour (embodying knowledge, skill and attitudes). The relations of production are the social relationships people enter into in the process of production, and are defined by who owns and controls the means of production.

In concrete terms, several different modes of production can be identified historically. They are differentiated according to the way in which the products of labour are distributed within society. In the earliest mode, primitive communalism, production through hunting and gathering and basic agriculture was at a very low level, land was held communally, and products were shared among the members of society. But once the development of settled agriculture had enabled the production of a surplus beyond immediate subsistence needs, the possibility arose of a social division of labour with one class appropriating the surplus product from the class of direct producers. The way this appropriation takes place is used to define subsequent modes of production:

> What distinguishes the various economic formations of society - the distinction between for example, a society based on slave-labour and a society based on wage-labour - is the form in which this surplus labour is in each case extorted from the immediate producer...[24]

The form of appropriation is determined by ownership of the means of production and therefore the nature of the relations of production provides the key to identifying a particular mode of production.

Marx and Engels used the concept to differentiate historical epochs, regarding the different modes as stages in the evolution of higher forms of society:

> In broad outlines Asiatic, ancient, feudal and modern bourgeois modes of production can be designated as progressive epochs in the economic formation of society.[25]

It is important to note that they did not regard these stages of social evolution in a unilinear way. Although human society began with the primitive communal mode of production, its evolution globally and historically has taken several different directions from that starting point. Sometimes a mode has remained relatively static for a long period, such as the Asiatic mode in China. Sometimes external forces have extinguished a mode, as in the case of the ancient mode of the Roman Empire. One mode, feudalism in Western Europe, underwent an internal process of development from the thirteenth century, resulting eventually in the capitalist mode of production. By the late nineteenth century this mode had spread so that it made an impact on the rest of the world. During the twentieth century, it has been superseded by the socialist mode of production in several parts of the globe. The historical development of modes of production has therefore been an uneven process.

There have been the following modes: primitive communalism, a variety of pre-capitalist modes, capitalism and socialism. But although it is possible to define the historical existence of different modes of production, none of them has ever existed on its own in isolation. At any given time there may be several modes evident in a society, although one will be dominant and thus define the character of the society. The totality of varying economic relations forms the basis of the social entity which Marx called the 'social formation'. It includes a configuration of modes: 'A formation embraces both the past and the future; dying modes of production; the dominant, defining mode; and seeds of coming modes.'[26]

Most of the work of Marx and Engels consisted of an analysis of the capitalist mode of production, which is characterised by a minority having ownership of the means of production and the majority being dependent for their subsistence on wage labour. They analysed how capitalism arose from pre-capitalist modes and drew the conclusion that it would eventually be superseded by socialism and communism, in which the means of production would be owned by society and therefore the basis of exploitation would be eliminated. Today there are two kinds of social formation, the capitalist and the socialist. But they can be considered in terms of another dimension, namely the level of development of the forces of production on a spectrum from advanced to underdeveloped. Hence I distinguish between advanced and underdeveloped capitalism (for example, the USA and Kenya) and between advanced and underdeveloped socialism (for example, the USSR and Mozambique). I use the term 'Third World' to refer to both kinds of underdeveloped economy.

The concept of the mode of production is central to historical materialism because it provides the means of differentiating societies according to the nature of their economy. This is of vital significance because of the role of the economy in Marxist theory:

> ...the economic structure of society always furnishes the real basis, starting from which we can alone work out the ultimate explanation of the whole superstructure of juridicial and political institutions as well as the religious, philosophical and other ideas of a given historical period.[27]

This concept of base and superstructure is one of some complexity and it is of great controversy within Marxism, especially over the precise extent to which economic factors determine the political and cultural levels, and the extent to which these have a reciprocal effect on the economy. It is a concept of particular importance for the Marxist analysis of adult education. The general processes which shape the individual's psychology are to be located within this framework. The specific institutional form of the shaping process, education, is one of the institutions of the superstructure.

In their metaphor of base and superstructure Marx and Engels were pointing out that the mode of production provides the foundation of political institutions and cultural processes. Their fundamental point was that these institutions and processes are not autonomous and self-created but are related to economic factors, such as the relationship between classes. In explaining the complex reality of society, the economic base provides the final clue to its nature. The base determines the form of superstructural institutions and ideas, in the sense of setting limits and exerting pressures on their development. But these institutions and ideas have a degree of autonomy and can in turn influence the economic base. Marx, for example, in

14

Capital. Volume 1 showed how the power of the state in England hastened the transformation of the feudal mode of production into the capitalist mode.[28]  The metaphor therefore does not imply a crude economic reductionism, that all aspects of politics and culture can be explained directly by the state of development of the forces of production or the relations of production.  The economy is not the only determining factor and there is a certain degree of reciprocal causality between the base and superstructure.  However, in the final analysis the distinguishing feature of Marxist social theory is that the 'ultimate explanation' of political and cultural phenomena is to be found in the material conditions of life.  This is the essential insight of the 'materialist conception of history' and the rationale for its analytical method:

> Empirical observation must in each separate instance bring out empirically, and without mystification and speculation, the connection of the social and political structure with production.  The social structure and the state are continually evolving out of the life-processes of definite individuals, not as they appear in their own or other people's imagination, but as they really are; i.e. as they operate, produce materially, and hence as they work under definite material limits, presuppositions and conditions independent of their will.[29]

The Marxist approach to adult education therefore argues that it must be analysed within its economic and political context.

Within the conceptual matrix of the mode of production and base and superstructure, the idea of class has an important place.  Class expresses a relationship to the means of production.  Certain groups in society own the means of production, other groups do not.  There are therefore different classes in different modes of production and each mode has its characteristic polarisation of antagonistic classes - for example, slave-owners and slaves in the ancient mode; landowners and serfs in feudalism.  Classes also reflect the division of labour in society, in which the division between mental and manual labour is primary.

The relationship between classes is one of contradiction, involving a shifting terrain of

domination and subordination.  The ownership of
economic property is a source of political power and
the property-owning class constitutes the ruling
class in society.  But the opposed economic
interests of the classes leads them into conflict.
In capitalism, for example, there is a fundamental
conflict over the relative size of the workers'
wages and the capitalists' profits.  Marx and Engels
regarded this struggle between classes as a major
source of social change.  However, they stressed
that while a class may be seen objectively to exist
in society (as a 'class-in-itself') its members do
not necessarily have a shared consciousness of their
common interests (and therefore it may not constitute a 'class-for-itself').  It is in developing
this class consciousness in the working class that
socialist organisations have a role to play,
creating the subjective conditions of conscious (as
opposed to spontaneous) class struggle which may
hasten social change in a socialist direction.

Identifying the objective existence of
different classes is an important part of the
Marxist method, because it can provide an
understanding of the nature of the economic base of
a given society (and hence provide insight into the
phenomena of the superstructure).  The empirical
procedure of class analysis in contemporary
capitalist social formations is based on
distinguishing between the following classes:

The bourgeoisie (or capitalist class), whose
members own means of production on a large scale
(such as banks, land, factories, and businesses).

The petty-bourgeoisie (or middle-class) which
contains two strata.  The members of the first
stratum own small-scale enterprises or employ
themselves (such as shopkeepers and small
producers).  The members of the second stratum help
to supervise and maintain the capitalist system
(such as government officials, teachers, technical
and management personnel in commerce and industry,
and professionals).

The proletariat (or working class), whose
members own no means of production and have to sell
their labour for wages in order to survive.  This
class occupies the subordinate position in all
sectors of the economy - industry, services,
agriculture, etc. - in both urban and rural areas.

The peasantry whose members possess means of agricultural production (such as land, implements, and animals) and rely primarily on their own labour and that of their family. This class can be subdivided into the strata of rich, middle, and poor peasants.

The semi-proletariat, whose members retain some means of agricultural production but who also spend a lot of time working for wages (such as many migrant workers in the Third World).

The lumpenproletariat, whose members have no means of production and engage in casual or illegal forms of employment.

Each of these classes has different economic interests, a fact which underlies conflicts which appear in political, legal and other spheres, including education. The Marxist approach thus locates adult education within the class structure of society and identifies how the different class interests influence its nature.

It is in relation to the classes in society that the concept of the state is important. Marx and Engels stressed that the state is not neutral and somehow 'above' society but rather it is a political institution through which the economically dominant class seeks to advance its own interests. They conceived the state as fundamentally an instrument of the ruling class - for example:

> ...the modern state, no matter what its form, is essentially a capitalist machine, the state of the capitalists, the ideal personification of the total national capital.[30]

Thus whilst there are different forms of the state in the capitalist mode of production (ranging from dictatorships to parliamentary democracies), its basic role is to maintain the conditions for capitalist accumulation and reproduction.

Marx and Engels, and subsequently Lenin, focussed primarily on the coercive nature of the state and its 'organised violence', paying attention to the armed forces, the police, the courts and prisons, the legislature, and the bureaucracy of government officials as the agents of state power.

However, later Marxist writers, influenced
particularly by Gramsci, have also considered the
state's ideological role in legitimating capitalism
and in engendering willing consent to the existing
social order. For example, Althusser in an
important essay distinguishes between 'repressive'
and 'ideological' state apparatuses, identifying
education as the most important of the ideological
state apparatuses.[31] Furthermore, recent Marxist
debates on the nature of the state have indicated
that the state cannot be conceived simplistically as
the tool of the ruling class. As with other
institutions of the superstructure, the state is a
terrain on which class struggle takes place, so that
ruling class control has to be continually defended
and renewed in the face of contradictions and
resistance, especially in the ideological
apparatuses. This concept of the state as both a
medium of class domination and a site of class
struggle is highly significant for the study of
adult education because of the increasingly central
role of the state in its provision.

The final concept of historical materialism for
consideration is that of imperialism. Marx and
Engels showed how capitalism had developed a world
market and they began to identify the tendency to
monopoly in capitalism, with smaller enterprises
being conglomerated into larger ones. In a major
theoretical advance, Lenin analysed how the
development of monopoly capitalism in the later
nineteenth century resulted in the export of capital
to economies outside Europe and the USA:

> As long as capitalism remains what it is,
> surplus capital will be utilised not for the
> purpose of raising the standard of living of the
> masses in a given country, for this would mean a
> decline in profits for the capitalists, but for
> the purpose of increasing profits by exporting
> capital abroad to the backward countries. In
> these backward countries profits are usually
> high, for capital is scarce, the price of land
> is relatively low, wages are low, raw materials
> are cheap.[32]

Lenin called this economic process of capitalist
accumulation in a world market 'imperialism'. It
was accompanied by the imposition of political power
by the capitalist nations so that they could
guarantee geographical areas against competition

18

from each other. In Africa, for example, the
'scramble' for colonies culminated in the 1885
Berlin Conference where the main capitalist powers
of Europe agreed to divide the continent into
different spheres of influence.

The first period of imperialism was
characterised by colonisation, that is, direct
political control of other nations by the ruling
class of the advanced capitalist nations. But since
the Second World War most colonies have become
formally independent and the present period can be
described as 'neo-colonialism' (with a continuing
dominance by the advanced capitalist states,
particularly the USA). The majority of the former
colonies have predominantly capitalist relations of
production and remain incorporated in the capitalist
world market. The multi-national companies play a
central role in the external control of their
economies. Foreign loans, aid and military
assistance by Western nations are provided with the
aim of preserving their capitalist structures.
Whenever a country attempts to break out of the
situation, economic, political and even military
intervention is undertaken, as in the cases of Cuba,
Vietnam, Angola and Nicaragua. In Marxist analysis,
imperialism is seen as a fundamental part of the
economic and political context of adult education in
the Third World. No study of adult education in
these countries is complete without a consideration
of these external influences.

The preceding pages provide a sketch of a very
extensive body of social theory whose interpretation
and application is the source of much debate within
Marxism.[33] However, the concepts of historical
materialism that I have introduced (namely, mode of
production and social formation, base and
superstructure, class and the social division of
labour, the state, and imperialism) are
indispensable for understanding the economic and
political context of adult education. Such a
structural understanding has explanatory power for
elucidating both the institutional pattern of adult
education provision and the nature of adult
education practices at the cultural level of social
processes, curriculum content and teaching methods.

My argument is that education as a cultural and
ideological institution is inextricably linked to
the economic and political structure of society. In
capitalist society education systems have developed
historically as a means of the ruling class ensuring

19

its control over other classes. The establishment
of mass schooling in the nineteenth century in
countries like England and the USA was a conscious
political response to the instability created by
industrialisation and the emergence of the working
class. Schooling was seen as a way of providing the
socialisation process necessary to fit people for
the new social relations of production of industrial
capitalist society. For example, nineteenth century
educators stressed 'moral' education and the
inculcation of 'order' rather than the acquisition
of skills. They sought to teach the new behaviour
(such as discipline, punctuality, acceptance of
authority outside the family) necessary for the new
social order.[34] Similarly, the ruling class of the
capitalist countries used education in their
colonies explicitly to strengthen their economic and
political control. A Governor-General of French
West Africa defined the aims of the colonial system
of education in these terms:

> Education is politics. It is an effective way
> of making our colonial policy acceptable to the
> Africans. It aims at producing the type of
> African who will always be our ally in all
> spheres of our colonial policies. The objective
> is to make sure that we have a few but well
> selected African elite who will become cogs in
> the machinery of our colonial system. On the
> other hand, it is education whose essence, in
> relation to the African masses, is to create a
> gap between Europeans and Africans so that the
> African elite is something intermediary,
> something neither African nor European. From
> the point of view of politics, the aim of
> education is to make the African feel that we
> are making efforts to improve his lot, to make
> the African believe that we are changing his
> life and his ways for the better and thus
> redeeming the African from slavery. From the
> point of view of economics, our colonial
> education is aimed at producing producers of the
> raw materials we need in Europe and consumers of
> the manufactured goods we make in Europe from
> these raw materials.[35]

State education systems can therefore be seen to
have been developed to serve capitalist interests
both in the advanced industrialised countries and
their colonies. Primarily their role was to

legitimate and stabilise the social relations of production of capitalism. Their concern with teaching literacy and technical skills was secondary.

Despite the arguments of twentieth century liberalism that education is capable of reducing inequalities, it is evident that an essential role of education in the political economy of capitalism remains one of reproducing class, gender and racial inequality. In contemporary capitalist social formations the education system continues to serve the interests of the ruling class, and acts to legitimate its rule and to train people to fit into the socio-economic hierarchy. For example, in England in the 1950s, the different kinds of secondary school clearly reflected different roles in the production process - secondary modern schools for manual workers, technical schools for skilled workers and technicians, grammar schools for managers and professionals, and public schools for owners. There is a growing body of literature which documents how education reproduces the social division of labour of the capitalist class structure from generation to generation. Evidence of this can be found in advanced capitalist countries, such as the USA[36], and in the underdeveloped countries of the former colonies, such as Ghana.[37] Although the relationship between education and the economic and power structure of society cannot be conceived in reductionist terms, its general form is clear - education is one way in which the ruling capitalist class seeks to advance its economic interests and consolidate its political position. This can be illustrated in adult education in advanced capitalism by the situation in England in the late 1970s when increased opportunities for recurrent education were advocated as a way of helping those who had been made unemployed to adapt to and accept their situation (thus legitimating structural unemployment and defusing discontent). It can be seen in underdeveloped capitalist countries in agricultural extension programmes which encourage cash crop production in the class interests of those (locally and abroad) who appropriate the surplus of the peasantry.[38] Another Third World example is to to be found in the programmes for small entrepreneurs, such as those organised in Africa by the US organisation Partnership for Productivity, which are specifically intended to develop a strong petty-bourgeois class. For capitalism, the economic role of adult education is to contribute to the processes of capitalist accumulation, the political role is to contribute to the legitimation of the existing distribution of power.

On the other hand, like other institutions of the superstructure, education must also be viewed as an arena of class struggle. While reproducing the capitalist mode of production it also reproduces the contradictions inherent in that mode. Recent Marxist analysis has considered how education is not only a mechanism for class reproduction but also a site of resistance and opposition. A good example of this kind of analysis is to be found in Willis' ethnographic study of an English secondary school _Learning to Labour_.[39] He describes the counter-culture of the working class children in the school who informally resist the institution and its rules (in a similar way to that of manual workers in the work-place). He shows how this resistance opposes the dominant ideology that the school mediates in its role of preparing labour for capitalism. But while the children penetrate to some extent capitalist ideology, these insights are only partial and in the end their opposition leads to an acceptance of the structure of capitalism, particularly the crucial split between mental and manual labour. Willis points out that because there is no political attempt to interpret the children's insights, develop in them a critical analysis of society, and mobilise them for political action for change, the significance of their understanding of capitalism and their experience of class solidarity is lost. This is a point elaborated by Giroux in his article developing the notion of resistance as the basis of a critical theory of schooling when he argues that a radical pedagogy must politicise student resistance so that it becomes part of a collective political struggle for social justice and emancipation.[40]

Generally speaking, the recent analysis of resistance has considered it in terms of spontaneous action within the education system. However, just as the ruling class has consciously used the education system to serve its interests, so the dominated classes have also fought purposefully for their own interests in education. A central demand of the labour movement in the nineteenth century in England was for mass education. In the mid-twentieth century, realising that state education was acting against working class interests through

the division of the secondary schools, the demand
was made for unified comprehensive schools.
Education therefore is a field of conscious and
organised class struggle as well as spontaneous
conflict. This is true in adult education as much
as in school education. When the Chartists in
England established their own workers' adult
education programmes in the 1830s, the capitalists
responded by setting up the Mechanics Institutes
with curricula designed to 'tranquilise the popular
mind' and to be 'a sedative to all sorts of
turbulence and disorder'.[41] The '150 hours'
programme in Italy provides a recent example.[42]
'150 Hours' is the amount of paid educational leave
that the Metalworkers Union got agreed in their
national contract in 1973. Since then over a
million workers throughout industry have had paid
leave for such activities as literacy, school
diplomas and technical training, as part of a
movement aiming at workers' control of industry and
society rather than individual advancement. This
achievement was based on the upsurge of strength of
the Left in Italy during the late 1960s and early
1970s. But just as the development of the programme
was based on the organised strength of the working
class, once the unions were weakened by the economic
recession of the late 1970s the anti-capitalist
political impact of the programme was blunted.
    The understanding that adult education is a
site of struggles between the classes in capitalist
social formations is the starting point for
clarifying its role in the achievement of socialism.
It is necessary at this point to give an account of
the nature of socialist society as I envisage it.
Socialist opposition to capitalism aims for a
fundamental change in society and it is important to
specify the direction of this change. This
specification is significant not only because it
provides a vision of the future on which to base
political and educational action but also because it
provides an end whose nature should influence the
means of its attainment. In the following sections
I will first give an outline of socialist society,
then present a theory of revolution which indicates
how capitalism might be tranformed, and finally I
will summarise the role of adult education in this
process of social transformation.

## THE NATURE OF SOCIALIST SOCIETY

Socialism is a complex notion which in everyday usage embraces a plurality of meanings. Although opposition to capitalism is the common denominator, the nature of socialist alternatives to capitalism varies. Even within the Marxist tradition there are disagreements on how to define socialist society, a difficulty compounded by the variety of historical experiences of those societies which, since the Russian revolution of 1917, have attempted to detach themselves from the international capitalist system and develop alternatives in practice. However, I think it is possible to provide an outline of socialist society, based on the writings of Marx and Engels and an assessment of historical experience. My starting point is that socialism in Marxist theory is generally conceived of as a period of transition between capitalism and communism - as Marx put it: 'Between capitalist and communist society lies the period of the revolutionary transformation of the one into the other.'[43] It is the full development of communism as the total negation of capitalism which provides the long-term goal to which the economic, political and cultural transformations are directed in the socialist mode of production. (It is this concept of socialism as a stage towards a future communism that distinguishes Marxism from other positions, such as that of the social democrats, and the reason why many Marxist political parties call themselves Communist.)

Marx and Engels identified within the capitalist mode of production fundamental contradictions which generate a conflict between the bourgeoisie and the proletariat. They envisaged that this class conflict would eventually lead to the proletariat taking state power and ending the class rule of the bourgeoisie. After this revolution, there would be a long period of social transformation, marked by continuing struggles at all levels of the social formation because aspects of capitalism would persist. The new society is not ready-made but emerges from capitalism and 'is thus in every respect, economically, morally and intellectually, still stamped with the birthmarks of the old society from whose womb it emerges.'[44] Only after a long transitional period would a fully communist society be established which would finally create the possibility

...of securing for every member of society, by means of socialised production, an existence not only fully sufficient materially, and becoming day by day fuller, but an existence guaranteeing to all the free development and exercise of their physical and mental faculties.[45]

This is the goal to which socialist political activity is directed and in the transitional period of socialism the proletariat uses state power to develop society in this direction.

Marxist theory and post-1917 historical practice suggest that socialist society has a number of defining characteristics at the economic, political and cultural levels. An important feature of historical experience is that socialism has not occurred in advanced capitalist social formations but in economically backward ones. Russia in 1917, China in 1949, Mozambique in 1975, for example, were all underdeveloped capitalist social formations (indeed, with remnants of pre-capitalist modes of production). The economic and cultural constraints on the practical development of socialist societies have therefore been immense, despite the political will of the parties in power. The objective conditions of scarce material and human resources have been an important influence on the nature of actual socialist development. It is therefore necessary to bear in mind the theory of the socialist mode of production as well as the practice.

The basis of socialism is to be found in its economic structure. The fundamental break with capitalism is made with the abolition of private ownership of the means of production and the ending of the dynamic of private capitalist accumulation. The process of bringing the means of production under social ownership and control and of eliminating individual ownership and control is central to the socialist transition. It involves the state taking over the major means of production and exchange by the nationalisation of large factories, plantations, banks and so forth. It also involves the development of co-operative ownership of smaller industrial and commercial enterprises and, particularly, the agricultural means of production.[46]

The process of socialisation is directed towards a steady elimination of private property in

the means of production and therefore the
termination of the economic basis of the capitalist
class structure. The change in ownership and
control involves a concomitant change in the social
relations of production, enabling the possibility of
democratic participation in decision-making about
production, distribution and consumption. In
theory, workers' control of industrial and other
work-places and peasants' control of agriculture
enables a high degree of self-management and
economic democracy. But in practice the low level
of technical and managerial knowledge of the working
class and peasantry at the time of the overthrow of
capitalism has tended to mean the development of a
technical and managerial elite with hierarchical
rather than participatory forms of management. [47]

The third aspect of economic change is that
great emphasis is put on the development of the
forces of production through industrialisation and
the mechanisation of agriculture. It is a sine qua
non of socialism that it must be built on material
abundance which requires highly developed forces of
production. A major problem historically has been
that socialists have come to power in predominantly
agricultural economies rather than advanced
industrial economies. The imperative of
industrialisation has been central to the early
years of socialist transition. The pace of
industrialisation and its relation to agricultural
development is an important area of debate within
Marxism because many view the programme of very
rapid industrialisation undertaken in the USSR in
the 1930s as negative in terms of its effect on
agriculture and, more widely, on political and
social life. However, the goal of developing the
productive forces remains central, the arguments
focussing on how to achieve it. The aim is to
provide the mass of the population with a materially
sufficient existence (including full employment and
extensive social services) and to achieve
the benefits of industrialisation without the costs
of exploitation and alienation inherent in
capitalism's development of the productive forces.

An important aspect of the development of a
socialist economy is economic planning. The aim of
production under socialism is to meet people's
needs, whereas the driving force of production under
capitalism is the making of private profit. To
achieve this, economic life has to be planned and
given central direction so that the anarchy created

by the market forces of capitalism with its cycle of expansion and recession is overcome:

> ...the social anarchy of production gives place to a social regulation of production upon a definite plan, according to the needs of the community and of each individual.[48]

Again, historical experience has revealed that the process of economic planning is a complex one and there is, for example, a tension between central planning and the need for decentralised decision-making inherent in the concept of economic democracy. And of course socialist economies have not been able to disengage totally from the capitalist world market and therefore continue to be subject to the cyclical crises of capitalist accumulation which complicate the planning process.

The economic basis of socialism, as I have described it above, is characterised by state and co-operative ownership of the means of production, democratic social relations of production, and increasingly developed force of production. The role of the state in creating these economic conditions (for example, through expropriating private owners and through central planning) exemplifies that it is the predominant institution within the political superstructure of existing socialist societies. The nature of the state was described by Marx as 'the revolutionary dictatorship of the proletariat'[49] and its form is intended to meet the needs of the transitional period by enabling the working class to take the measures necessary for realising its own class interests.

Following Lane[50], I will distinguish five major political institutions which are commonly found in socialist societies (though obviously with national variations). The first is the party which, whatever its formal name (whether the Communist Party of the Soviet Union, the Polish United Workers Party or the Yemeni Socialist Party, for example) adheres to a self-proclaimed Marxist ideology. It is a selective political organisation, recruiting the most politically conscious and active people and it takes the role of providing political leadership for the working class and its allies and of representing their interests. It has its own internal democratic structure with different levels of elected representation, culminating in the national Congress of the Party. The party sets policy and monitors its implementation by the administrative bodies of the government at all levels.

The second institution is the government, which is comprised of the bureaucracies responsible for economic planning, industrial affairs, social services and so forth, normally arranged as ministries and co-ordinated by a Council of Ministers. The government bureaucracies (at national and local level) are answerable to a third institution, the hierarchy of popularly-elected political councils. This democratic system of councils is open to all members of society (not just party members) and seeks to mobilise the mass of people in political participation. In the USSR these councils are called soviets and build up to the Supreme Soviet, the chief legislative body. In Cuba, since the 1975 Constitution, they are known as Organs of Popular Power and delegates are elected at district, provincial and national levels. Fourthly, within this system of participation and control there are the mass organisations which are designed to represent the sectional interests of particular groups in society, such as organisations for women, youth and students, trade unions, and peasant associations. Finally, in many socialist societies there are other political parties which are allowed to continue in existence insofar as they accept the social order. In China in 1963, for example, there were eight other parties besides the Communist Party.[51]

The changes in the superstructure (which include other alterations, for example to the legal system) are designed to produce control of state power by the working class and its allies so that they can undertake economic and social development in their own interests. In theory, an institutional system of participatory democracy in the political sphere is established to parallel that in the economic sphere. In practice, severe problems have arisen because of the objective conditions in which Marxist parties have come to power and because of certain theoretical positions on the nature of socialist development.

The problems of objective conditions include economic underdevelopment and the shortage of human resources. This has led to a key role being played by the government bureaucracy in economic development and the concomitant growth of an elite formed by those with technical and managerial

expertise. This elite, derived initially from the
petty bourgeoisie and bourgeoisie of the previous
capitalist social formation, is not subject to
elections and has tended to perpetuate itself,
particularly through education.[52] The power of the
administrative bureaucracy has acted to restrict
political participation. Another objective problem
has been that socialist revolutions have immediately
been met by internal capitalist resistance and by
external imperialist intervention, which has led to
militarisation and a disproportionate role in public
life of the armed forces and police. Both these
trends have contributed to the development of
authoritarianism at the expense of democratisation.
The quality of democratic life under socialism
remains the central problem for practical solution –
in a telling phrase, White comments on North Korea
'where remarkable social and economic progress has
gone side by side with political stultification.'[53]
     What needs to be recognised is that the
problems of democratisation not only stem from
objective conditions at the time of revolution (such
as low levels of education and the absence of
democratic traditions) but also from theoretical
approaches to socialist development and, especially,
to the role of the party. The issue can be somewhat
crudely conceptualised in the polarisation between
socialism 'from above' and socialism 'from below'.
The model of socialist construction provided by the
historical experience of the USSR since the late
1920s has been essentially one of socialism 'from
above', with an emphasis on state direction and a
stress on the development of the productive forces.
The major alternative to this model has been
provided by China at certain periods in its
development (such as 1958-1960 and 1966-1969) when
the emphasis has been on the mass mobilisation of
workers and peasants and democratisation of the
relations of production. In one model, the party
uses its power to direct popular activity, and in
the other, it seeks to be a catalyst enabling people
to transform society through their own collective
and conscious activity. This polarisation is rather
crude (especially when sloganised as Bolshevism
versus Maoism), both in terms of political theory
and the analysis of historical experience, but it
does highlight a major problem of socialist
construction. Clearly what is required is a form of
political practice that combines dialectically both
the elements of party leadership and popular power,

a practice whose precise shape will be conditioned by the particular circumstances in which it takes place.

The problems of political life in existing socialist societies revolve around a number of contradictions, such as those between central planning and participation, party direction and popular power, technical expertise and political consciousness, development of the productive forces and democratisation of the social relations of production. These tensions cannot be easily resolved and they surface time and again in the vicissitudes of socialist construction. However, the long term goal of communist society must not be lost sight of and here Marx and Engels envisaged that the state's political function as an instrument of class rule would be unnecessary and its role would be reduced to administrative functions:

> State interference in social relations becomes, in one domain after another, superfluous, and then dies out of itself; the government of persons is replaced by the administration of things, and by the conduct of processes of production.[54]

The progressive dispersion of state power and the growth of participatory democracy must provide the direction for socialist political development.

Finally, there are cultural transformations associated with the socialist mode of production. These transformations are intended to engender the modes of thinking and the social practices which will facilitate the building of socialism. On the intellectual level, great priority is given to the dissemination of Marxism and to the development of scientific and technological knowledge so that people can understand and control their social, natural and productive environment. On the level of values, co-operation, egalitarianism and mutuality are encouraged whilst sexism, racism and ethnic discrimination are particular targets of attack. Indeed, the goal is set of creating a new kind of person with the intellectual capabilities, technical skills and political awareness to control production and society democratically. Emphasis is also placed on developing a sense of national identity in order to resist the cultural forces of imperialism, but simultaneously the global nature of monopoly capitalism is stressed so that internationalism and

30

solidarity with the worldwide struggle against capitalism are encouraged.

Obviously a key institution for achieving such cultural and ideological changes is education and in all socialist societies there has been a massive quantitative expansion of education. In theory, the objectives of education are to provide a high level of general knowledge and technical training, to combat individualism and encourage co-operative attitudes, to develop political consciousness and, above all, to break down the division between mental and manual labour which is the basis of class society. However, the exact nature of education has varied historically according to the different economic and political situations. Whyte, for example, has drawn parallels between the Russian and Chinese experience.[55] In the USSR from 1917 to 1928 and in China from 1966 to 1969, political emphasis was given to changing the relations of production and this was reflected in closer links between education and production, downgrading of exams and academic competition, greater opportunities for workers and peasants, more politicisation, more active modes of learning, and more equal teacher-student relations. Conversely, in other periods in both countries when emphasis has been on developing the forces of production, education has tended to stress academic performance, exams, centralisation, and dilution of the relationship between education and production. The latter approaches were justified at the time by a concern for improvements in the quality of education but objectively they represented a trend towards stratification and hierarchical order. As such, they indicated how the bureaucratic elite sought to use education for its own legitimation and reproduction. Education within the socialist mode of production thus reflects the contradictions present in this transitional social formation.

Nevertheless, education is a crucial cultural condition for the development of socialism and within this adult education has a particularly important role to play as the imperatives of socialist construction cannot be delayed until a future generation emerges from school. Indeed it is the practical activity of adults in the years after the revolution that shapes the emergent society. Hence all socialist societies have given very high priority to adult education on a large scale, as exemplified by the mass literacy campaigns of Cuba

31

and Nicaragua, and by the USSR's enormous system of part-time study at all levels. The role of adult education is to develop political consciousness on the one hand, and general knowledge and technical expertise on the other.

In sum, socialism involves a transformation of the economic base and of the superstructure. The experience of such widely different countries as the USSR, Yugoslavia, China, North Korea and Cuba, indicates that the period of socialism is one of many contradictions, caused by the legacy of capitalism and the external pressure of imperialism. Thus whilst all these countries have made rapid economic development and have achieved a good measure of social equality, the development of economic and political democracy has often been curtailed. However, socialism in practice certainly provides a viable alternative to capitalism. Its historical achievement has been to provide the mass of the people with tangible improvements in their standard of living and with a comparatively greater degree of social equality. The theoretical ideal of greater economic and political democracy remains to be achieved in practice. Nevertheless, it is a democratic ideal that capitalism is structurally unable to provide. And, most importantly, socialism opens up the possibility of all-round human development that the class structure and social division of labour of capitalism prevents. It is constructing the social conditions that will enable the full development of human potential which is the ultimate goal of Marxist socialism, the aim being 'a higher form of society, a society in which the full and free development of every individual forms the ruling principle.'[56]

A THEORY OF REVOLUTION

In order to achieve this goal of human emancipation, capitalism has to be overthrown. Marx and Engels emphasised that the issue is 'not the improvement of existing society but the foundation of a new one.'[57] Thus Marxist socialists do not pose as their goal the amelioration of society within a basically capitalist framework (as do the social democrats) but rather they advocate the fundamental transformation of society. It is this transformation that constitutes a revolution, that is, an overturning of the existing economic and

political order. It is signified by the working
class taking political control of the state:

> The passing of state power from one class to
> another is the first, the principal, the basic
> sign of a revolution, both in the strictly
> scientific and in the practical, political
> meaning of that term.[58]

It is in this sense that Marxism is a theory of
revolutionary socialism, proposing the changeover
from the rule of the capitalist class to that of the
working class. Marxism identifies the source of
this changeover within the nature of capitalism
itself. Inherent in this mode of production is a
conflict of interest between the owners of the means
of production who appropriate surplus value and the
direct producers whose labour power creates that
value. The process of capitalist development itself
engenders an increasingly unified working class:

> Along with the constant decrease in the number
> of capitalist magnates, who usurp and
> monopolise all the advantages of this process
> of transformation, the mass of misery,
> oppression, slavery, degradation and
> exploitation grows; but with this there also
> grows the revolt of the working class, a class
> constantly increasing in numbers and trained,
> united and organised by the very mechanism of
> the capitalist process of production.[59]

Thus the very dynamics of capitalist accumulation
generate class conflict. The economic exploitation
of the workers can only be ended when they as a
class own the means of production. There are
therefore objective reasons why the capitalist mode
of production is unstable.

It is within this context that subjective human
activity takes place. The basic economic antagonism
of the classes is expressed in class struggles in
the work-place, in the institutions of the
superstructure, and in the domain of culture. The
capitalist class defends its own economic interests
by seeking to manage the instability and contain the
contradictions politically. In so doing it veers
between persuasion and coercion. At times it even
makes concessions, as in the granting of trade union
rights, the extension of suffrage, and the
development of social services. But whatever form

this activity takes, it is intended to prevent the working class from freeing itself from its subordination. On the other hand, the working class seeks to further its own interests in all the different levels of the social formation, economic, political and cultural. The capitalist social formation is therefore characterised by class struggles which take place continuously with varying degrees of consciousness and organisation.

The most important subjective dimension of socialist revolution is to be located in the concept of class consciousness, that is, the awareness of members of a class of their common interests and how to advance them. The process of developing class consciousness for socialism involves the growing understanding that the emancipation of the working class (and other subordinated classes) necessitates the overthrow of capitalism and the evolution of the practical commitment and ability to achieve this. The development of this consciousness is fundamentally an educational task of enabling people people to understand the nature of capitalist society and to gain the knowledge, skills and values necessary to overthrow it. Thus an important component of the struggle for socialism is the general, technical and political education of adults from the working class and its allies.

Such educational activity has to be linked to forms of organisation if it is to have an impact. Different kinds of organisation have been developed to advance the interest of subordinated classes within capitalism, such as trade unions, co-operatives, peasant leagues and so forth. The most important is the independent working class party which provides an instrument for the development of class consciousness and its organised expression as a force in society.

The ideal type of party to represent the interests of the working class has long been an issue of debate amongst Marxists, who have tended to split into advocates of a small vanguard party of special cadres (epitomised by Lenin) and advocates of a broad mass party (epitomised by Luxemburg). To some extent, the nature of the party is determined by conditions, so that in repressive conditions a cadre party which can operate clandestinely is a necessity, whereas in the more open conditions of a bourgeois democracy a mass party becomes a possibility. However, to a large extent it is also influenced by differing

conceptions of the relationship of the party to the
working class. Lenin stressed the party's role in
directing working class activity and in bringing
class consciousness to the working class 'from
outside', whereas Marx and Engels placed more
emphasis on political organisation developing
conjointly with class consciousness and on the
working class having the prime responsibility for
its own emancipation:

> When the International was formed we expressly
> formulated the battle-cry: The emancipation of
> the working classes must be conquered by the
> working classes themselves, we cannot therefore
> co-operate with people who openly state that
> the workers are too uneducated to emancipate
> themselves and must be freed from above by
> philanthropic big bourgeois and petty
> bourgeois.[60]

This is clearly a warning against the dangers of an
elite which, in trying to bring socialism 'from
above', substitutes itself for the collective action
of the working class.
However, this quotation should not be construed
as excluding a role for intellectuals in working
class organisations. In fact, within the process of
development of class consciousness there is an
important role for intellectuals who, by virtue of
their education and their distance from the
production process, are able to penetrate the
reality of capitalist society and provide a
theoretical analysis of its nature. These
theoretical insights, crystallised in Marxism, are
essential for developing the emergent political
awareness that arises spontaneously from the
individual's everyday experience of exploitation,
powerlessness and oppression in the work-place and
the community. The role of the party is to fuse
theory and the social experience of individuals into
collective action for change. Thus intellectuals
have a significant role, as Marx and Engels pointed
out earlier in the letter quoted above:

> It is an inevitable phenomenon, rooted in the
> course of development, that people from what
> hitherto has been the ruling class should also
> join the militant proletariat and supply it
> with educative elements. We clearly stated

> this in the [Communist] Manifesto. But here two points should be noted:
>
> First, in order to be of use to the proletariat movement these people must bring real educative elements into it...
>
> Secondly. If people of this kind from other classes join the proletarian movement, the first condition must be that they should not bring any remnants of bourgeois, petty-bourgeois etc prejudices with them but should whole-heartedly adopt the proletarian outlook.[61]

Socialist intellectuals (including committed adult educators) therefore have the task of introducing 'educative elements' into the struggle of subordinated classes, helping the development of class consciousness and class organisation. The essential point is that a working class party is identified by its commitment to advancing the objective interests of the proletariat, not by the social origins of its members.

The primary conflict within the capitalist social formation is between the capitalist class and the proletariat. The organisation of the working class is therefore central to the struggle for socialism and hence working class parties have a fundamental role. The exact nature of the party has to take into account the particular circumstances of its operation. Within these circumstances the party, as Miliband has argued, must solve the problem of achieving an organic unity with the working class in a way that enables it to provide leadership without becoming isolated, and that enables it to be integrated with a mass base without losing its capacity to lead.[62] The aim of the party must be to gain the support of the majority of the population for socialism. In doing so it obviously needs to form alliances with other classes and other social movements. In underdeveloped societies, for example, the need to form an alliance with the poorer peasants has long been recognised. In struggles which have an anti-imperialist dimension, other classes with a nationalist interest may enter into alliance. In the advanced capitalist countries, broad social movements (such as the feminist, anti-racist, ecological and anti-nuclear movements) also often have an anti-capitalist dimension.

The purpose of all organised political activity by the working class and its allies is to achieve state power, because the state reflects the political power of the ruling class, serving (however indirectly) to foster and legitimate capitalist accumulation. The nature of political tasks will vary according to the nature of the social formation (for example, the class structure of underdeveloped capitalism is different to that of advanced capitalism) and according to the nature of the state (for example, military dictatorship is different to parliamentary democracy). The important thing about the political tactics of socialism is that they should embrace a wide variety of different forms of struggle at the economic, political and cultural levels. The nature of these struggles will alter according to the circumstances. In certain situations, a cultural organisation may be the spark awakening class consciousness, in others an election campaign, in others industrial action, in yet others an armed struggle for land rights. Marxists must be undogmatic and take a multi-dimensional perspective of the political means for reaching the goal of socialism. The aim is to achieve the conscious support of the majority of the population for the overthrow of capitalism.

My conclusion from this brief presentation of a Marxist theory of revolution is that the development of the subjective conditions of socialist revolution has two central components - organisation and education. This conclusion is fundamental to my understanding of the role of adult education in the struggle for socialism.

ADULT EDUCATION FOR SOCIALISM

The discussion in the previous section shows that I believe adult education to have a significant role in establishing the cultural and ideological conditions for socialist revolution. I have argued that the general, technical and political education of adults from the subordinated classes within capitalism is in fact vital if significant numbers of the population (not just cadres) are going to understand the nature of capitalist society and develop the capabilities to overthrow it. Hence it is important to conceptualise adult education in capitalist social formations as a site of class struggle. The ruling class seeks to use adult

37

education as a force for reproducing the status quo, encouraging forms of adult education which serve the needs of the capitalist labour market and which legitimate the social order. On the other hand, the working class and its allies see the possibility of adult education becoming a force for social change. Two aspects of this political economy of adult education need a final clarification - the precise scope of adult education for socialism, and its institutional context.

First, what is the scope for action in adult education as part of the struggle for socialism? This question, as Young and Whitty have pointed out, is often considered in terms of the dichotomy of whether, in relation to society, education is determined or determining.[63] In one view, the nature of education totally reflects the demands of capitalism and therefore there is no scope within education for activity which will contribute to social change. In the other view, the social structure is regarded as the product of people's activity and can therefore be changed by its members, thus education which changes people's consciousness will lead to social change. It has been a pervasive dichotomy within the discussion of those seeking to change capitalism. It arose, for example, within debates among Italian socialists in the 1910s and 1920s and the significance of Gramsci's contribution (as we shall see in Chapter Two) is that he suggested how to overcome the determined position of 'economistic extremism' and the determining position of 'cultural opportunism', both of which he regarded as signs of immature thinking.[64] He himself argued for the importance of educational action linked to economic and political struggle. When a similar debate revived amongst Marxists in the 1970s it was not surprising that Gramsci's work should have been an important point of reference for those trying to go beyond the dichotomy.

There can be no doubt from the Marxist perspective I have presented in this chapter that education in the first instance is determined. Its nature is very much dependent on the conditions of the wider society and particularly the social and political inequalities arising from the economic base. Furthermore, state intervention in education is weighted towards the reproduction of the capitalist status quo. But, as I have indicated before, the contradictions of the wider society also arise within education, making it a site of class conflict. It thus becomes an area of activity through which it is possible to develop class consciousness. Hence if educational action is coupled to socialist struggles in the wider society it can be a force for social change, contributing to the subjective processes which challenge capitalism. This general argument has been well made by Frith and Corrigan in their paper 'The Politics of Education' and they conclude:

> We must take educational debates out of their exclusively educational contexts (where the bourgeoisie still set the limits of discussion), and place them in the context of organised socialist politics.[65]

It is by relating educational action to organised socialist politics that the dichotomy can be transcended.

The example of the previously mentioned '150 hours' programme in Italy in the 1970s provides an appropriate illustration - the trade unions sought to transform state provision of adult education so that it would equip the working class on a large scale with the capacity to understand and change society. My conclusion is that socialist adult educators face a configuration of limitation and possibility in their educational activities. The scope of possibility can only be enlarged by an educational practice which seeks connections with organised economic and political struggles to transform capitalist society.[66]

Related to the above points, a second issue for clarification is that of the institutional context of adult education for socialism. The question here is whether socialist adult education in capitalist society should be confined to independent organisations or whether it can also take place within state-funded programmes. This is a question which has often arisen in discussions of adult education and socialism. In Britain, for example, there was a bitter debate in the mid-1920s between the National Council of Labour Colleges (NCLC) and the Workers Educational Association (WEA) around the NCLC's charge that the WEA's receipt of state funds limited its independence. The NCLC argued that the workers must retain control of their own education and have their own educational institutions if they were to ensure a socialist adult education with a

Marxist content.

In my opinion, the question involves another false dichotomy. Clearly independent institutions which are controlled by trade unions, co-operatives, working class parties, peasant associations and so forth are vital institutions in which socialist adult education has a wide scope and in which education and organisation can be organically unified. Such autonomous institutions must provide the leading edge of socialist adult education. But the logic of my argument that state education is a site of class struggle means that efforts to practise socialist adult education within state-funded programmes are also vital. In fact, in underdeveloped capitalist countries in particular, the independent sector is often so small and insecure that action within state-funded adult education may constitute the main thrust of socialist efforts. Obviously the context of state-funded institutions poses many obstacles and limitations and confines the scope of activity. But undoubtedly space exists and must be utilised and enlarged. The important factor, as enunciated above, is that struggles within state institutions must in some way be related to the wider struggles in society and not remain isolated.

It is perhaps inevitable that the time and place for socialist adult education within capitalism will never seem exactly right. The problems, restrictions and obstacles will always loom large, maybe obscuring the inherent contradictions which undermine capitalism from within and which socialist activity seeks to exacerbate. The situation was captured by Marx in a characteristic paradox when he was recorded as having said:

> ...on the one hand a change of social circumstances was required to establish a proper system of education, on the other hand a proper system of education was required to bring about a change of social circumstances.[67]

Faced with this situation, adult educators must not be immobilised but must start from wherever they are. The question, in practical terms, is how?

The central purpose of this book is to help adult educators committed to socialism develop the educational practices which are consonant with their political commitment. This makes the unity of theory and practice a central goal and puts great importance on the need to match ends and means. Hence it incorporates the belief that the struggle against capitalism must prefigure socialism by enabling people to experience for themselves what the socialist alternative to capitalism means in practice. The essential attitudes and practices of socialism - equality, co-operation, participation, democratic control and so forth - must be embodied all anti-capitalist activity so that the social relations of the future are developed in the present. Similarly, the essential intellectual capabilities and technical skills required to take control of production processes and of the institutions of society have to be developed in the struggle against capitalism. The socialist revolution is not an event, not simply the moment of taking state power, but a long process which both precedes and follows that moment. It is not a coup d'etat by a small elite. Rather it is a process in which many people change themselves and their social relations as they act together to change society: 'In revolutionary activity the changing of oneself coincides with the changing of circumstances.'[68] Thus the principles of socialist adult education must be implemented within capitalist society, however imperfectly. It is only through such activity that the socialist culture necessary for socialist construction after the revolution can be created. This means that socialist adult educators have to develop forms of adult education which will counter the experience of capitalism and engender new ideas, skills, values and social practices (just as feminists seek to develop forms of adult education that will counter the dominance of patriarchy[69]).

In this chapter I have located adult education within its structural context in society. Also I have argued for the validity and significance of adult education's role in the struggle for socialism. The rest of the book focusses on clarifying the nature of the alternative forms of adult education practice that are required for this role to be fulfilled effectively. In order to do this, I begin with a Marxist theory of learning and in Chapter Two I draw on Marxist philosophy, social theory and psychology. This enables me in Chapter Three to formulate a set of principle which can guide a Marxist approach to adult learning. On the basis of these principles I then undertake a critique of orthodox approaches to adult learning and make an assessment of the pedagogy of Freire. In the last two chapters I consider practical examples of adult education for socialism and reach conclusions about a socialist pedagogy for adult education.

NOTES

1.  K.P.Cross, <u>Adults as Learners</u> (San Francisco: Jossey-Bass, 1982), p. 52.
2.  Advisory Council for Adult and Continuing Education, <u>Continuing Education:  From Policies to Practice</u> (Leicester: Advisory Council for Adult and Continuing Education, 1982), p. 52.
3.  B.A.P. Mahai, 'Health and nutrition education through radio study group campaigns: the Tanzanian experiences,' <u>Adult Education and Development</u> 19 (1982):136.
4.  C. da Rocha Reufels, 'Mobral:  Literacy for Brazil,' <u>Adult Education and Development</u> 20 (1983): 79.
5.  B.L. Hall,'Continuity in adult education and political struggle,' <u>Convergence</u> Vol XI, No. 1 (1978): 8-15.
6.  Ibid., p. 14.
7.  There has been a debate within North American adult education over the concept of pedagogy since 1970 when M. Knowles published his book <u>The Modern Practice of Adult Education</u> (Chicago: Association Press, 1970) with the subtitle 'Andragogy versus Pedagogy'. He proposed that andragogy was a more suitable term to denote the teaching of adults because it drew attention to the fact that 'adults are different from youth as learners' (p. 305). This proposal was subsequently challenged, for example by C.O. Houle in <u>The Design of Education</u> (San Francisco: Jossey-Bass, 1974) on the grounds that 'education is a single fundamental human process' (p. 221) and the learning of young and old have essential similarities. The present state of the debate is summarised by K.P. Cross (Ibid., pp. 222-228).
    In my view, depite the etymology of pedagogy deriving from the Greek for child, the word remains an adequate term to describe the principles and methods of teaching in general, that is, in all contexts and with all age groups.  This is consistent with my position that adult education is only part of a greater whole, there being a basic

unity in the total educational process. By implication therefore, my discussion of a socialist pedagogy in the contxt of adult education not only draws on the theory and practice of other branches of education but also, I hope, has a resonance beyond the teaching of adults.

8. H.A. Giroux, Ideology, Culture and the Process of Schooling (Sussex: Falmer Press, 1981), pp. 63-89.

9. Ibid., p. 63.

10. Ibid., p. 83.

11. M. Yarnit, 'Second chance to learn, Liverpool: class and adult education', in Adult Education for a Change. Ed. J.L. Thompson (London: Hutchinson, 1980), p. 180.

12. R.N. Berki, Socialism (London: Dent, 1975).

13. V.I. Lenin, 'Our Programme', in V.I. Lenin, Collected Works. Vol. 4. (Moscow: Progress Publishers, 1964), pp. 211-212.

14. M.W. Apple, Ed., Cultural and Economic Reproduction in Education (London: Routledge and Kegan Paul, 1982).

15. S. Frith and P. Corrigan, 'The politics of education', in Society, State and Schooling. Eds. M. Young and G. Whitty (Ringmer: Falmer Press, 1977), p. 255.

16. T.M. Norton and B. Ollman, Studies in Socialist Pedagogy (London: Monthly Review Press, 1978).

17. G. Kitching, Rethinking Socialism (London: Methuen, 1983).

18. Ibid., p. 165.

19. K. Marx, 'Preface to a Contribution to the Critique of Political Economy', in K. Marx and F. Engels, Selected Works. Vol. 1 (London: Lawrence and Wishart, 1950), p. 329.

20. S. Bowles and H. Gintis, Schooling in Capitalist America (London; Routledge and Kegan Paul, 1976).

21. See, for example, H.A. Giroux, Ibid, Chap. 3, and M.W. Apple, Ibid., pp. 7-9.

22. K. Marx and F. Engels, The German Ideology. Ed. C.J. Arthur (London; Lawrence and Wishart, 1970).

23. F. Engels, 'Socialism: Utopian and Scientific', in K.Marx and F. Engels, Selected Works. Vol. 2 (London: Lawrence and Wishart, 1950), p. 94.

24. K. Marx, Capital. Vol. 1 (Harmondsworth:

Penguin, 1976), p. 325.

25.   K. Marx,'Preface to a Contribution to the Critique of Political Economy', in K. Marx and F. Engels, Selected Works Vol. 1 (London: Lawrence and Wishart, 1950), p. 329.

26.   D.R. Gandy, Marx and History (Austin: University of Texas Press, 1979), p. 151.

27.   F. Engels, Ibid., p. 124.

28.   Marx, Capital. Vol. 1 (Harmondsworth: Penguin, 1976), pp. 915-916.

29.   K. Marx and F. Engels, The German Ideology. Ed. C.J. Arthur (London: Lawrence and Wishart, 1970), pp.46-47.

30.   F. Engels, Ibid., p. 136.

31. L. Althusser,  'Ideology and ideological state apparatuses', in L. Athusser, Lenin and Philosophy (New York: Monthly Review Press, 1971).

32.   V.I. Lenin, 'Imperialism, the Highest Stage of Capitalism', in V.I. Lenin, Collected Works. Vol. 22 (Moscow: Progress Publishers, 1964), p. 241.

33.   Relevant overviews of these concepts and debates can be found in D.R. Gandy, Ibid., and in A. Brewer, Marxist Theories of Imperialism. A Critical Survey (London: Routledge, Kegan and Paul, 1980).

34.   See R. Johnson, 'Notes on the Schooling of the English Working Class 1780-1850', in Schooling and Capitalism. Eds., R. Dale, G. Esland and M. Macdonald (London: Routledge and Kegan Paul, 1976).

35.   A. Moumouni, Education in Africa (London: Andre Deutsch, 1968), p. 24.

36.   S. Bowles and H. Gintis, Ibid.

37.   L. Weis, 'Education and the reproduction of inequality - the case of Ghana,' Comparative Education Review Vol 23, No. 1 (1979): 41-51.

38.. G. Filson and G. Green, Towards a Political Economy of Adult Education in the Third World (Toronto: International Council for Adult Education, 1980), pp. 59-60.

39.   P. Willis, Learning to Labour (Aldershot: Gower, 1977).

40.   H.A. Giroux, 'Theories of reproduction and resistance in the new sociology of education - a critical analysis', Harvard Educational Review Vol. 53, No. 3 (1983): 257-293.

41.   S. Shapin and B. Barnes, 'Science, nature and control in interpreting Mechanics Institutes', in Schooling and Capitalism. Eds., R. Dale, G.

Esland and M. Macdonald (London:  Routledge and Kegan Paul, 1976), p. 60.

42.  M. Yarnit, '150 hours: Italy's experiment in mass working class adult education', in Adult Education for a Change.  Ed. J.L. Thompson (London: Hutchinson, 1980).

43.  K. Marx, 'Critique of the Gotha Programme', in K. Marx and F. Engels, Selected Works. Vol. 2. (London:  Lawrence and Wishart, 1950) p. 30.

44.  Ibid., p. 21.

45.  F. Engels, Ibid., p. 140.

46.  See J. Myrdal, Report from a Chinese Village (London: Pan, 1975) for one account of socialist development in agriculture.

47.  P. Sketchley and F.M. Lappe, Casting New Molds (San Francisco Institute for Food and Development Policy, 1980) illustrates an attempt to develop democratic management in a steel mill in Mozambique.

48.  F. Engels, Ibid., p. 137.

49.  K. Marx, Ibid., p. 30.

50.  D. Lane, The Socialist Industrial State (London: Allen and Unwin, 1976), p. 75.

51.  Ibid., p. 24.

52.  A. Westoby, 'Education, inequality and the question of a communist "new class"', in Education and the State. Vol. 1. Eds. Dale, R. et al. (Lewes: Falmer Press, 1981).

53.  G. White, 'Revolutionary socialist development in the Third World: an overview', in Revolutionary Socialist Development in the Third World.  Eds., G. White, R. Murray and C. White. (Sussex: Wheatsheaf Books, 1983), p. 11.

54.  F. Engels, Ibid., p. 138.

55.  M.K. Whyte, 'Educational reform: China in the 1970s and Russia in the 1920s', Comparative Education Review Vol. 8. No. 1. (1974): 112-128.

56.  K. Marx, Capital. Vol. 1. (Harmondsworth: Penguin, 1976), p. 739.

57.  K. Marx and F. Engels, 'Address of the Central Committee to the Communist League', in K. Marx and F. Engels, Selected Works. Vol. 1. (London: Lawrence and Wishart, 1950) p. 102.

58.  V.I. Lenin, 'Letters on Tactics', in V.I. Lenin, Collected Works.  Vol. 25. (Moscow: Progress Publishers, 1964), p. 44.

59.  K. Marx, Ibid., p. 929.

60. K. Marx and  F. Engels, 'Circular Letter',

in K. Marx and F. Engels, <u>Selected Works</u>. Vol. 2.
(London: Lawrence and Wishart, 1950), p. 440.

61.   Ibid., p. 439.

62.   R. Miliband, <u>Marxism and Politics</u> (Oxford:
Oxford University Press, 1977).

63.   M.  Young and G.  Whitty,  Eds.,
<u>Society, State and Schooling</u> (Ringmer: Falmer Press,
1977), pp. 1-15.

64.   Q. Hoare and G.N. Smith, Eds., <u>Selections
from   the   Prison  Notebooks  of  Antonio  Gramsci</u>
(London: Lawrence and Wishart, 1971), p. xxix.

65.    S. Frith and P. Corrigan, Ibid., p. 266.

66.   See M.W. Apple, <u>Education and Power</u>
(London: Routledge and Kegan Paul, 1982), especially
in Chapter 6.

67.   Quoted in R.F. Price, <u>Marx and Education
in Russia and China</u> (London: Croom Helm, 1977). p.
69.

68.   K.  Marx and F.  Engels, <u>The German
Ideology</u>. Ed. C.J. Arthur (London:  Lawrence and
Wishart, 1970), p. 29.

69.   J.L.  Thompson,  <u>Learning Liberation</u>
(London: Croom Helm, 1983).

Chapter Two

**MARXISM AND LEARNING**

In the previous chapter I discussed the economic and
political context of adult education and I argued
that socialist adult educators require approaches
and teaching methods which are consistent with their
political philosophy. In this chapter I seek to
articulate a Marxist view of learning which will
provide the basis for a socialist pedagogy. I
therefore present an exposition of aspects of
Marxist theory relevant to human learning. There is
no ready-made Marxist theory of learning and so my
presentation is necessarily selective and
interpretative, reflecting my own position within
the Marxist tradition. This chapter is an attempt
to construct from Marxist philosophy, social theory
and psychology a coherent position on which to base
a set of principles to guide a Marxist approach to
adult education. It is a theoretical chapter and
leads on to Chapter Three which discusses the
practical significance of this theory for adult
education.
     The Marxist tradition in philosophy and other
fields is a broad and complex one, comprised of
different tendencies, some of which are in conflict.
This is to be expected in a theory which regards
contradiction as a source of development and which
is used as a guide for practical political activity
in a wide variety of contexts. It is therefore
better, in my view, to regard Marxism as a
conceptual framework of analysis rather than a
timeless dogma (which has been its fate in some
hands). In the words of Raymond Williams, Marxism
is 'active, developing, unfinished and persistently
contentious'.[1] Marx and Engels, and later writers
such as Lenin and Gramsci, have been subject to a
wide range of interpretations by writers working

within the Marxist tradition on issues of theory and political strategy.

Perhaps the most significant source of contention is to be found within the very intellectual enterprise on which Marx engaged. He attempted to synthesise aspects of the philosophical, political, and economic thought of his time into a new social theory that went beyond the separate elements from which it was built. Later interpretations have not always fully appreciated the transmutation of the original elements. The most prominent case of this is in relation to Marx's basic philosophical position. Marx sought to transcend the dichotomy between the idealist philosophy of Hegel and the materialist philosophy of Feuerbach. But subsequent writers have often emphasised idealism at the expense of materialism, or vice versa, leading to the two most contradictory tendencies within Marxism. One stresses a form of materialism which leads to a theory of economic determinism and a political position which tends to passivity because of the supposedly 'inevitable collapse of capitalism'. This tendency has been present since the late nineteenth century and developed historically within the Second International (the organisation linking socialist movements between 1889 and 1914). It is now often called 'official' Marxism and is identified with the official theoretical stand of the Soviet Union, particularly during the period of Stalin. The other tendency is a reaction against this and stresses a form of idealism which emphasises the role of human will and the power of human action. Historically, it arose in response to the political reformism of the Second International and it is associated particularly with the writings of Korsch and Lukacs in the early 1920s (and later with those of the 'Frankfurt School'). It is often called 'Hegelian' or 'humanist' Marxism and it has been an important factor in the renaissance of Marxist scholarship of the last twenty-five years.

The main debates within Marxism are usually influenced by adherence to variants of these two basic tendencies. Pareto's analogy is appropriate. He 'once likened Marx's statements to bats - you can see something in them that looks like a mouse and something that looks like a bird.'[2] Partial views see either the materialist body or the idealist wings. But in my opinion there is an authentic Marxist bat, a transcendence of this dichotomy, and my own position within the Marxist tradition seeks to avoid a one-sided emphasis on either determinism or voluntarism. The consequence of this position, as indicated in the previous chapter, is that I ascribe an important role to conscious political activity (and to adult education) as part of the subjective dimension of the struggle for socialism but I also recognise this role to be circumscribed by the objective conditions of the economic structure of society.

The conceptual framework for considering learning that is presented in this chapter is therefore a selection from a wide and diverse body of theory. It reflects my own position but I support it as strongly as possible with reference to the actual writings of Marx and Engels, whom I regard as the joint founders of Marxism.[3] In this chapter I present first a philosophical theory of knowledge (based on Marxist materialism) and secondly a sociological perspective on knowledge (based on the idea of knowledge as a social product). I then consider the contribution of Marxist psychology to the understanding of human learning.

My starting-point is a consideration of the philosophy of materialism. In the words of Engels 'The great basic question of all philosophy...is that concerning the relation of thinking and being.'[4] The answer to this question provides the foundation for a Marxist perspective on learning.

MARXIST MATERIALISM

Materialism is fundamental to Marxist philosophy and to a Marxist theory of knowledge but the exact nature of Marxist materialism needs clarification. Basically, materialism maintains that there are objects which exist independently of the mind and therefore phenomena of the human consciousness are ultimately due to material factors. While on the one hand materialism is distinct from idealist philosophy (which argues that there is a spirit which exists prior to and separate from nature), on the other hand there are different kinds of materialism. The inability to distinguish between different forms of materialism has been a source of misunderstanding and controversy within Marxism.

A common denominator of materialism is the 'realist' position that objects (reality) have an existence independent of subjects (people) and the mind reflects this external reality. But many materialists also take a 'naturalist' position and emphasise the physical nature of people, arguing that the mind itself is a product of matter. Some materialists carry this argument further and say that all the world is reducible to matter. They make no qualitative distinction between the different ways in which matter is organised (for example, between living organisms and inorganic matter) and reduce thought to physical motion (of chemicals or molecules or whatever). The differences between these forms of materialism have far-reaching ramifications and it is therefore important to see how they relate to Marxist materialism.

What, then, is the philosophical position of Marx and Engels? Its origins can be found in their analysis of the prevalent intellectual currents in Germany in the early 1840s. The predominant philosophy was that of Hegel, who believed in a spiritual absolute. He regarded existing phenomena as embodiments of a spiritual ideal. For example, he wrote that '...man's existence has its centre in his head i.e. in Reason, under whose inspiration he builds up the world of reality.'[5] In their early works Marx and Engels attacked this idealist philosophy. At first they found the weapon for their attack in Feuerbach's writing on religion.

Feuerbach had developed an approach which reversed traditional theology. He argued that god was a projection of man and not vice versa. He took the premise of logic that every proposition has a subject and a predicate and developed a critique of theology by reversing the relation of subject and predicate. Thus 'god created man' became 'man created god'. He turned philosophical attention from god to people and asserted the primacy of reality over thought, writing that 'The true relation of thought to being is this: being is the subject, thought the predicate. Thought arises from being - being does not arise from thought.'[6] Marx and Engels accepted this basic materialist approach.

Marx also identified the antecedents of their position in eighteenth century philosophy. In The Holy Family he gives an account of how French materialism developed and how it built on the work of earlier English philosophers such as Bacon, Hobbes and Locke.[7] It is important to note that here Marx criticised Hobbes, for example, for producing a mechanical 'one-sided' materialism because this indicates that he realised the limitations of previous forms of materialism. This criticism was soon extended to Feuerbach as well, in the Theses on Feuerbach[8] and The German Ideology[9].

In the Theses on Feuerbach Marx expressed in highly condensed form his criticism of Feuerbach and other materialist philosophers for failing to grasp the active nature of human thinking and thus positing a purely contemplative relation between perception and reality, subject and object. Marx advocated a 'new' materialism that would introduce a social dimension to the question of people's relationship to the material environment. This position is elaborated in The German Ideology, which shows how thought arises from an active relation to the environment, starting from the premise that 'life is not determined by consciousness but consciousness by life'.[10] Consciousness is not the product of a spiritual essence (idealism) or of biological determinism (mechanical materialism) but is a result of the social and natural conditions of life and the activity involved in changing them.

The German Ideology represents the first systematic exposition by Marx and Engels of their 'materialist conception of history' and contains the basic philosophical position that informs their subsequent work. This position goes beyond a simple dualism of nature and thought by examining the relationship between the objective natural and social environment and subjective human activity. In this relationship the role of labour (conceived as the interaction between people and nature) is central because in this activity people change nature, create social relationships, and develop ways of thinking. The development of tools and of language led to the differentiation of people from animals, people 'begin to distinguish themselves from animals as soon as they begin to produce their means of subsistence.'[11] In other words, material production provides the basis for human culture. Marx and Engels therefore reject a materialism which reduces people to passivity and equates their behaviour with that of animals. They stress that human activity - labour, or production in the broadest sense - is purposive and not merely a reflexive response to external conditions. They thus transcend a separation of nature and thought and a rigid distinction between object and subject. Engels in a late work expressed their position thus:

> Natural science,like philosophy, has hitherto entirely neglected the influence of men's activity on their thought; both know only nature on the one hand and thought on the other. But it is precisely the alteration of nature by men, not solely nature as such, which is the most essential and immediate basis of human thought, and it is in the measure that man has learned to change nature that his intelligence has increased.[12]

It is in this sense that Marxist materialism can be called dialectical because although historically nature preceded human existence, once human beings had evolved there arose a reciprocal relationship between consciousness and reality, thought and being.

It can be seen that the materialism of Marxism is not a reductionist one. While accepting the primacy of nature, it assigns human activity a distinctive role in the process of cognition. Thought originates in matter, both in the sense of being a reflection of external reality and insofar as it is produced by the neuro-physiological activity of the brain. But it is not reducible to matter, a viewpoint Marx and Engels regarded as 'vulgar' or 'mechanical' materialism because it excluded the historical and social dimension of thought. Engels posed the question 'One day we shall certainly 'reduce' thought experimentally to molecular and chemical motions in the brain; but does that exhaust the essence of thought?'[13] in order to refute it.

We can conclude by saying that Marx and Engels emphasised a materialist approach against the prevailing current of Hegelian idealism but they also criticised the materialism of Feuerbach for its reductionism and lack of social context. As Timpanaro has put it, in the expression 'historical materialism' the noun is a polemic against Hegel and the adjective a polemic against Feuerbach.[14] This position leads logically to a specific theory of knowledge. Lenin summarised the fundamental difference between materialism and idealism like this - 'Are we to proceed from things to sensation and thought? Or are we to proceed from thought and sensation to things?'[15] Marxist materialism clearly proceeds from things to thought but by being historical and dialectical it does so in a particular way. The epistemological implications of this view of thinking and being are discussed in the next section.

## THE REFLECTION THEORY OF KNOWLEDGE

The two basic trends in philosophy that Engels and Lenin identify lead to distinctively different theories of knowledge. Idealism leads to a position which regards knowledge as the creation of the mind independent of external things and which posits a priori truth. Lenin quotes a nineteenth century English scientist who wrote 'The laws of science are products of the human mind rather than factors of the external world.'[16] This is a typically idealist view because it makes the mind primary and nature secondary, and it suggests that there are innate categories of knowledge inherent in the mind. A materialist view regards knowledge differently, as a process by which thought comes to correspond more accurately with external realities. The laws of science, then, are regarded as ever-improving ways of expressing the autonomous laws which are inherent in nature. The law of gravity, for example, provides an explanation for some aspects of the physical motion which actually occurs in nature.

The natural and social world, therefore, is not a mental construct. The basic postulate of materialism that things exist independently of the mind means that the starting-point of a materialist theory of knowledge is that mental phenomena reflect external reality. As Marx put it in an afterword to Capital.Volume 1, ideas are 'nothing else than the material world reflected by the human mind and translated into forms of thought.'[17] For Marxist materialism, this process of reflection is not (as for Locke) one in which a totally passive and blank consciousness has sense-impressions imprinted upon it. In a Marxist theory of knowledge the processes of cognition are conceived as being more complex than just a mirroring of reality. The brain, the organ of thought, does not just receive sense-perceptions as images but is capable, through the medium of language, of elaborating perception as ideas, of 'translating' reflected reality into 'forms of thought'. Behaviour is not simply a question of stimulus and response. The idea of reflection in Marxism does not imply a mere mirror-image because the process of thought is seen as a product of active interaction between the mind and reality, subject and object.

It is this interaction that I referred to earlier as dialectical. I had shown how the relationship between mind and matter prior to Marx and Engels had generally been seen in one of two ways, either in a dualist perspective which regarded them as totally separate and distinct (idealism) or in a reductionist perspective which saw the mind as nothing but a form of behaviour of matter (mechanical materialism). Marx and Engels went beyond dualism and reductionism to argue for the mutual interdependence of mind and matter, a unity of opposites. It is this relationship that is called dialectical, embracing as it does ideas of reciprocity and inter-connectedness. Ruben has pointed out that this does not presuppose a symmetry between the elements - matter is primary and hence the theory is known as dialectical materialism.[18] But once that is given, then the relationship of reciprocity is important. For example, the process of cognition is influenced by the needs and interests of the subject. A starving person perceives food differently to a chef; a manager perceives the production line differently to a worker.

Lenin placed great emphasis on dialectics as distinguishing a Marxist theory of knowledge from that of other kinds of materialism 'the fundamental misfortune of which is its inability to apply dialectics to the theory of reflection, to the process and development of knowledge.'[19] Indeed it is only through a dialectical approach that a reflection theory of knowledge can encompass the role of human activity and the social dimension of knowledge. The reflection of reality is not static, and people in changing the world through their activity also change their thinking as it comes to correspond with the new situation. In Lenin's words:

> The reflection of nature in man's thought must be understood not 'lifelessly', not 'abstractly', not devoid of movement, not without contradiction, but in the eternal process of movement, the arising of contradictions and their solutions.[20]

The role of human activity - praxis - in the process of knowing is therefore very significant and I will now discuss it at length before going on to a consideration of the social nature of knowledge.

PRAXIS

The word praxis has a history in philosophy which stretches back to Aristotle. But its precise meaning has not been stable and its usage has varied with different philosophers. The question of meaning has been rendered more problematic by its usual translation in English as 'practice'. The utilitarian connotations of 'practice' simply as doing or action are unhelpful when discussing exactly what 'practice' means within the Marxist tradition. I have therefore decided to use 'praxis' to draw attention to the particular, non-mundane meaning of the concept, though I recognise that in most English translations of writers such as Marx, Lenin and Mao, the word 'practice' is used. It is important to make this point at the beginning of this section because of the significance of the concept in Marxist philosophy, in which it draws attention to the role of human activity and creativity in the processes of historical development. Indeed, for Marxist epistemology, as we have seen, the idea of praxis is central to a reflection theory of knowledge which does not reduce the individual to a passive receptor of sensory information. It is essential to the manner in which Marx went beyond previous materialist philosophy, to the extent that Gramsci, for example, thought it appropriate to describe Marxism as ' the philosophy of praxis'.[21]
But the exact extent of the significance which should be attached to praxis is the cause of much controversy, raising as it does the tension within Marxism between voluntarism and determinism, freedom and necessity, that I discussed above. To what extent is human activity conditioned by the necessities inherent in the natural and social environment? This is the key question relating to the debate over praxis.
In my opinion, praxis is an integral part of Marx's philosophy. Basically it refers to the human activity through which people shape and are shaped by the world around them. The most important form of activity is labour, in which people act upon the natural environment and create social relationships as well as objects. Praxis is a distinctively human characteristic because a person's interaction with

the natural and social environment is a conscious activity. It has purpose and intention in a way that animal behaviour lacks. As Marx put it in Capital.Volume 1:

> A spider conducts operations which resemble those of the weaver,and a bee would put many a human architect to shame by the construction of its honeycomb cells. But what distinguishes the worst architect from the best of bees is that the architect builds the cell in his mind before he constructs it in wax. At the end of every labour-process, a result emerges which had already been conceived by the worker at the beginning...[22]

The idea of praxis at the level of individual behaviour therefore conceptualises the connection between consciousness and reality, between thought and action.

The concept of praxis in Marx's writings emerges reasonably clearly, particularly in his early works. But the interpretation of its importance to Marxist philosophy as a whole is a source of debate and polemics. Some writers argue that it is the central concept, 'the key for understanding his basic outlook from his early speculations to his mature thought.'[23] These writers represent the 'humanist' interpretation of Marxism opposed to notions of determinism. On the other hand, writers such as Hoffman have argued that the work of people like Lukacs, Korsch and Sartre who stress praxis is an idealist distortion which ends up in subjectivism. Hence, far from identifying the 'authentic core' of Marxism, the 'praxis critique...represents a fundamental attack on the scientific content of Marx's writing.'[24]

The argument veers between a stress on human consciousness as simply a response to objective reality and an emphasis on human activity as the agent of social change. Ironically, it was precisely this dichotomy that Marx sought to transcend in going beyond both Hegel and Feuerbach. My own position is summarised in Marx's comment in The Eighteenth Brumaire:

> Men make their own history, but they do not make it just as they please; they do not make it under circumstances chosen by themselves, but under circumstances directly encountered,

given and transmitted from the past.[25]

This quotation clarifies the falseness of the polarity in the praxis debate. Marx states clearly that, on the one hand, human beings are active agents within the processes of history, they 'make their own history'. Their ideas, their actions, their subjective behaviour, create and produce history. But he also states emphatically that, on the other hand, this activity does not take place in the abstract. Prior to activity, there are objectively existing circumstances (i.e. the realities of the natural and social environment) which provide the context in which activity occurs. The material existence of these circumstances has primacy and they pre-date the human activity of a given time, thereby determining what is possible. It is within these limits of necessity that there is scope for human creativity and freedom. Natural laws can be grasped and used, so that, for example, through the understanding of gravity flight becomes possible. Similarly, social reality can be comprehended and changed by social action. In sum, the primacy of material life, of objective reality separate from human consciousness, does not preclude the role of the subjective from human activity. The concept of praxis is based on this conclusion. It has important implications for the theory of knowledge.

As we saw above, the epistemology of idealist philosophy argues that knowledge is created abstractly by consciousness, the product of a spiritual essence. In contrast, mechanistic materialist philosophy regarded knowledge simply as the mental reproduction of objects as ideas. Marx accepted the basic premise of the materialist position, namely that there is a world external to people which is only knowable through the senses, but he criticised the idea of sense perception as being a passive contemplative process:

> The chief defect of all hitherto existing materialism (that of Feuerbach included) is that the thing, reality, sensuousness is conceived only in the form of the object of contemplation, but not as sensuous human activity, practice, nor subjectively.[26]

Here in the Theses on Feuerbach Marx established praxis as an important component of his epistemology. Lenin re-emphasised this when presenting more systematically a reflection theory of knowledge in <u>Materialism and Empirio-Criticism</u>[27] and the <u>Philosophical Notebooks</u>[28]. Here he argued that the process of cognition is not passive, not 'a dead mirroring'.[29] Rather it involves an active relationship to the external world in which perception, abstraction and the testing of knowledge in practice play a part. Thus praxis is a distinctive element in Marxist approaches to learning - in Lenin's words 'The standpoint...of practice should be first and fundamental in the theory of knowledge.'[30]

There are three aspects of the relationship of knowledge and praxis to be taken into account. First, praxis is the source of knowledge. The starting point of mental activity is the data of the external world perceived by the physical senses. As people enter into an active relationship with their environment they obtain perceptions. Their activity in production furnishes information particularly about the natural environment, and their social relationships provide information about society. Of course, not all information individuals get is through direct experience, they also learn indirectly from books, tradition and so forth. But what is indirect for them is ultimately based on the direct experience of someone else. Thus people's interaction with their environment is the basis of knowledge.

The initial results of perception are fragmentary and unsystematic but the brain is able to analyse, interpret and synthesise perceptual knowledge and make a transition via generalisation of experience to abstraction and theory, which expresses the connections between isolated phenomena and suggests explanations for events. These judgements represent a qualitative change in knowledge, a movement from sensation to conceptualisation.

The second aspect is that praxis provides the criterion for measuring the correctness of knowledge, for testing the extent to which ideas correspond to reality. New activity becomes the way in which the truth and meaningfulness of judgements and theories can be discovered. As Marx wrote in another of the <u>Theses on Feuerbach</u>:

> The question whether objective truth can be attributed to human thinking is not a question

> of theory but is a practical question. Man
> must prove the truth i.e. the reality and
> power, the this-sidedness of his thinking in
> practice.[31]

However, such truth is incomplete and partial, and
knowledge is continually growing and developing.
Praxis is the process by which knowledge is deepened
and moves from less complete to more complete, from
error to truth.

Thirdly, praxis is the objective of knowledge.
Learning is not a contemplative process but one
which provides the basis for new activity.
Judgement and theory become the guides to re-
entering into the cycle of relating to the external
environment. Activity is therefore conscious and
purposive. Learning is thus a dialectical process
of perception, abstract thought and active
application. The clearest expression of this
Marxist approach to praxis and knowledge is to be
found in Mao's short essay On Practice. He provides
a succinct summary of the role of praxis in human
learning:

> Practice, knowledge, again practice and again
> knowledge. This form repeats itself in endless
> cycles, and with each cycle the content of
> practice and knowledge rises to a higher level.
> Such is the whole of the dialectical
> materialist theory of knowledge, and such is
> the dialectical theory of the unity of knowing
> and doing.[32]

The process of learning, the development of
knowledge, is a spiral which unifies theory and
practice.


THE SOCIAL NATURE OF CONSCIOUSNESS AND KNOWLEDGE

The concept of praxis draws attention to the
significance of human activity and intentionality in
acquiring knowledge, showing that it is not a
passive process but one in which the individual is
actively involved. This process is dialectical
because while knowledge arises from material
reality, the understanding of this reality is shaped
by ideas. It is in this sense that a Marxist theory
of knowledge is antagonistic to empiricist theories
which deny the role of ideas and theory (indeed, of

language itself) in apprehending the random data presented by the world. What must be emphasised at this stage is that the notion of activity is in no way individualist. As people interact with nature in order to meet their physical needs, they necessarily enter into social relationships. This means that for Marx and Engels, praxis is essentially social:

> Not only is the material of my activity given to me as a social product (as is even the language in which the thinker is active): my own existence is social activity...[33]

The implications of this stress on the social character of existence are two-fold. First, Marx and Engels regard the formation of the individual's cognitive powers - consciousness - as having an indispensable social dimension. Secondly, they locate the production of knowledge within its social context. I will discuss each of these ideas in turn.

Marx and Engels developed their conception of human nature in their early works such as <u>Economic and Philosophic Manuscripts of 1844</u> and <u>The German Ideology</u>. Here they recognised the fact that people's biological structure generates certain needs (for example, for food and sex) which make people similar at one level to animals. But they argued that human being have uniqueness as a species as a result of their ability to undertake purposive action to meet these needs. People cannot be reduced simply to biological activities because in satisfying their needs they create social relationships which are distinctively human. It is the interaction between people and their physical environment in a way which necessitates social relationships that Marx and Engels call 'production' (and which is characterised by 'labour'). They maintain that the central element in the creation of human psychological attributes is production (which Marx in this quotation calls 'industry'):

> We see how the history of industry and the established objective existence of industry are the open book of man's essential powers, the perceptibly existing human psychology.[34]

It is the activity of labour that develops a specifically <u>human</u> nature. This nature cannot be conceived abstractly but must be located in the society of which the individual is the product: 'the human essence is no abstraction inherent in each single individual. In its reality it is the ensemble of the social relations.'[35] They therefore consider that the senses - the organs of consciousness - are a social product: 'The forming of the five senses is a labour of the entire history of the world down to the present.'[36]

The fundamental point made in these early writings is that there is not an unchanging human nature and a fixed set of human capabilities: 'all history is nothing but the continuing transformation of human nature.'[37] Thus although people inherit a biological structure, its capabilities are only realised in their actual social existence. The important factor is therefore the way in which class relationships affect social existence. The mature Marx in Capital.Volume 1 makes it clear that it is the particular mode of production which shapes ways of being and thinking, referring to 'human nature as historically modified in each epoch'.[38] In a well-known chapter in this volume on 'The Division of Labour and Manufacture'[39] he shows the psychological effects of the transition from handicraft production to manufacture, as the skilled worker increasingly became more and more specialised in a narrow area of work and eventually became just a machine attendant. The worker became 'one-sided', a 'crippled monstrosity', who developed 'one faculty at the expense of all others'. Indeed the worker became separated from knowledge and science and merely a 'fragment of himself', an automaton. In the next chapter on 'Machinery and Large-scale Industry'[40], Marx shows how the development of the factory on a wide scale increased this deskilling process and reduced further the intellectual content of work. In a very vivid way, Marx demonstrates how the human potentiality of the worker is stifled by capitalism. Capital.Volume 1 provides a concrete example of the Marxian thesis that the ultimate determinant of consciousness is the mode of production.

The ideas outlined by Marx and Engels in their early works were taken up again thirty years later by Engels in an unfinished document entitled The Part Played by Labour in the Transition from Ape to Man. In this piece Engels reiterates the idea that people become distinguished from animals through labour, which is 'the prime basic condition for all human existence, and this to such an extent that, in a sense, we have to say that labour created man himself.'[41] He traces the development of humankind with reference to the increasing dexterity and skill of the hand, which is 'not only the organ of labour, it is also the product of labour' because its abilities were developed by undertaking increasingly complicated operations. Essentially, labour is different from animal activity by being characterised by the use of tools. The development of labour brought people together in joint activities and thus necessitated the development of language. In turn, labour and speech provided the stimuli for the development of the brain and of the sense organs and an 'increasing clarity of consciousness, power of abstraction and of judgement'. This account is a classic statement of the Marxian analysis of the development of people's capacity to know. It suggests that while the human brain is the product of an evolutionary process which differentiated people from animals (for example, the brain size is much larger), once this had occurred the significant thing is the use to which the brain has been put, ideas being continually extended in the process of controlling nature and organising society. These suggestions are at once materialist and historical in their explanation of consciousness.

To summarise, we can say that Marx and Engels conceptualise the psychology of the individual in social and historical terms and situate it within a given mode of production:

> What they are, therefore, coincides with their production, both with what they produce and with how they produce. The nature of individuals thus depends on the material conditions determining their production.[42]

As we have seen, by 'material conditions' they mean not only the natural world but also the social relations of production. It is these social relations which provide the context in which consciousness appropriates reality, in which knowledge arises as a social product. Ideas and beliefs are produced within a specific socio-economic situation, they do not have a total autonomy of their own. In the final analysis knowledge is dependent on people's involvement in production and class struggle. It is the relationship between knowledge and the social structure that I now wish to discuss.

The most important source for considering this question is in Marx's succinct formulation of the relationship in his Preface to a Contribution to the Critique of Political Economy:

> The sum total of these relations of production constitutes the economic structure of society, the real basis, on which arises a legal and political superstructure and to which correspond definite forms of social consciousness. The mode of production of material life conditions the social, political and intellectual life process in general.[43]

We saw in Chapter One how this concept of the base and superstructure leads logically to a position which locates educational activities in an economic and political context. Here we can see how even knowledge - part of the 'intellectual life process' - is conditioned by the economic basis of society.

Raymond Williams has presented a very subtle discussion of the issue.[44] In much Marxist analysis the base and superstructure have come to be regarded as elements which are separate spatially and temporally, and the base has been accorded a simplistically deterministic role. Williams shows how Marx's metaphor is really one of inter-connected parts of a totality (which is the social formation). Also he points out that the 'economic basis' in fact includes the social relations of production and therefore cannot be considered in a reductionist sense as consisting of purely economic forces. He argues convincingly that while intellectual production does correspond in general terms to a given mode of production (such as feudalism or capitalism), the 'dynamic and internally contradictory' nature of a mode of production (for example, as manifested in class struggle) means that ideas do have a certain autonomy. Furthermore, as Engels emphasised in his letter to Bloch, ideas can have a reciprocal action of the base.[45] Williams thus provides a welcome corrective to trends within Marxism which reduce all ideas to a 'preceding and controlling' economic situation. He shows how Marx's concept of determination is a complex one and while it is fundamental to Marxism that the material conditions set limits and exert pressures on the production of ideas, equally this does not entail a

predetermined and predictable outcome. Marx, in
typical fashion, suggests there is dialectical unity
of determinism and interaction, and only in the
final instance are intellectual production and
knowledge dependent on the economic basis of
society.

Because the basis includes the social relations
of production, it is the class structure which is of
special significance for a Marxist sociology of
knowledge. The general conclusion of Marx and
Engels' argument on knowledge as a social product is
that in class society the very nature of ideas has
an inescapable class dimension. The knowledge held
by the individual has a class character:

> Upon the different forms of property, upon the
> social conditions of existence, rises an entire
> superstructure of distinct and peculiarly
> formed sentiments, illusions, modes of thought
> and views of life. The entire class creates
> and forms them out of its material foundations
> and out of the corresponding social relations.
> The single individual derives...them through
> traditions and upbringing...[46]

The analysis of the class nature of knowledge has
been elaborated in Marxist theories of ideology,
which discuss the products of consciousness, that
is, ideas, values, theories, beliefs, and their
expression in language.


IDEOLOGY

Ideology is a widely used term both inside and
outside Marxism and one which is susceptible to a
wide variety of meanings. The problem of definition
arises in the work of Marx and Engels itself as they
did not produce a systematic theory of ideology and
left ambiguities which have led to divergent
emphases by their interpreters. However, I think it
is possible to give a coherent view of the concept
which indicates its complexity but which is not
contradictory.

At a surface level of meaning, ideology is
simply a system of ideas and beliefs. It is evident
from the preceding section that a Marxist viewpoint
will relate ideology to the social structure and
indicate a correlation between different classes and
the ideas they hold. On the whole, different

classes will view the world differently according to their distinct experience of life. One dimension of the concept of ideology therefore takes account of the way in which a class holds ideas which arise spontaneously from its way of life. But in a class-divided society, the ruling class has the economic and political power to consciously disseminate ideas which will justify and support its own class interests. A second dimension of ideology thus recognises that a system of ideas comes to predominate in society because it is used by the ruling class to serve its interests. Both these processes of idea formation contain pressures which lead to false ideas and distorted views of reality, so that a third dimension of ideology refers to a system of illusory ideas. I will now elaborate these three dimensions of meaning.

The first dimension was introduced in the previous section where we saw that 'the mode of production of material life conditions...the intellectual life process'. People's ideas, beliefs and values arise from their position within the social relations of production. Althusser in his essay 'Ideology and Ideological State Apparatuses'[47] has been particularly helpful in re-emphasising the view of Marx and Engels that ideology is not simply an abstract system of thought but what he calls a 'lived relation'. People's everyday experience of life is shaped by their position in the division of labour and this social experience is the source of their view of the world. The submission to the foreman's orders, the comradeship of the shopfloor, the monotony of the production line are aspects of daily life which influence a worker's thinking, just as the issuing of instructions, the camaraderie of the boardroom, and desk-work in the office influence that of a manager. People internalise a system of ideas and beliefs - an ideology - which is created by the conditions of their social existence, particularly in the labour process but also in other spheres of their life, such as the community they live in. The fundamental point here is that the ideology has an experiential element. It is produced and re-produced by the routines and relationships of daily life as experienced from a particular class position.[48] Marx illustrates this very clearly in the chapter entitled 'Simple Reproduction' in Capital. Volume 1, which he closes with the comment:

The capitalist process of production,

> therefore, seen as a total, connected process,
> i.e. a process of reproduction, produces not
> only commodities, not only surplus value, but
> it also produces and reproduces the capital-
> relation itself; on the one hand the
> capitalist, and on the other the wage-
> labourer.[49]

In this process at the heart of the capitalist mode
of production, its requirements come to be
conceptualised by both worker and capitalist as
'natural'. Wage labour, the market, property,
contracts and so on seem normal and immutable, the
way things have always been, the way things should
be. Habits, customs, practices, assumptions, even
language itself, all embody unexamined ideas that in
fact reflect the mode of production. As Mepham has
pointed out, 'it is not the bourgeois class which is
the source of ideology, but bourgeois society
itself.'[50]

However, if the ruling class is not the source
of ideology, it certainly plays a significant role
in the articulation and dissemination of ideas which
serve its class interests. The origins of this
second dimension of the concept are to be found in
The German Ideology:

> The ideas of the ruling class are in every
> epoch the ruling ideas i.e. the class which is
> the ruling material force of society is at the
> same time the ruling intellectual force. The
> class which has the means of material
> production at its disposal, has control at the
> same time over the means of mental production,
> so that thereby, generally speaking, the ideas
> of those who lack the means of mental
> production are subject to it.[51]

Here Marx and Engels make it clear that a system of
ideas and beliefs can be used to advance class
interests in the conflict between classes. Indeed,
in the Preface to a Contribution of a Critique of
Political Economy referred to earlier, Marx writes
about 'the legal, political, aesthetic, or
philosophic - in short, the ideological forms in
which people become conscious of this conflict and
fight it out.'[52] The sphere of ideas is therefore
one characterised by class struggle. The ruling
class seeks to justify its economic position by
saturating society with ideas which support the

status quo.

It undertakes this, in the words of the earlier quotation, through its 'control...over the means of mental production'. It uses a number of social institutions to propagate and reinforce the ideology which serves its interests. Althusser suggests that these institutions (which he terms 'ideological state apparatuses') include the churches, education, the family, the legal system, trade unions, the media and cultural organisations.[53] He attaches greatest importance to educational institutions, which he regards as being central to capitalism in the way the Catholic church was to feudalism. The knowledge and attitudes transmitted by education are characterised by their selectivity and their role in serving bourgeois society.

However, because the sphere of ideology is one of class struggle, the ruling ideas are never totally dominant. A given social formation may include a complex of modes of production and consequently a variety of ideologies despite the general dominance of bourgeois thought. (For example, pre-capitalist ways of thinking are still generated in some rural areas of the Third World which have not yet been fully incorporated into capitalism.) Also, the life experience of the subordinated classes can in various ways contradict the dominant ideology and weaken its effect. The contradictions at the heart of the capitalist mode of production have ideological impact – for example, a sense of working class solidarity and shared exploitation can create a dissonance with the prevailing ethos of individualism and private profit. There is therefore an unevenness in the extent to which the 'ruling ideas' in fact dominate the consciousness of subordinated classes. Certainly, these classes are not completely trapped within ruling class ideology and the possibility of oppositional ideas and beliefs always exists. Actually the very notion of 'ideas which serve class interests' means that there are ideas which serve the interests of the dominated classes. For instance, the role of Protestantism in the struggle of the emergent bourgeoisie against the dominant feudal aristocracy in various parts of Europe is well known. The concept of 'ruling ideas' therefore does not suggest that individuals can achieve no critical distance from them. All it does imply is that the sheer social weight of these ideas transmitted through a variety of institutions makes a critical position difficult to achieve. (The perceived potential of Marxism, for example, to serve the interests of the working class has been matched historically by the ferocity of bourgeois reaction.) To summarise, we can say that ideology implies a degree of conscious imposition of particular ideas by the ruling class but that this is never totally effective.

So far I have suggested that ideologies are acquired through lived experience and through the theoretical propagation of certain social institutions. The third dimension of the concept considers how these processes lead to a system of ideas and beliefs which are illusory. This is a basically pejorative sense of ideology and the term was used frequently by Marx and Engels in this way to suggest 'inverted thought' - in a famous phrase they said 'in all ideology men and their circumstances appear upside down'.[54] The question is, how does this distortion of ideas come about? The answer has two aspects, as suggested by the two dimensions I have just considered.

The first aspect is that the reality which people experience is in itself in certain senses false. Just as the earth appears flat in ordinary experience, so facets of society are often mystified. This idea runs throughout the work of Marx and Engels. In the 1840s Marx wrote about 'alienation', a process by which the products of people's activity begin to have a life of their own and appear as autonomous and objective. He started with an analysis of religion as alienation (whereby people create the idea of god to explain certain natural phenomena and then come to regard god as a separate existence, an alien being to be worshipped) and in the Economic and Philosophic Manuscripts of 1844 extended the idea to labour. This alienation profoundly affects the workers, firstly by distorting their relationship to their products - 'the object which labour produces - labour's product - confronts it as something alien, as a power independent of the producer.'[55] For example, the workers' labour produces large houses for the rich capitalists while they remain in hovels, yet the connection between the two is not grasped. Secondly, it distorts the relationship of the workers to their work, so that work is not self-directed but a form of 'forced labour'. Thirdly, it leads to estranged relationships with other people. Finally, it results in 'self-estrangement'. In this way people's activity, the products of their labour, and their social relationships, all come to appear as alien, the result of an external force.

Later, in Capital.Volume 1, this idea is to be found in the concept of 'fetishism', a process by which objects come to appear as though they have natural properties when in fact they are produced by people and their social relations. For example, value appears as an inherent property of a commodity rather than as a social relationship of exchange. Thus people conceive social relationships to be objects and they reify social reality - 'Their own movement within society has for them the form of a movement made by things, and these things, far from being under their control, in fact control them.'[56] This kind of 'fetishised' thinking is generated by the capitalist mode of production in particular (for example, the exploitation of labour is more transparent in the feudal mode of production).

It is through these processes of alienation and fetishism that the products of human activity (whether intellectual, political or economic) come to appear as external objects on which people are dependent. Religion, the state, money, are all experienced as somehow independent of human creation. Thus the very reality which people experience can be understood as a distortion, a product of self-estrangement. The surface of phenomena therefore conceals the essential nature of society. In Ruben's apt comparison, just as 'in the natural world, the sun appears to move round the earth, but the matter is essentially the reverse',[57] so in social reality there is a gap between appearance and essence. But the surface reality cannot be regarded as simply imaginary, it is what people actually experience.

Distorted thought therefore arises from the experience of a reality which in certain respects conceals the essence of social relationships. For example, the apparent 'freedom' of the worker to sell labour power in fact conceals the lack of alternative means of subsistence. But there is also a systematic distortion arising from how the ruling class supports its interests in a way which serves to conceal the inequality and exploitation inherent in its domination of society. Ideology in this sense refers to claims made on behalf of one part of society which appear to be beneficial to all. In class society, the minority ruling class represents its partial interests as being universal interests.

The virtue of private enterprise, for instance, is held to advance the general good when in fact it benefits the few at the expense of the many. Thus the 'ruling ideas' can be seen to offer a partial representation of reality and to the extent that they are imposed on and internalised by the dominated classes, these classes come to have a false understanding of society, accepting ruling class interests as their own.

The third dimension of ideology therefore highlights how ideas form a barrier to understanding the real nature of class society. The task facing dominated classes is how to penetrate beyond surface appearances. Marx's own intellectual work was a deliberate effort to unmask ruling ideas and reveal the essence of the capitalist mode of production, an attack on 'vulgar' political economy which provided only superficial explanations. He wrote that 'The forms of appearance are reproduced directly and spontaneously, as current and usual modes of thought; the essential relation must first be discovered by science.'[58] The role of Marxist social science is to show the real relationships behind surface appearances.

But Marx was clear that intellectual activity alone was insufficient - 'Ideas can never lead beyond an old world order but only beyond the ideas of the old world order.'[59] The important conclusion to be drawn is that ideas cannot be countered only at the level of rational argument. The explicit effort to debate and rebuff the ideas of the ruling class as disseminated in institutions such as education and the media is important but will be of limited effect. This is because people's ideas and beliefs also arise out of their lived experience. Hence action is needed to change the economic and political structures within which people experience their lives and which act to reproduce their ways of thinking. In Marx's words, the communist workers of Manchester or Lyons:

> ...do not believe that by 'pure thinking' they will be able to argue away their industrial masters and their own practical debasement. They are most painfully aware of the differences between being and thinking, between consciousness and life. They know that property, capital, money, wage-labour and the like are no ideal figments of the brain but very practical, very objective products of

their self-estrangement and that therefore they
must be abolished in a practical, objective way
for man to become man not only in thinking, in
consciousness, but in mass being, in life.[60]

The struggle for socialism must therefore involve
not only the criticism of ideas, values and beliefs
held and disseminated by the ruling class but also
action to change the social circumstances which
continually regenerate these ideas in the experience
of the dominated classes. In other words, to change
their consciousness, people need both different
ideas and different experience. The implications
of this are explored in the next section on the
concept of hegemony.


## HEGEMONY

We saw in the previous section how the concept
of ideology elucidates the way in which the social
structure influences the development of knowledge in
the individual. In particular, it contributes to an
understanding of how people come to hold ideas and
values which, seen objectively, are not in the
interests of themselves and their class. The
central aim of socialist education is to change this
consciousness, so that people become critically
aware of their situation and see their potential for
changing it.
The concept of hegemony helps to clarify the
processes involved in the formation and change of
consciousness. It deepens the theory of ideology by
extending the analysis of how consciousness is not
only the product of ideas but also the result of a
total social process. The concept was elaborated by
Gramsci and it constitutes his distinctive
contribution to Marxist theory.
Gramsci developed the idea in his Prison
Notebooks.[59] The fragmentary nature of these notes
means that there is no coherently expressed theory
of hegemony. Indeed, as Anderson has pointed out,
there are ambiguities in Gramsci's presentation.[60]
However, I think that it is possible to synthesise
the main elements of the idea as it emerges from use
in different contexts. Its origins lie in Gramsci's
attempt to analyse the defeat of the workers'
movement that took place in the period after 1918 in
such Western European countries as Germany and
Italy. He sought to explain  the phenomenon of

reformism, the willing incorporation of the working class within capitalist society even in a period of economic crisis. Deterministic Marxist views concluded that the contradictions in economic life - the experience of exploitation - should lead inevitably to working class militancy. Consequently, they found it difficult to explain the political passivity of the workers, and the resilience of capitalism. Gramsci, on the other hand, took as his starting point the position that the realm of ideas, values and beliefs has a certain autonomy from the economic structure of society. His theory of hegemony was concerned with analysing the ideological and cultural level of society, in order to provide a guide to political action to overthrow capitalism.

He examined how the ruling class exerts its control in society. Most Marxist analysis focusses on the state as the main organ of class rule and one which is based on coercion - 'a special organisation of force...an organisation of violence for the suppression of some class' in the words of Lenin.[63] Gramsci studied how control takes place not only through force but also through other means, such as ideology, philosophy, culture and psychological processes. He therefore distinguished between what he called 'political society' (where power is 'domination' based on force) and 'civil society' (where power is 'direction' based on consent). 'Political society' comprises of public institutions such as the courts, the army and the government bureaucracy, whereas 'civil society' includes organisations such as the church, the media, trade unions and educational institutions. He made this distinction for analytical purposes, recognising that in reality the two spheres interpenetrate.[64] But he did so in order to explore more thoroughly the way in which dominated classes internalise the world-view of the ruling class so that they give consent to being subordinated, often for long periods. In such periods of stability, class control is exercised primarily in 'civil society' through a diversity of processes which constitute what Gramsci called hegemony. It has been defined clearly by Gwyn Williams:

> ...an order in which a certain way of life and
> thought is dominant, in which one concept of
> reality is diffused throughout society in all
> its institutional and private manifestations,

informing with its spirit all taste, morality,
customs, religions, particularly in their
intellectual and moral connotations.[65]

An example of a hegemonic institution often cited by
Gramsci is the Catholic church in Italy, which
diffuses its world view widely in different aspects
of life, largely through its priests, who exercise
intellectual and moral leadership.
    Gramsci stressed the extent to which the
ideology of the dominant class can permeate people's
lives so that it becomes 'common sense', an
unconscious and uncritical way of seeing the 'world'.
Thus domination and subordination are created and
reproduced not only by the imposition of
systematised ideas but also by institutional
behaviour, social relationships, and daily
experience. The central question is therefore how
to change this consciousness, how to engender an
alternative view of the world that will free the
workers and other dominated classes from their
hegemonic subordination and enable them to work for
the overthrow of capitalism and the development of
socialism. This can be answered within the context
of Gramsci's thinking on revolution.
    He saw revolution (i.e. the achievement of
state power by the working class and its allies) as
a process, rather than a single event, in which the
coercive power of the ruling class is defeated.
Like Lenin, he saw a role for ideological
preparation and political organisation as well as
armed action. Conceptually, he distinguished the
two elements of revolution as the 'war of position'
(i.e. the gradual development of the consciousness
and political strength of the working class in order
to put the ruling class under siege) and the 'war of
movement' (i.e. the decisive moment of direct
confrontation). Anderson has noted that if these
elements are separated, it could lead to either
reformism or adventurism.[66] But Gramsci saw them as
interdependent, though in his writing he focussed on
the 'war of position' because of a tendency for
Marxists to neglect this element. The 'war of
position' is based on undermining the legitimacy of
the ruling class by creating a counter-hegemony so
that 'the great masses have become detached from
their traditional ideologies and no longer believe
what they used to believe previously'[67] and thus the
ruling class can no longer rule by consensus but
only by coercion.

For Gramsci, then, revolution is a popular
movement in which the masses take an active role
because they have developed a consciousness which
challenges the existing economic and political
order. It involves a fundamental change in the
consciousness of the masses. In emphasising this he
develops an idea to be found in The German Ideology:

> Both for the production on a mass scale of this
> communist consciousness, and for the success of
> the cause itself, the alteration of men on a
> mass scale is necessary, an alteration which
> can only take place in a practical movement, a
> revolution: this revolution is necessary,
> therefore, not only because the ruling class
> cannot be overthrown in any other way, but also
> because the class overthrowing it can only in a
> revolution succeed in ridding itself of all the
> muck of ages and become fitted to found society
> anew.[68]

It is important to note that Gramsci, while
focussing on the cultural and ideological level,
does not abstract hegemony from the economic basis
of society - 'for though hegemony is ethical-
political, it must also be economic, must
necessarily be based on the decisive function
exercised by the leading group [i.e. class] in the
decisive nucleus of economic activity.'[69] His
emphasis on consciousness and on the need for
ideological struggle in no way negates the need for
economic and political action. Indeed he shows that
when the ruling class cannot achieve control through
consent, it turns to coercion so that for a
revolution to succeed there will need to be counter-
coercion. What he is arguing is that there is need
for different forms of struggle and not simply a
concern for the direct seizure of state power. For
revolution to be more than a coup, the mass of
people will need to be involved in undermining
capitalism in all its manifestations. As a process
requiring conscious activity, the revolution needs
intellectual and cultural preparation. In arguing
this he deliberately elaborated an idea of Marx:

> The weapon of criticism certainly cannot
> replace the criticism of weapons; material
> force must be overthrown by material force; but
> theory, too, becomes a material force once it
> seizes the masses.[70]

Gramsci did not ignore the need for force ('the war of movement') but he gave attention to the comparatively neglected area of how 'theory'(i.e. counter-hegemony) can seize the masses.

His conclusion is that for a revolution to take place (especially in advanced capitalist countries where bourgeois ideology is deeply rooted in the everyday experience of the people) a necessary condition is that the working class begins to develop its own hegemony. For Gramsci, the ruling ideology is never totally hegemonic and uncontested. Ideology is therefore an area of struggle in which conscious action can be taken. The dominated classes need their own view of the world, their own set of values, in a word their own culture, in order to erode continuing capitalist rule by consent. And once having achieved state power, they will need to spread their own hegemony throughout society to develop an authentic socialist culture. (There are clear parallels here with the ideas of Lenin and Mao on a cultural revolution being necessary for the consolidation of the socialist mode of production.) The role of 'intellectuals' in society is therefore of great significance.

Gramsci identified the 'intellectuals' as the main agents for diffusing different conceptions of the world in society. He used the term in a broad sense to refer to all those with a 'technical' or 'directive' function in society. The group therefore includes people such as bureaucrats, managers, politicians and teachers, and not just scholars as in other uses of the word. In fact he distinguishes between 'traditional' intellectuals (such as scholars and artists) and 'organic' intellectuals, who are more closely related to the class structure of society. Capitalism, for example, generates the kind of intellectuals necessary to organise and control production and run society:

> Every social group [i.e. class], coming in to
> existence on the original terrain of an
> essential function in the world of economic
> production, creates together with itself,
> organically, one or more strata of intellectuals
> which give it homogeneity and an awareness of
> its own function not only in the economic but
> also in the social and political fields. The
> capitalist entrepreneur creates alongside
> himself the industrial technician, the

specialist in political economy, the organisers
of a new culture, of a new legal system etc.[71]

Gramsci thought that the 'traditional' intellectuals
did not always have identical class interests
to those of the ruling class, whereas 'organic'
intellectuals closely represent class interests.
    He was concerned that the working class usually
relied on 'traditional' intellectuals for
leadership. He regarded this as a problem because
such leaders were inherently unreliable, as
ultimately their class interests did not coincide
with those of the working class. A central task of
political activity (in factory councils, the party,
newspapers and so forth) was therefore to provide
the education which could develop a new group of
'organic' intellectuals of the working class, with
the technical ability to control production and the
political awareness to organise society. It is
these 'organic' intellectuals who must develop a
counter-hegemony that contributes both to the
overthrow of capitalism and the construction of
socialism. In this way the working class becomes
the instrument of its own emancipation and not
simply an inert mass under elite direction.
    Gramsci's theory of hegemony is of central
importance to my consideration of adult education
and socialism because of its focus on how capitalist
ideology is internalised and how it can be
counteracted. In the final analysis, these are
epistemological questions:

        ...the theoretical-practical principle of
        hegemony has also epistemological
        significance...The realisation of a hegemonic
        apparatus, in so far as it creates a new
        ideological terrain, determines a reform of
        consciousness and of methods of knowledge: it
        is a fact of knowledge, a philosophical fact.[72]


THE CONTRIBUTION OF PSYCHOLOGY

    So far in this chapter I have considered
aspects of Marxist philosophy and social theory
which I think throw light on the processes of
learning. In this section I look at work in the
field of psychology which has been informed by
similar considerations in order to see what

contribution Marxist psychology makes to the understanding of learning.

The only extensive development of a Marxist psychology, as we shall see below, has been in the Soviet Union. It is interesting to note, for example, that there is no well-developed and distinctive Chinese tradition.[73] Prior to the Chinese revolution of 1949, Western theories dominated and in the period after 1949 Soviet approaches prevailed until the Sino-Soviet split of 1962. Only briefly in the early 1960s was there an attempt to develop a psychology based on indigenous traditions and Mao Tse Tung's philosophy as well as Marxism-Leninism. During the Cultural Revolution of 1966-1976 psychology was proscribed and it was not officially rehabilitated until 1979. It is therefore not possible to identify a specifically Chinese approach in psychology, as one might in economics or medicine for example.

It is also noticeable that in Western Europe and North America, very little psychology has been based on Marxist principles, although the writers of the 'Frankfurt School' have tried to synthesise Marx and Freud, and a 'radical' trend which emerged in the 1970s showed Marxist influences.[74] However, the main focus of this radicalism has been the field of mental illness and psychiatry, so that Brown's book Towards a Marxist Psychology has a narrower compass than the title suggests.[75] The only sustained Marxist work in the broad field of psychology has been that undertaken in the critique of intelligence testing, for example by Simon.[76] But compared to the renaissance of Marxist scholarship in other areas in the last twenty years (such as sociology, economics, political theory, literary criticism) there has been surprisingly little activity in psychology. Thus although writers on topics like 'alienation'[77] and Marx's concept of 'human nature'[78] signpost possibilities for Marxist psychological theory, very little has emerged, with the major exception of Seve's Man in Marxist Theory and the Psychology of Personality.[79] Riegel's theory of 'dialectical psychology' acknowledges the influence of Soviet work and uses some terminology and concepts which have a Marxist flavour. But he specifically distances himself from Marxist dialectics with its emphasis on materialism, writing that 'dialectical theory neither needs to be materialistic or idealistic; it can encompass a manifold of different conceptions.'[80] My conclusion, therefore, is that the Marxist standpoint in Western psychology is very undeveloped. Where it does occur it is primarily theoretical and there seems to be no experimental work based on Marxist principles. In particular, I have come across very little on the psychology of learning.[81]

However, if there is very little to be found in Chinese or Western psychology, the Soviet tradition proves to be exceptionally rich. Since the revolution of 1917, there has been a consistent effort in the Soviet Union to develop a psychology which is consonant with Marxist theory. One major influence on this development has been not only the works of Marx and Engels, but also the interpretations provided by Lenin, especially in his book Materialism and Empirio-Criticism which dealt directly with issues of psychology. The other significant influence has been the work on physiology by Pavlov, which Lenin granted special state support in 1921. Pavlov was not a Marxist but his scientific work was regarded as congruent with Marxist principles, demonstrating the materialist basis of psychological behaviour.

During the 1920s and early 1930s a lot of theoretical discussion took place in the attempt to evolve the principles which should define a Marxist psychology. This debate involved criticism of Western psychology (for example, behaviourism and Gestalt psychology) as well as of the empirical work being undertaken in the Soviet Union itself (for example, psychometric testing, which was discontinued in 1936). After this period of intense controversy a basic consensus was reached on the essential principles which should provide the theoretical framework for psychological research. Ananiev in an important lecture in 1947 entitled 'The Achievements of Soviet Psychology'[82] summarised these principles. Simon has presented Ananiev's summary as follows:

> (1)     Mental processes are properties of the brain, the highest form of organic matter; it is impossible to understand mental processes without knowledge of the cerebral processes which underlie mental activity.
>
> (2)     Consciousness is a reflection of the objective world; in explaining mental processes, therefore, the psychologist must

take into account the objective reality they reflect.

(3)    Neural-mental activity is conditioned by the form of existence of living beings and changes with changes in the form of existence. Therefore, the development of human consciousness is conditioned by changes in the material life of society and must be studied, not in the abstract, but in a concrete historical setting.

(4)    Consciousness is formed in practical activity and revealed in the course of activity. Changes in the content and form of practical activity can, therefore, influence changes in the organisation and development of mental processes.[83]

It can be seen from these four points that each refers to a key theme, namely, materialism, reflection, social consciousness, and activity. These are, as one would expect, themes that have arisen earlier in the chapter in my own analysis of Marxist theory. For Ananiev, they are the guiding principles of Soviet psychology.

The other foundation of this psychology was provided by Pavlov, who died in 1936.  Although his work was criticised in the Soviet Union during the late 1920s because it was thought to be reductionist, when its full complexity was realised it was given great prominence because it provided an understanding of the physical basis of psychological processes, the 'material substratum' of mental activity.  During the 1950s Pavlov's theories had a predominant role and although today they are of less central concern, they remain basic to Soviet approaches.  It is therefore worth giving a brief account of some aspects of his theory, not least because of the faulty impressions often held in the West, where there is ignorance of his work with human beings for example.  Macleish has pointed out that 'American behaviourism grossly misunderstood and misrepresented the work of Pavlov'[84] yet it is this view that tends to prevail.

Pavlov's work spread over a period of forty years and therefore encompassed a number of internal developments.  But at its centre was the study of physiology and the nature of conditional reflexes. These new reflexes are established on the basis of

79

inborn reflexes as a result of the organism's interaction with the environment. In his famous experiment, the dog's inborn reflex of salivating in response to food provided the basis for the conditional reflex of salivating in response to a bell. The conditional reflex is a learned one and is a temporary and variable connection between the organism and the environment, which can disappear if not reinforced, whereas unconditional reflexes are inherited and relatively constant. (The word conditional is usually rendered in English as 'conditioned' although this has erroneously deterministic connotations because in fact Pavlov stressed the dependence of the reflex on changing circumstances and conditions.[85])

Pavlov sought to explain behaviour in terms of physiological analysis of the central nervous system. His theories presented an explanation of the biochemical basis of mental activity based on an enormous amount of experimental data (primarily from animals but also from people). He developed a conception of the organism as an integral whole, denying a mind/body dualism. He regarded the organism as a single system in continuous interaction with the changing environment, this state of dynamic equilibrium being maintained particularly through learned (i.e. conditional) responses to the surroundings. The nature of response activity he explained in the theory of reflexes, which argues that these processes of the central nervous system are regulated by the cortex, and which proposes laws of cerebral functioning.

He did not deny the existence of inner mental activity but believed that it could be explained as an aspect of higher nervous activity, whose highest level he took to be speech:

> In the animal, reality is signalised almost exclusively by stimulations and the traces they leave in the cerebral hemisphere...This is the first system of signals of reality common to man and animals. But speech constitutes a second signalling system of reality which is peculiarly ours, being the signal of the first signals...It is precisely speech that has made us human.[86]

Pavlov therefore suggested that human behaviour is not only a response to direct signals from the environment but also a response to speech, signals of these first signals. He wrote that the word 'is just as real a conditioned stimulus as any other' and with language 'a new principle of nervous activity is introduced, the abstraction and generalisation of innumerable signals' and it is this new system which makes the second signalling system 'the highest regulator of human behaviour'.[87]

His theory of human behaviour is thus one of considerable complexity, its significance lying in its empirical demonstration of the material, biochemical basis of mental processes in the functioning of the central nervous system and the brain. (As Lenin recognised, this clarifies the physical dimension of the reflection theory of knowledge.) Finally, it should be noted that Pavlov regarded the higher nervous system as extremely 'plastic', that is, capable of being moulded or shaped. He therefore stressed the capacity for learning inherent in the human organism. He wrote:

> The chief, strongest, and most permanent impression we get from the study of higher nervous activity by our methods, is the extraordinary plasticity of this activity, and its immense potentialities; nothing is immobile or intractable, and everything may be always achieved, changed for the better, provided only that the proper conditions are created.[88]

Obviously, this has profound significance for education, whose task is to provide the best conditions for learning to take place.

The philosophical principles of Marxism and the scientific theory of Pavlov provide the foundations of Soviet psychology. This is the background to the work that has been undertaken on the psychology of human learning. A major review entitled 'The Psychology of Learning, 1900-1960' by Bogioavlenski and Menshinskaia indicates the scope of the experimental work that has been done in this area, very often in educational situations in close conjunction with teachers.[89] (Unfortunately, no reference is made to adult learning and development, but I think that the approach is of general relevance.)

The study of learning starts from the point that the physiological structure only provides the necessary internal capability for the development of psychological abilities. All normal children therefore have innate intellectual potential but

mental abilities themselves are not intrinsic and
are in fact formed by the conditions of life, which
are social.  In particular, these abilities are
formed through activity, through interaction with
the changing natural and social environment.  In
this, education has a central role, not because it
somehow 'draws out' what is already in the child,
but because it contributes to the  actual process of
mental development.  Thus the planned learning that
takes place in education must be based on an
understanding of developmental stages and of how
children move from one stage to another, so that
activity is organised in such a way as to create
these transitions.  Intelligence is regarded not as
an inherent and fixed quality, but as one which
develops within changing conditions of activity.
Learning difficulties arise when one stage has not
been satisfactorily mastered, thus blocking
capability at a higher stage. But these problems can
be solved by remedial action.  Special attention has
been given to the role of language in mental
development, for example its part in complex forms
of thought (the movement from perception to
abstract, conceptual thinking) and in making
learning a conscious activity.  Within this general
framework, Bogoiavlenski and Menchinskaia report on
a wide variety of experimental studies into such
topics as understanding, abstraction  and
generalisation, habit formation, attention, the role
of activity in learning and individual differences.

Perhaps the most influential work on human
learning has been that of Vygotsky (who died in
1934) and his two colleagues Luria and Leontiev, who
were active from the 1920s into the 1970s.  In
effect, their work elaborated the area of higher
psychological functioning and the role of
language which Pavlov had referred to but had not
studied in detail.  Their studies were based on the
premise that the existence of different levels of
human behaviour means that while there is a
biochemical basis to all behaviour, higher forms of
activity are also characterised by their social
nature. Psychology, therefore, should be consistent
with physiology but not solely dependent on it.
Their work explored how natural processes (such as
sensory activity) 'became intertwined with
culturally determined processes to produce the
psychological functions of the adult.'[90]  Thus
whereas biological evolution over millions of years
led to the emergence of homo sapiens, the historical

development of the human race has not involved any physical changes to the structure of the brain but only the socio-cultural development of different forms of consciousness.

Luria records how he and Vygotsky and Leontiev worked together from the late 1920s on key areas of cognitive psychology (- perception, memory, problem-solving and motor activity -) trying to devise experiments within a Marxist framework.[91] With their students, they built up a large body of empirical data on many of these topics. The context of their work was set by Vygotsky's 'instrumental' 'cultural' and 'historical' approach, which was derived from the Marxist conception of labour, tools and language (which Engels had sketched in The Part Played by Labour in the Transition from Ape to Man). 'Instrumental' referred to the use of mental tools which mean that complex psychological functions have a mediated nature. They are not a simple stimulus-response process but incorporate auxiliary stimuli produced by people themselves (i.e. sign systems, such as language) so that responses to stimuli are indirect. The 'cultural' aspect signified the fact that these systems are socially produced. The mental tools which people use in interacting with the environment and in directing their own thought processes are of social origin. The 'historical' element stressed that these tools (such as writing and number systems) are a product of social history so that language, for example, puts individuals into contact with a vast reservoir of knowledge beyond their own direct experience.

The titles of Vygotsky's major English-translation works - Thought and Language and Mind in Society - neatly encapsulate his central concerns. In his own words:

> Thought and language, which reflect reality in a way different from that of perception, are the key to the nature of human consciousness.[92]

and

> The internalisation of socially rooted and historically developed activities is the distinguishing feature of human psychology, the basis of the qualitative leap from animal to human psychology.[93]

His experimental programme with concept development in children and the neuropsychology of mental abnormalities has been expanded in many directions by his colleagues and their students, whose work, in a variety of ways, developed his perspective on human behaviour and significantly influenced Soviet learning theory.

I therefore think it is fitting at this stage to present a rather detailed account of Luria's book Cognitive Development. Its Cultural and Social Foundations because it provides a unique study of an aspect of adult psychology based on Marxist principles and empirical research.[94] The study was undertaken in 1931-1932 but was not published as a book in the Soviet Union until 1974, subsequently being published in English in 1976. It seems to have been totally ignored in the English-language literature on adult education and yet in my opinion it is a book of great significance.

Luria carried out the research in remote areas of Central Asia at a time when the socialist transformation of society was just beginning to reach the villages and mountain pastureland. It was a time when the feudal mode of production, buttressed by Islam, was being transformed by the collectivisation of agriculture, the development of industry, and the introduction of education, including courses for adults. It therefore presented an excellent opportunity to study empirically the proposition that consciousness changes when the fundamental forms of social life change. The basis of the research was the Marxist position proposed by Vygotsky:

> ...the view that higher cognitive activities remain socio-historical in nature, and that the structure of mental activity - not just the content but also the general forms basic to all cognitive processes - change in the course of historical development.[95]

The period of rapid socio-economic transformation provided the chance to observe a moment when the processes of history had been telescoped and the mode of production was changing and engendering a new class structure and culture.

Luria and his associates conducted fieldwork with five groups of people: a) illiterate Muslim women from remote villages who wore the veil and could not meet men from outside the family circle; b) illiterate peasant men in remote areas who were still engaged in individual production; c) women with no formal education who had attended short courses on teaching infants; d) active collective farm workers and young people who had attended short adult education courses; and e) women teacher trainees with a few years' schooling. Groups (a) and (b) were living in as yet untransformed socio-economic conditions, while the other groups had begun to experience the changes involved in the transition to a socialist economy. Through interviews, the research team studied six aspects of cognitive activity - perception, generalisation and abstraction, logical assumptions, reasoning and problem-solving, imaginative processes, and self-analysis and self-awareness. The research methodology and the data from the investigations are carefully reported.

The research bears out the proposition that cognitive activity is of social origin. For example, people share the same physiological basis for colour perception but there are cultural differences in the classification of colours, deriving from the practical interests of the group. It is the same with the perception of shapes. Luria found that the first two groups used different systems of classification to those whose conditions of life had begun to change. In broad terms, the perception of the first two groups was under the influence of object-oriented practical activities (geometrical figures being identified as a tent or milk bucket, for example), while the other groups tended to use abstract concepts (such as square, circle, triangle). This basic divide in cognitive activity according to life experience ran throughout the results of the research, though of course some individuals, particularly the women of group (c), were at a transitional stage. The main difference was between situational (practical) and abstract (theoretical) thinking, a difference arising from the conditions of daily life, not innate capacity.

Luria argues that there are no invariable categories of thought but that mental processes are social products, so that the mode of thought changes when the conditions of people's lives change. The most important changes in life-experience that he identifies are the changes in the nature of work (i.e. the labour process) and the acquisition of literacy. The new collective work relations require

joint planning, evaluation of progress, discussion
of personal efficiency and so on. The significance
of literacy lies not simply in the acquisition of
knowledge but 'in the creation of new motives and
formal modes of discursive verbal and logical
thinking divorced from immediate practical
experience.'[96] The social changes mean that the
mental world of people not only has a new content
but also takes on 'new forms of activity and new
structures of cognitive functioning.'[97] He
therefore concludes from the study that people's
consciousness is changed by the process of social
transformation and the part they play in it -'The
basic theses of Marxism regarding the historical
nature of human mental life are thus revealed in
their concrete forms.'[98] It can be seen from my
description that the book is a very important
example of a Marxist psychology of adult cognitive
development.

However, I have not come across Soviet studies
on adult learning and development in relation to
adult education. But insofar as some conclusions
might be drawn from the general approach of Soviet
psychology to learning, I think the following points
may be applicable to adult learning. First, the
'plasticity' of the central nervous system suggests
a strong capacity for learning that continues into
adulthood. The work of Luria and Leontiev in
rehabilitating the war-injured in the early 1940s
provides a graphic illustration of this capacity.
Secondly, the idea that intelligence is not an
inherent, static capability but is formed during
personal development also suports a positive
approach to the learning capacity of adults. The
concept that the unsuccesful mastery of lower stages
inhibits higher stages of learning may contribute to
an understanding of adults who performed poorly in
school, enabling diagnosis and remediation.
Leontiev reports an interesting experiment with
supposedly tone-deaf children to develop their sense
of pitch, a 'missing link' which had made them
perform poorly in singing classes.[99] Thirdly, the
role of activity in learning suggests a certain kind
of approach to the teaching-learning process.
Leontiev and Rozonava report on experiments into
memorisation with adults which indicate the
important role of activity (goals, intention,
orientation) in memory.[100] Fourthly, the importance
of conscious learning is suggested by Pavlov's
discovery that 'connections can only be formed and

retained to those stimuli which possess a definite meaning and importance for the organism.'[101] Finally, Luria's fieldwork in Central Asia strongly emphasises the social context of the formation of consciousness, the effect of life-experience on how adults think. It also indicates that the 'mental tool' of literacy may be very decisive in the shaping of consciousness. Overall, it does not seem unreasonable to extend the optimism of Soviet psychology about the role of education in child development to an optimism about its role in adult development.

CONCLUSION

In this chapter I have presented aspects of Marxist philosophy, social theory and psychology in order to construct a coherent view of how Marxist theory approaches the question of learning. To do so, I began with a philosophical theory of knowledge which centred on the concepts of dialectical materialism, reflection and praxis. The main conclusion here was that human activity within a given natural and social environment forms the concrete historical context of consciousness. Processes of thought and the development of knowledge are the result of this interaction between the mind and objective reality. It is in purposively acting upon the environment in order to change it that people change their thinking and behaviour. Hence praxis is the key to learning, which can be considered as a dialectical process of perception, abstract thought and practical application, a constant cycle of practice-theory-practice.

Secondly, I considered consciousness and knowledge from a sociological perspective. The formation of the individual's cognitive powers was portrayed as an essentially social process in which labour has a central part. Thus the mode of production is significant because it shapes ways of being and thinking. The Marxist view of the individual's psychology is one which conceptualises its development within a social context. Knowledge is regarded as a social product conditioned by the economic basis of society and ideas, values, theories, beliefs and so forth therefore have a class nature. This view is elaborated in the concepts of ideology and hegemony which theorise the relationship between thought and the social structure. The conclusion was reached that for people to change their thinking, they need both different ideas and different experience, re-emphasising the theoretical-practical nature of learning.

Finally, I examined the contribution of Marxist psychology, which has been derived from Marxist theoretical principles, such as materialism and activity. I have drawn conclusions in the previous section but it is worth emphasising the sharp differentiation made between animal and human learning, a distinction made primarily on the basis of the social and historical origins of cognitive processes and the unique role of language.[102]

This chapter contained the elements of a Marxist theory of learning. Although it is not a theory of adult learning as such, I think it provides the basis for drawing up principles with which to guide a Marxist approach to adult education, a task I turn to next.

NOTES

1. R. Williams, Marxism and Literature (Oxford: Oxford University Press, 1977), p. 4.
2. J.V. Femia, Gramsci's Political Thought (Oxford: Clarendon Press, 1981), p. 57.
3. The relationship of the ideas of Marx and Engels is the source of much debate, the 'humanist' Marxists arguing that Engels laid the foundations for the mechanistic and positivistic Marxism that eventually led to Stalinist totalitarianism. See, for instance, N. Levine's book The Tragic Deception: Marx Contra Engels (Oxford; Clio Books, 1975) which counterposes the two with the aim of distinguishing Engels' 'distortions' from 'core Marxism'. In my view these differences have been exaggerated and there is a basic affinity between the two. See, for example, D.D. Weiss 'The Philosophy of Engels Vindicated,' Monthly Review Vol, 28, No 8 (1977): 15-30.
4. F. Engels, 'Ludwig Feuerbach and the end of classical German philosophy', in K. Marx and F. Engels, Selected Works. Vol. 2 (London: Lawrence and Wishart, 1950), p. 344.
5. Quoted in D. Mclellan, Marx before Marxism (London: Macmillan, 1980), p. 17.
6. Quoted in D. Mclellan, The Young Hegelians and Karl Marx (London: Macmillan, 1969), p. 99.

7.    K. Marx and E. Engels, <u>The Holy Family</u> (London: Lawrence and Wishart, 1976), pp. 154-166.

8.    K. Marx, 'Theses on Feuerbach', in K. Marx and F. Engels, <u>The German Ideology</u>. Ed., C.J. Arthur (London: Lawrence and Wishart, 1970).

9.    K. Marx and F. Engels, <u>The German Ideology</u>. Ed., C.J. Arthur (London: Lawrence and Wishart, 1970).

10.    Ibid., p. 47.

11.    Ibid., p. 42.

12.    F. Engels, <u>Dialectics of Nature</u> (Moscow: Progress Publisher, 1976), p. 231.

13.    Ibid., p. 248.

14.    S. Timpanaro, <u>On Materialism</u> (London: New Left Books, 1975), p. 40.

15.    V.I. Lenin, <u>Materialism and Empirio-Criticism</u> (Peking: Foreign Languages Press, 1976), p. 34.

16.    Ibid., p. 184.

17.    K. Marx, <u>Capital</u>.Vol. 1. (Harmondsworth: Penguin, 1976), p. 102.

18.    D-H. Ruben, <u>Marxism and Materialism</u> (Sussex: Harvester Press, 1977), p. 118.

19.    V.I. Lenin, 'Philosophical Notebooks, in V.I. Lenin, <u>Collected Works</u>. Vol. 38. (Moscow: Progress Publishers, 1972), p. 362.    26.

20.    Ibid., p. 195.

21.    A. Gramsci, <u>Prison Notebooks</u>, Eds., Q. Hoare and G.N. Smith (London: Lawrence and Wishart), p. 381.

22.    K. Marx, <u>Capital</u>. Vol. 1. (Harmondsworth: Penguin, 1976), p. 284.

23.    R.J. Bernstein, <u>Praxis and Action</u> (Philadelphia: University of Philadelphia Press, 1971), p. xi.

24.    J. Hoffman, <u>Marxism and the Theory of Praxis</u> (London: Lawrence and Wishart, 1975), p. 156.

25.    K. Marx, 'The Eighteenth Brumaire of Louis Bonaparte', in K. Marx and F. Engels, <u>Selected Works</u>. Vol. 1. (London: Lawrence and Wishart, 1950), p. 225.

26.    K. Marx, 'Theses on Feuerbach', in K. Marx and F. Engels, <u>The German Ideology</u>. Ed. C.J. Arthur (London: Lawrence and Wishart, 1970), p. 121.

27.    V.I. Lenin, <u>Materialism and Empirio-Criticism</u> (Peking: Foreign Languages Press, 1976)

28.    V.I. Lenin, 'Philosophical Notebooks', in V.I. Lenin, <u>Collected Works</u>. Vol. 38. (Moscow: Progress Publishers, 1972).

29.    Ibid., p. 372.

30. V. I. Lenin, Materialism and Empirio-Criticism (Peking: Foreign Languages Press, 1976), p. 155.

31. K. Marx, Ibid., p. 121.

32. Mao Tse Tung, 'On Practice', in Mao Tse Tung, Selected Readings (Peking: Foreign Languages Press, 1971), p. 82.

33. K. Marx, Economic and Philosophic Manuscripts of 1844 (Moscow: Progress Publishers, 1977), p. 99.

34. Ibid., p. 104.

35. K. Marx, 'Theses on Feuerbach', in K. Marx and F. Engels, The German Ideology. Ed., C.J. Arthur (London:Lawrence and Wishart, 1970), p. 122.

36. K. Marx, Economic and Philosophic Manuscripts of 1844 (Moscow: Progress Publishers, 1977), p. 103.

37. K. Marx, The Poverty of Philosophy (Moscow: Progress Publishers, 1975), p. 135.

38 K. Marx, Capital. Vol. 1. (Harmondsworth: Penguin, 1976), p.759.

39. Ibid., pp. 455-491.

40. Ibid., pp. 492-639.

41. F. Engels, 'The part played by labour in the transition from ape to man', in K. Marx and F. Engels, Selected Works. Vol. 1. (London: Lawrence and Wishart, 1950), p. 74.

42. K. Marx and F. Engels, Ibid., p. 42.

43. K. Marx, 'Preface to a Contribution to the Critique of Political Economy', in K. Marx and F. Engels, Selected Works. Vol. 2. (London: Lawrence and Wishart, 1950).

44. R. Williams, Ibid., pp. 75-94.

45. F. Engels, 'Engels to J. Bloch', in K. Marx and F. Engels, Selected Works. Vol. 2. (London: Lawrence and Wishart, 1950).

46. K. Marx, 'The Eighteenth Brumaire of Louis Bonaparte', in K. Marx and F. Engels, Selected Works. Vol. 1. (London: Lawrence and Wishart, 1950), p. 247.

47. L. Althusser, 'Ideology and ideological state apparatuses', in L. Althusser, Lenin and Philosophy (New York: Monthly Review Press, 1971).

48. It is worth pointing out that while Marxism accords pre-eminence to relations of class, it also recognises that bodies of ideas and values can be shared by other groups in society, such as those defined by gender or race.

49. K. Marx, Capital. Vol. 1. (Harmondworth: Penguin, 1976), p. 724.

50.   J. Mepham, 'The theory of ideology in Capital' Radical Philosophy 2 (1972): 12-19.
51.   K. Marx and F. Engels, The German Ideology. Ed., C.J. Arthur (London: Lawrence and Wishart, 1970), p. 64.
52.   K. Marx, 'Preface to a Contribution to the Critique of Political Economy', in K. Marx and F. Engels, Selected Works. Vol. 1. (London: Lawrence and Wishart, 1950), p. 329.
53.   L. Althusser, Ibid.
54.   K. Marx and F. Engels, Ibid., p. 47.
55. K. Marx, Economic and Philosophic Manuscripts of 1844 (Moscow: Progress Publishers, 1977), p. 25.
56. K. Marx, Capital.Vol. 1. (Harmondsworth: Penguin, 1976), pp. 167-168.
57.   D-H. Ruben, Ibid., p. 127.
58.   K. Marx, Ibid., p. 682.
59. K.   Marx, Economic and Philosophic Manuscripts of 1844 (Moscow: Progress Publishers, 1977), p. 148.
60.   Ibid., pp. 66-67.
61.   A. Gramsci, Ibid.
62. P.   Anderson, 'The antimonies of Antonio Gramsci,' New Left Review Vol. 100 (1977): 5-80.
63.   V.I. Lenin, 'The State and Revolution', in V.I. Lenin, Collected Works. Vol. 25 (Moscow: Progress Publishers, 1964), p. 402.
64.   A. Gramsci, Ibid., p. 160.
65. G.A.   Williams, 'The concept of 'egemonia' in the thought of Antonio Gramsci: some notes on interpretation,' Journal of the History of Ideas (1960): 587.
66.   P. Anderson, Ibid.
67.   A. Gramsci, Ibid., p. 276.
68.   K. Marx and F. Engels, Ibid., pp. 94-95.
69.   A. Gramsci, Ibid., p. 161.
70.   K. Marx, Critique of Hegel's Philosophy of Right. Ed., J. O'Malley (Cambridge: Cambridge University Press, 1970), p. 137.
71.   A. Gramsci, Ibid., p. 57.
72.   Ibid., p. 57.
73.   L.B. Brown, Psychology in Contemporary China (Oxford: Pergamon Press, 1981).
74.   See, for example, P. Brown, Ed., Radical Psychology (London: Tavistock, 1973) and N. Heather, Ibid.
75.   P. Brown, Towards a Marxist Psychology (New York: Harper Colophon, 1974).
76. B. Simon, Intelligence, Psychology and

Education (London: Lawrence and Wishart, 1978).
77. B. Ollman, Alienation (Cambridge: Cambridge University Press, 1971).
78. N. Geras, Marx and Human Nature (London: New Left Books, 1983).
79. L. Seve, Man in Marxist Theory and the Psychology of Personality (Sussex: Harvester Press, 1978).
80. K.F. Riegel, Foundations of Dialectical Psychology (New York: Academic Press, 1979), p. 16.
81. A significant exception is the article by G.S. Coles, 'Adult illiteracy and learning theory: a study of cognition activity,' Science and Society Vol. XLVII No. 4. (1983-84): 451-482.
82. Referred to in J. Macleish, Soviet Psychology (London: Methuen, 1975), p. 169.
83. B. Simon, Ed., Psychology in the Soviet Union (London: Routledge and Kegan Paul, 1957), p. 8.
84. J. Macleish, Ibid., p. 119.
85. B. Simon, Ibid., p. 12.
86. Quoted in J. Macleish, Ibid., p. 119.
87. Quoted in B. Simon, Ibid., p. 116.
88. Quoted in B. Simon , Intelligence, Psychology and Education (London: Lawrence and Wishart, 1978), p. 135.
89. D.N. Bogioavlenski and N.A. Menshinskaia, 'The psychology of learning, 1900-1960', in Educational Psychology in the USSR, Eds., B. Simon and J. Simon (London: Routledge and Kegan Paul, 1963).
90. A.R. Luria, The Making of Mind (Cambridge: Harvard University Press, 1979), p. 43.
91. A.R. Luria, Ibid.
92. L.S. Vygotsky, Thought and Language (New York: Wiley, 1962), p. 153.
93. L.S. Vygotksy, Mind in Society (Cambridge: Harvard University Press, 1978), p. 57.
94. A.R. Luria, Cognitive Development. Its Cultural and Social Foundations (Cambridge: Harvard University Press, 1976).
95. Ibid., p. 8.
96. Ibid., p. 133.
97. Ibid., p. 163.
98. Ibid., p. 164.
99. A.N. Leontiev, 'The nature and formation of human psychic properties', in B. Simon, Ed., Psychology in the Soviet Union (London: Routledge and Kegan Paul, 1957), pp. 228-230.
100. A.N. Leontiev and T.V. Rozanava, 'The

formation of associative connections: an experimental investigation', in Psychology in the Soviet Union, Ed., B. Simon, (London: Routledge and Kegan Paul, 1957).

101. B. Simon, Ed., Psychology in the Soviet Union (London: Routledge and Kegan Paul, 1957), p. 25.

102. This view is well summarised in A.R. Luria, Language and Cognition (New York: Wiley, 1981), Chapter 1.

Chapter Three

## PRINCIPLES OF A MARXIST APPROACH TO ADULT EDUCATION

Educational practices are significantly influenced
by ideas about human psychology and how people
learn.   These ideas may be unsystematic or even
unformulated, but they influence the educator's
choice in doing things one way rather than another.
The authoritarian teacher, for instance, is acting
on certain presuppositions about people and the
learning process.   In my opinion, many adult
educators actually operate without a coherent
approach to learning and teaching, not least because
of the relative paucity of studies relating to the
psychology of adult learning.   (By contrast, the
teachers of children have the benefit of a variety
of learning theories from which to choose and their
application in teaching methods has been spelt out.)
When adult educators do consciously refer to a body
of psychological theory, they tend to be eclectic.
I think that this is a particularly serious problem
for those who are involved in adult education with
the purpose of advancing socialist goals.   This is
because a dissonance can arise between their
political theory and their adult education practice,
thus inhibiting the attainment of the  very goals
which they are aiming at.   The purpose of this book,
as elaborated in Chapter One, is to point towards a
way of harmonising theory and practice.
     In order to do this I have presented in the
previous chapter an analysis of Marxist philosophy,
social theory, and psychology so that I can propose
a coherent set of principles on which to base a
Marxist approach to adult education.   I now wish to
formulate the principles which I think arise from
Marxist theory.   Some elements of these principles
are compatible with other theories, but taken
together I think the principles represent a

94

distinctively Marxist position.   They are as
follows:

### PRINCIPLE ONE

Marxist materialism is dialectical and
historical.   It posits the existence of a
reality independent of the mind and rebuts the
notion of innate ideas and a priori truths.   It
regards mind as a form of matter but it does
not consider that mental activity can be
reduced to material processes.   Hence although
human beings have a biological structure which
shares many characteristics with animals, human
mental behaviour is different, being
distinguished by its social and cultural
nature.

### PRINCIPLE TWO

The neuro-physiological structure of human
beings is very plastic and people therefore
have an immense capacity for learning.
Intelligence is not a static, innate
characteristic but is developed during the
individual's experience of life.

### PRINCIPLE THREE

Human cognitive activity is basically a
reflection of external reality.   This process
of reflection is not one of simple stimulus and
response because it is mediated by mental
tools, especially language, which is a
distinguishing feature of the human species.
Language enables the transition from perception
to conceptual thinking.   Other significant
mental tools are writing and number systems.

### PRINCIPLE FOUR

Human nature develops in the process of
interaction with the environment.   Activity
upon the natural surroundings also creates
social relationships.   This process, conceived
in the broadest sense as production, is
characterised by labour.   The mode of
production and its accompanying social
relationships are the context in which
consciousness is formed.

PRINCIPLE FIVE

Consciousness includes the individual's cognitive powers of perception, attention, memory, understanding, problem-solving and so on. Cognitive behaviour is shaped by the conditions of life because consciousness has a social nature. Changes in these conditions (particularly the mode of production) can therefore change not only what people think but also the ways in which they think, that is, both the content and the form of thought.

PRINCIPLE SIX

The specific determinant of consciousness is praxis, or activity. Human activity involves purpose and intention, and knowledge arises and deepens within a continuous process of activity, conceptualisation, and renewed activity. Praxis takes place within situations transmitted from the past but can change these situations and create new ones. Thus people are the conscious agents of social change within the constraints of historically constructed objective conditions. All praxis is essentially social.

PRINCIPLE SEVEN

Knowledge is a social product and the knowledge held by individuals is influenced by the class structure of society. Ideas and beliefs - ideology - arise out of people's daily experience (especially of production and of class struggle) and from the propagation of particular views by the ruling class. Hence individuals of the dominated classes often hold ideas and values which are contrary to their own class interests.

PRINCIPLE EIGHT

The processes of hegemony enable the ruling class to exert a dominant influence over the ideas of other classes. To challenge ruling class hegemony, it is necessary to unmask ruling ideas so that people can penetrate surface appearances and see the reality beneath. This is both an intellectual and a practical task, because the transformation of consciousness requires both a change in ideas and a change in the conditions which produce these ideas. The indispensable theoretical guide for this task is provided by Marxism.

PRINCIPLE NINE

Socialist revolution requires the development of a counter-hegemony by the working class and its allies. This is a process involving mass activity in cultural and ideological struggles which are linked to and support the organisations (particularly working class parties) involved in the struggle for economic and political power. In this process, intellectuals have an educational role to play by helping the dominated classes to develop the intellectual capabilities, technical expertise and political awareness necessary to create a new society.

These nine principles provide a guide to action for socialist adult educators. At this point I will provide a preliminary sketch of the implications for adult education practices of the nine principles formulated above. This sketch will be given more detail and depth in the subsequent chapters, which analyse orthodox approaches and the pedagogy of Freire, and which consider socialist pedagogy and adult education.

It is my view that every adult education practice is the consequence (often unwitting) of a certain philosophical position. My first principle therefore makes explicit in a general way the theoretical postulates which underlie a Marxist approach to adult learning. It thus provides the philosophical foundation for the other eight principles. But these tenets of dialectical and historical materialism also provide the criteria for assessing the theoretical bases of different approaches. For example, linear programmed learning kits based on Skinner's behaviourist psychology ultimately derive from a position of materialist reductionism that is open to criticism from a Marxist perspective. The principle thus provides a reference-point for critique, suggesting forms of adult education which should be avoided.

The second principle emphasises the adult's ability to learn. It encourages a highly positive approach by the adult educator towards the task of helping adults to learn. Obviously, it counters common-sense ideas about people being 'too old to learn' and the attitudes contained in the saying 'you can't teach an old dog new tricks'. Indeed it also opposes psychological theories which regard cognitive development as ending in childhood, arguing for the developmental nature of adulthood and a persisting capacity for learning. (There are parallels here with Allman's recent advocacy of a developmental psychology of adulthood.[1])

Similarly, it questions the ideas about intelligence as a genetic endowment which have become deeply rooted in educational thinking. The work of Burt in the 1920s propounded a theory of intelligence as an inborn intellectual ability which is relatively fixed and which can be measured objectively. The theory regarded intelligence as remaining static:

> 'This intelligence quotient', wrote R.B. Cattell...in a well-known textbook A Guide to Mental Testing (1936), 'remains constant for any given individual both during childhood and in adult life.'[2]

Since the 1930s, this view has been pervasive in educational circles, with IQ tests being used to stream children and justify divisions within school education. It has been challenged because it provides an ideological legitimation of education's role in reproducing the capitalist social division of labour, and the challenge has led to demands for undivided education (as in the movement for comprehensive schooling in Britain in the 1950s and 1960s). Simon in 'Intelligence, Race, Class and Education' presents a cogent Marxist critique of the hereditary theories of intelligence.[3] However, despite these challenges (including the discrediting of the scientific procedures of Burt by Kamin [4]), this concept of intelligence remains widespread. For instance, Lovell, in his recent book Adult Learning has a section on intelligence which, although more sophisticated than crude genetic determinism, still presents intelligence testing, for example, as unproblematic.[5]

The Marxist approach embodied in the second principle rejects a static notion of the mind and of inherited intelligence, and focusses on the processes of cognitive development that result from

98

life experience. It stresses that human cognitive ability can be developed. It thus contains an explicit belief in the great learning potential of all adults (rejecting ideas of 'bright' and 'dull' people) and an implicit belief in the role of education (as a specific form of life experience) to realise that potential. The task of adult education is to create intellectual development. This principle is therefore the basis for opposition to the kind of antagonism to formal education associated with Illich, who diminishes the part of education in learning:

> ...learning is the human activity which least needs manipulation by others. Most learning is not the result of instruction. It is rather the result of unhampered participation in a meaningful setting. Most people learn best by being 'with it', yet school makes them identify their personal cognitive growth with elaborate planning and manipulation.[6]

While Illich's overall description of the effects of present educational institutions has some force, it has been subjected to criticism by several Marxist writers who draw attention to his failure to locate the problems of education within a clear analysis of the capitalist mode of production.[7] His attack on education in general, and on adult education specifically in Imprisoned in the Global Classroom[8], has influenced some adult educators to question the validity of their work, leading them to question all forms of adult education rather than those forms associated particularly with capitalism. A Marxist approach places great emphasis on the role of education in adult cognitive development, while encouraging the establishment of adult education organisations and practices which are consonant with socialism.

The third principle draws attention to the role of language in learning and to the particular significance of literacy as a mental tool. The role of language warrants concern in two respects. First, there are class differences in the usage of any given language as a mother tongue. Secondly, many adult learners either have a foreign language as their medium of education (particularly in the former colonial countries of the Third World) or need to use a foreign language in their daily life (for example, as migrant workers).

Principles of a Marxist Approach

The implications of the class dimension of language for school education have been studied at length in Britain in the last twenty years. At the centre of this study is the controversial work of Bernstein, much of which is contained in the three volumes of <u>Class, Codes and Control</u>.[9] Latterly, he has focussed on 'educational transmissions' as part of the process of the reproduction of the social division of labour in capitalist society, and on the role of language within these 'transmissions'. One of the influences on Bernstein's approach has been Marxist theory, although the extent of this influence has been questioned by Marxist writers such as Sharp.[10] Certainly Bernstein raises very central issues of language, cognition and educational processes in relation to the class basis of society. The ramifications for adult education in the mother tongue have not been explored in depth.

Similarly, the implications of the second area of concern, that of adult learning and foreign languages, have perhaps had inadequate recognition. Gelpi has discussed the problems of life-long education and migrant workers in Europe at the level of policy, correctly emphasising the elements of power and domination involved in language policy.[11] But at the level of actual adult education practices there seems to have been little research. What learning and conceptual problems are likely to arise in adult education programmes which, say, use English in Uganda or Setswana in the Seyei speaking areas of north-western Botswana? Organisers do not always take these issues into account, sometimes because of the dictates of national language policies which discriminate against the use of some languages in education, sometimes from lack of consideration of their importance. The implication of Marxist theory is that questions of language are in fact of great importance to adult education processes.

Within the general significance of linguistic issues, that of literacy has a special place, considered here not in terms of its social and political aspects, but in terms of the psychological functioning of the individual. Literacy is a mental tool developed from language - it is in Oxenham's words a 'technology' which has an impact on the user.[12] Vygotsky, for example, stressed the role of mastery of the written language in complex mental processes suggesting (though not elaborating)

significant differences between the literate and
non-literate.[13] It seems, for instance, that
literacy provides an aid to the planning and
organisation of mental activity, enabling
interaction with one's own thoughts and access to
the thought of others, and also contributing to a
sense of being able to control the environment,
rather that simply respond to it. The importance of
understanding such differences cannot be overemphasised given the number of adult education
programmes, particularly in the Third World, in
which the participants are not literate. Here I am
referring not to actual literacy programmes but to
other programmes such as agricultural extension,
health education campaigns or political education
courses which are not directly concerned with
teaching literacy and in which participants are
often not literate.

The psychology of the non-literate is therefore
worthy of great concern. It cannot be assumed
that the cognitive behaviour of literates and non-
literates is similar, although many programmes do in
fact make this assumption. The dissimilarity has
been considered in terms of perception (for example,
in relation to visual aids[14]) but other activities
such as memory and conceptualisation require study.
Understanding the world-view and cognitive behaviour
of non-literates is therefore essential for adult
educators who work with them. General theoretical
insights may perhaps be derived from the increasing
work of Marxist anthropology on pre-capitalist modes
of production.[15] A specific anthropological study
of the consequences of writing on 'modes of thought'
is Goody's The Domestication of the Savage Mind,
which is not in the Marxist tradition but which
(despite its dubious title) does discuss relevant
issues of literacy and cognition from a position
which includes an awareness of Marxist
perspectives.[16]

The next two principles can be considered
together by focussing on their common denominator,
which is that they give priority to the mode of
production as the shaping context in which
psychological processes take place. Just as the
labour theory of value is at the centre of Marx's
economic analysis so we can make the analogy that a
labour theory of knowledge characterises a Marxist
approach to learning. By this I mean that the most
important influence on consciousness is the labour-
process and the specific forms it takes within

particular modes of production. The adult learner's daily existence is situated within a definable mode of production and it is incumbent on socialist adult educators to have a clear analysis of the nature of the social formation within which they are working.

This also means studying the nature of the labour-process.[17] As Gelpi has put it 'An analysis of work in contemporary society is the precondition for all educational strategy',[18] and he himself has raised important questions about the relationship between life-long education and work, considered in terms of the division of labour, the impact of technology, the organisation of work processes, worker alienation and so on. His writing is primarily concerned with these issues at the level of educational and social policy though he is aware of their significance for the processes of education. For example, he refers to the 'weekend college' experiment at Wayne State University in the USA and its stress on the fact that 'the system for the mediation of knowledge must adapt itself to the psychological and cultural reality of the adult worker-student.'[19] It is the 'psychological and cultural reality' of the adult as shaped by the labour-process and the particular mode of production that a Marxist approach to adult education makes central to its teaching methods.

E.P. Thompson's historical study of the restructuring of the sense of time that occurred with the development of industrial capitalism in England provides a concrete example of how a change in the labour-process changes the way people think.[20] He documents how the task-oriented time of the independent peasant and self-employed craftsperson was replaced by the subjection to measured time of the wage-labourer. The implication of such an analysis for adult education is that adult educators in Zambia, for instance, would have to take into account the cognitive differences between a group of peasants in the remote rural areas of the west and a group of mine-workers in the north when developing adult education programmes. In my experience, such differentiations are seldom made in practice and the orthodox psychology of adult learning does not deal with them in theory. For example, an article on 'Psychology and Adult Education' by Thomas in a recent handbook <u>An Introduction to the Study of Adult Education</u> intended for developing countries and adopting a 'cross-cultural approach', does not discuss such issues, giving the impression that the cognitive structure of adult education learners is unchanging with time and culture.[21] The adult learner is wrongly portrayed as an abstract and universal individual.

The next principle is that of praxis, which clearly leads to educational approaches which emphasise an active role for the learner. But it is essential to distinguish this Marxist concept of activity from ideas of 'learning by doing' and 'discovery learning' which derive from empiricism. Praxis avoids tendencies to reduce knowledge simply to personal experience based on interaction with the environment and it accords a significant role to theory. Thus while a Marxist approach emphasises the value of the learner's experience, it also places stress on the theorisation of experience, a task in which the teacher has an important part to play. The dialectic of theory and practice is fundamental. Take for example Boydell's account of 'experiential learning' in adult education which describes the processes by which learning is achieved by the learners gaining insight into their perceptual experience, usually in an experiential situation which the teacher has structured (such as case-studies or role-plays), though also from real life.[22] His account pays insufficient attention to theory, both in regard to how the processes of perception themselves have a theoretical component and in terms of the role of theory in 'making sense' of experience. A Marxist approach seeks to situate activity within the context of the learners' awareness of their own socially shaped perception and of an analysis of experience based on a critical, theoretical position towards social reality.

Forms of active learning must therefore take into account the position that experience does not take place in a vacuum. Processes of perception, language, and knowledge are all social products. Our understanding of the implications of praxis for adult education must be complemented by consideration of the concepts of ideology and hegemony which are contained in the next two principles. These concepts highlight the nature of the qualitative leap from perceptual information to judgement. Whereas empiricist appproaches to knowledge focus on the surface appearance of phenomena, on 'the facts', a Marxist approach seeks to develop knowledge which can go beyond appearances to grasp the essential structure of reality.

The seventh and eight principles therefore consider adult education in terms of resistance to the dominant ideology. Boggs, in discussing Gramsci's Marxism, has neatly encapsulated this task:

> ...the struggle for ideological hegemony has two phases: to penetrate the false world of established appearances rooted in the dominant belief systems and to create an entirely new universe of ideas and values that would provide the basis for human liberation.[23]

This summarises the role of adult education in the ideological struggle, though I see the struggle as having two dimensions rather than 'phases' (which suggest sequentiality rather than simultaneity). Because ideology is a product of both ideas and experience, a Marxist approach to adult education needs to encompass both dimensions.

The first dimension implies a particular approach to the intellectual content of the curriculum. This stance recognises the curriculum as being characterised by selectivity, involving choices of what to teach which are ideological in nature. It is consonant with the extensive Marxist analysis of the school curriculum that has been developed over the last decade by writers like Whitty and Young in Britain and Apple in the USA.[24] This work has drawn attention to how the choice of knowledge presented in the curriculum is part of the process of hegemony, of the ideological and cultural reproduction of capitalist society. Griffin in his book Curriculum Theory in Adult Education has begun to extend this analysis to adult education.[25]

The corollary of this stance is that a Marxist approach to curricular practice in adult education stresses a critical theoretical perspective that aims to demystify social reality (exposing exploitation and oppression for example) and to challenge common-sense ideas and assumptions (about industrial relations, dress-making, health, literature or whatever). The emphasis is on 'unmasking ruling ideas' wherever they occur and this presupposes the adult educator's commitment to Marxism as the theoretical perspective which most satisfactorily and comprehensively explains capitalist society. This commitment derives from a political choice made on the basis of allegiance to the class interests of the proletariat and its allies. It does not imply a narrowly dogmatic outlook, but in the final analysis it certainly opposes relativism and pluralism as props of bourgeois class interests.[26] The curriculum, from this viewpoint, must therefore be geared to the development of the theoretical 'penetration of established appearances' and the testing of this in practice.

The second dimension is concerned with the experiential aspect of counter-hegemony and the building of an alternative hegemony in practice - 'an entirely new universe of ideas and values'. This underlines the need to develop specifically socialist practices of adult education. Socialists need to build an anti-capitalist culture both before the overthrow of the bourgeois state (and indeed as a contributory factor to that overthrow) and afterwards in the process of building socialism. Such a culture is produced by transforming the experiences of everyday life, including the experiences of adult education. If hegemony is the result of lived social relationships and not simply the dominance of ideas, then the experience inherent in educational situations (i.e. the totality of knowledge, attitudes, values and relationships) is as significant as the purely intellectual content. Thus socialist values of democratic control, participation, co-operative work and so on must be embodied in adult education processes.

This turns inside out the critical analysis of education as reproducing the capitalist relations of production by institutionalising corresponding 'social relations of education' that Bowles and Gintis made in <u>Schooling in Capitalist America</u>.[27] Their 'correspondence principle' suggested that schools are characterised by a hierarchy of authority and control which corresponds to the division of labour under capitalism, and the form of education (more than the content) thus prepares students ideologically to fit into the social hierarchy. The kinds of educational practice which concretise this correspondence have been studied by others as a 'hidden curriculum' through which capitalist values and beliefs permeate the everyday life of educational institutions. The experience of education encourages the internalisation of values such as competition, individualism, deference to authority and the importance of consensus. (It is

necessary to reiterate that the pressure towards
reproduction of these values does not go
uncontested.[28] As I put it in an earlier section,
the reproduction of capitalism entails the
reproduction of its contradictions also, and this is
reflected in education, for example, in the
hostility of working-class children to schools and
the low level of participation by adult workers in
adult education in Britain.)

Apple provides an interesting case study in his
analysis of a kindergarten, which shows how the
specific content of lessons is relatively less
important than the experiences in the classroom such
as enforced obedience and definitions of normality
and deviance.[29] Keddie, in discussing adult
education as an 'ideology of individualism', argues
that adult education shares these characteristics
with other parts of the education system.[30] Such
analysis presents negatively the insight into
educational experience which I want to transform
into a positive axiom. A Marxist approach to adult
education advocates an 'explicit curriculum' which
seeks to realise in adult education processes
socialist values and beliefs and to establish new
'social relations of education' alongside a
socialist content.

The seventh and eight principles imply that
adult education is part of the ideological struggle
and acknowledge the consequences of this for both
the content and form of adult education. The ninth
and final principle confirms this inescapable
political dimension. Gramsci wrote 'Every
relationship of hegemony is necessarily an
educational relationship'.[31] Thus all adult
education is political, contributing either to the
creation and re-creation of hegemony or to the
establishment of a counter-hegemony. Neutrality is
not possible. The adult educator - an intellectual
in Gramsci's terms - is necessarily a part of the
class forces at play in society. The socialist
adult educator accepts this responsibility and works
consciously for the development of a socialist
hegemony. The context of this was discussed fully
in Chapter One when I presented a theory of
revolution and adult education which connected
cultural and ideological struggle organisationally
with the struggle for economic and political power.
In practical terms, this means an approach to adult
education which ensures links with the organisations
of the working class and its allies (such as

parties, trade unions, peasant associations, co-operatives and national liberation movements) and which aims to develop the intellectual capabilities, technical expertise, and political awareness necessary to create a socialist society. This is the final implication of the Marxist approach which I have presented in this chapter - adult education has the potential to develop people who are, in the Chinese expression, both 'red and expert', both willing and able to build a new society.


NOTES

1.    P. Allman, 'The nature and process of adult development', in Education for Adults Vol. 1. Ed., M. Tight (Beckenham:  Croom Helm, 1983).
2.    Quoted in  G.  Esland, E202 Schooling and Society. Block IV. Processes of Selection (Milton Keynes: Open University Press, 1977), p. 17.
3.    B.  Simon, Intelligence,  Psychology and Education (London: Lawrence and Wishart, 1978), pp. 237-263.
4.    L. Kamin, The Science and Politics of I.Q. (London: Wiley, 1975).
5.    R.B. Lovell, Adult Learning (London: Croom Helm, 1980), pp. 98-102.
6. I. Illich, Deschooling Society (Harmondsworth: Penguin, 1973), p. 44
7.    See, for example, the following:
M.W. Apple, 'Ivan Illich and "Deschooling Society": the politics of slogan systems', in Social Forces and Schooling, Eds., N. Shimahara and A. Scrupski (New York: David McKay, 1975).
R. Dale, E202 Schooling and Society. Unit 31. Block VI. Alternatives? (Milton Keynes: Open University Press, 1977), pp.32-41.
H. Gintis,'Towards a political economy of education: a radical critique of Ivan Illich's "Deschooling Society"', Harvard Education Review 42(1)(1972): 70-96.
M. Sarup, Marxism and Education (London: Routledge and Kegan Paul) pp. 137-139.
Basically Illich's radical position derives from an anarchist tradition rather than a socialist tradition.
8.    I. Illich and E. Verne, Imprisoned in the Global Classroom (London: Writers and Readers Publishing Co-operative).
9.    B. Bernstein, Class, Codes and Control.

Vols 1-3 (London: Routledge and Kegan Paul, 1971, 1973, 1977).
    10.   R.  Sharp,   Knowledge, Ideology and the Politics of Schooling (London: Routledge and Kegan Paul, 1980), pp. 44-66.
    11.   E. Gelpi, A Future for Lifelong Education. Vol, 2. (Manchester: University of Manchester, Department of Adult and Higher Education), pp. 79-96.
    12.   J. Oxenham, Literacy (London: Routledge and Kegan Paul, 1980), p. 41.
    13.   L.S. Vygotsky, Mind in Society (Cambridge: Harvard University Press, 1978).
    14. D.A. Walker,   Understanding   Pictures (Amherst: University of Massachusetts, 1979).
    15.   For overviews of this development see the following:
D. Seddon, Relations of Production (London: Cass, 1978).
J.S. Kahn and T.R. Llobera, The Anthropology of Pre-Capitalist Societies (London: Macmillan, 1981).
    16. J. Goody, The Domestication of the Savage Mind (Cambridge: Cambridge University Press, 1977).
    17.   The analysis of the labour-process under advanced capitalism has had a lot of attention in the last ten years since the publication of H. Braverman's pioneering book Labour and Monopoly Capital (London: Monthly Review Press, 1974).   Three recent books document the lively debate sparked off by Braverman's publication:
C.R. Littler, The Development of the Labour Process in Capitalist Societies (London: Heinemann, 1982).
P. Thompson The Nature of Work (London: Macmillan, 1983).
S.   Wood,   The Degradation of Work?   (London: Hutchinson, 1982).
Although the central emphasis here is the labour-process in work situations, it should be noted that Marxist analysis regards the mode of production as influencing people in a myriad ways even when they are not 'in employment' as such.   For example, women undertaking house work are involved in a labour-process which has a characteristic capitalist form.
    18.   E. Gelpi, Ibid., p. 51.
    19.   Ibid., p. 61.
    20.   E.P. Thompson, 'Time, work-discipline and industrial capitalism,' Past and Present Vol. 38 (1967): 56-97.
    21. D. Thomas,'Psychology and Adult Education', in An Introduction to the Study of Adult Education,

Eds., L. Bown and J.T. Okedara (Ibadan: University Press, 1981), pp. 92-113.

22. C. Boydell, Experiential Learning (Manchester: University of Manchester , Department of Adult and Higher Education, 1976).

23. C. Boggs, Gramsci's Marxism (London: Pluto, 1976), p. 42.

24. G. Whitty and M. Young, Eds., Explorations in The Politics of School Knowledge (Nafferton: Nafferton Books, 1976).
M.W. Apple, Ideology and Curriculum (London: Routledge and Kegan Paul, 1979).

25. C. Griffin, Curriculum Theory in Adult and Lifelong Education (London: Croom Helm, 1983).

26. I am well aware that this position appears very controversial, especially as it contradicts the liberalism inherent in much adult education theory and practice in Western capitalist democracies. (See, for example R. Shaw's angry review 'Attacking the liberal tradition' Times Higher Educational Review (1980) of J.L. Thompson's book Adult Education for a Change (London: Hutchinson, 1980) which contained views questioning the liberalism of British adult education.) My position challenges the basic assumption of liberal adult educators who regard themselves as neutral, apolitical and unbiased in their teaching. My fundamental point is that 'neutrality' is in fact impossible and liberalism is actually an ideology that supports the capitalist status quo, concealing bias in a dishonest way. In particular, for the socialist adult educator, the relativism that regards all viewpoints as equally valid and reasonable is unacceptable - class oppression, sexism and racism have to be challenged in all their manifestations. In those capitalist societies which do not have a liberal democratic political system, the issue is far less mystifying as there is very little central ground. It is more obvious that the adult educator is either on one side or the other (as Freire found in Brazil in 1964 when he was imprisoned for his adult literacy work). For a critique of the 'fetished separation of education and politics in liberal theory' see Sharp, Ibid., pp. 166-167.

27. S. Bowles and H. Gintis, Schooling in Capitalist America (London: Routledge and Kegan Paul, 1976), pp. 131-2.

28. M.W. Apple, Education and Power (London: Routledge and Kegan Paul, 1982).

Principles of a Marxist Approach

29. M.W. Apple, <u>Ideology and Curriculum</u> (London: Routledge and Kegan Paul, 1979), pp. 51-57.
30. N. Keddie, 'Adult Education: an ideology of individualism', in <u>Adult Education for a Change</u>, Ed., J.L. Thompson (London: Hutchinson, 1980)
31. A. Gramsci, <u>Prison Notebooks</u>, Eds., Q. Hoare and G.N. Smith (London: Lawrence and Wishart, 1971), p. 350.

Chapter Four

## A CRITIQUE OF ORTHODOX APPROACHES TO ADULT LEARNING

A concern with learning is at the centre of all
educational activity. Educational processes are
designed to help learning occur, so that a
relatively permanent change in the individual's
behaviour or disposition takes place as a result of
the experience. The aim of education is to provide
the situations in which learning can take place most
effectively. Of course, incidental learning is
taking place all the time, from a child's discovery
that a match can burn its fingers to an adult's
acquisition of knowledge about international
politics from a news broadcast. But such learning
has severe limitations on its effectiveness. For
example, it is usually inefficient, as when one
tries to learn about microchip technology from
random articles in the newspaper, and its scope is
restricted, so that one would not want to learn to
fly a plane by trial and error. Adult education,
therefore, is about the systematisation of learning.
Delker's point is well made:

> Adult learning is a major continuing mode of
> adult behaviour permeating the major categories
> of human experience and the major sectors of
> society. It takes place in a 'natural societal
> setting'. Adult education refers to
> organised and sequential learning experiences
> designed to meet the needs of adults. It takes
> place in the context of 'learning
> organisations'. To be sure, all adult
> education then involves adult learning, but all
> adult learning is not adult education.[1]

Even if one does not agree precisely with his

concept of education, it is definitionally sound to consider adult education in terms of planning and organisation being introduced into the individual's learning process. In certain circumstances, individuals themselves can introduce this organisation, but generally external help is of significance. It is this help which the adult educator should provide.

The centrality of learning means that adult education practices are based on philosophical and psychological ideas about human nature and how people learn. Adult educators are therefore working explicitly or implicitly on the basis of a theory of learning. They hold a personal view of the learning process which provides them with a guide for their educational activities. This viewpoint may be derived from a variety of sources, such as their own experience, a professional tradition imbided from colleagues, or the study of psychology. Insofar as it provides a set of general principles it can be said to constitute a personal theory of learning. The important point is that this theory will dominate the adult educator's approach to the teaching-learning situation. The purpose of this chapter is to identify the theories of learning which underlie conventional adult education and subject them to criticism from the Marxist position developed in the first three chapters. Conventional adult education practice rests on the adoption of orthodox approaches to adult learning. This orthodoxy is problematic from a Marxist perspective because it can be shown that these theories embody a range of ideological assumptions. The political effect of adopting these theories (whether singly or in an eclectic combination) is to contribute to the hegemony of capitalism and to legitimate the bourgeois social order. It is therefore necessary to clarify these theories so that the political consequences of the practice they engender can be clearly grasped.

It is interesting to note that Bigge in Learning Theories for Teachers[2] and Elias and Merriam in The Philosophical Foundations of Adult Education[3] concur on the identification of three options that the educator has in espousing a personal position, whether in the psychology or philosophy of education. Their three options are:

a) To adhere to one existing systematic theory.

b) To compromise and take an eclectic position which borrows elements from a variety of theories.

c) To develop a new position that benefits from other theories but is consistent in itself.

In adult education, within option (a) the dominant learning theories are the behaviourist, humanistic and cognitive. It seems to me that the second and third options are in fact both a kind of eclecticism, option (c) simply being a more sophisticated form in its attempt to develop a conscious synthesis of different positions. Option (b) represents a naive, pragmatic form of eclecticism. I therefore regard conventional adult education as being characterised in practice by an adherence to one of three major learning theories (i.e. behaviourist, humanistic, cognitive) or by eclecticism.

The principles formulated in the previous chapter provide an approach to adult education processes which is internally coherent and theoretically consistent with a socialist political position. They constitute a Marxist theory of learning which can provide a guide to action for socialist adult education and a reference-point for the evaluation of other approaches to adult learning. In this chapter I wish to consider orthodox approaches, while in the next chapter I will look specifically at one radical approach, that of Paulo Freire. In these discussions, the Marxist position I have established will therefore be used in a normative way in relation to other theories. As I made clear earlier, there is not a Marxist psychology of adult learning developed enough to present a body of experimental evidence to counter that of other theories. However, I do not regard this as an obstacle, given the extent to which theories of learning embody philosophical standpoints as much as empirical data. As Allport has put it:

Theories of learning (like much else in psychology) rest on the investigator's conception of the nature of man. In other words, every learning theorist is a philosopher, though he may not know it.[4]

In actual fact, the orthodox learning theories which

A Critique of Orthodox Approaches

have been influential in shaping conventional adult
education are also limited in terms of their experimental evidence of <u>adult</u> learning. Indeed, as far as
adult learning is concerned, despite the rapid
growth of research into the psychology of adults
during the 1970s (particularly in the USA), a recent
British review of research on the psychology of
adult learning and development concluded that 'the
research into the processes of adult learning is
relatively sparse, given the importance of the subject. Too many references are to research concerned
with children or with institutionalised elderly'.[5]

The starting-point of this chapter is that a
theory of adult learning underlies all adult
education practices, leading to different
perspectives on teaching methods and on the
curriculum (and even on the organisation of adult
education institutions). If adult education is
going to be an effective force for socialism, then
socialist adult educators must be aware of the
ideological dimensions of other theories and of
eclecticism, so that their own practice represents a
conscious application of Marxist theory. The
following critique of orthodox approaches is
intended to contribute to this necessary awareness.


THE BEHAVIOURIST APPROACH

One of the most dominant schools of thought in
learning theory is behaviourism. The behaviourist
school is wide-ranging and includes a variety of
viewpoints. But it has a common approach to
learning which it sees in terms of the development
of connections in the organism between stimuli and
responses. Its origins are to be found in the work
of Watson and Thorndike in the USA in the first part
of the twentieth century.

Watson (who was influenced by Pavlov's early
work) rejected introspection as an approach to
psychology, regarding the observation of overt
behaviour as the only scientific method. He
conceptualised people as similar to machines,
considering the idea of the mind as irrelevant:

Behaviourism...holds that the subject matter of
human psychology is the behaviour or activities
of human beings. Behaviourism claims that
'consciousness' is neither a definable nor a
useable concept.[6]

114

He thus differed from Pavlov, who did not deny the existence of inner mental activity but sought to explain the physiological processes underlying mental phenomena. Based on laboratory experiments with animals and children, Watson portrayed learning as a process by which stimulus and response bonds are established when a successful response immediately and frequently follows a stimulus.

Thorndike also developed the notion of stimulus and response and through his animal experiments arrived at a set of 'laws of learning' which he thought applicable to human learning. He concluded that effective stimulus-response connections are 'stamped in' on the person's nervous system, while ineffective responses are 'stamped out'. Two of his main laws were those of 'exercise' and 'effect'. The 'law of exercise' emphasised that bonds are strengthened by the repetition of a stimulus-induced response and weakened by the reduction of response. The 'law of effect' stressed the importance of the effects of a response because satisfying results reinforce the response and annoying results weaken it. Repetition, reward and punishment are therefore important ingredients of learning.

It is very interesting that in 1928 Thorndike published a book entitled Adult Learning which investigated the relation of age to the ability to learn. He presented documentary and experimental evidence for the continuing 'plasticity' of adults and made a strong case for the provision of adult education. The empirical data is mainly the result of tests on adults learning reading and writing, high-school subjects, and type-writing in existing situations with no special teaching methods. However, some of the experiments were based on behaviourist principles (such as one teaching subjects to draw lines of the correct length when blindfolded). The book provides an example of the conscious desire of some behaviourist psychologists to contribute to more effective forms of education. The book's purpose was to guide 'adult education in all its multifarious forms' so that it had 'a better scientific basis both for selecting students and for training them'[7], although it only hinted at prescriptions for improving teaching methods:

> Adult education suffers no mystical handicap because of the age of students. On the other hand, it is not freed by the nature of its

115

> clients from any of the general difficulties -
> of adaptation of individual differences,
> stimulation of interest, arrangement for
> economy in learning each element, and
> organisation of the subject of study so that
> each element of learning shall help all the
> others as much as possible and interfere with
> them as little as possible.[8]

The important point is that Thorndike considered the
behaviourist approach to learning and teaching to be
just as relevant for adults as for children.

The early behaviourists described learning in
animals and humans as similar and saw it as based on
the essentially passive organism developing
responses to stimuli. These ideas have been
developed by later generations of behaviourists who
continue to take a mechanistic outlook and to
consider learning as the formation of habits through
conditioning which links desired responses to
stimuli. Within the behaviourist school there are
different views about the exact nature of the
stimulus-response relationship that takes place in
the learning process. However, the most important
theorist has been Skinner. Central to his theory is
the idea of operant conditioning based on positive
reinforcement, which he developed from experiments
with rats, dogs and pigeons.

In operant (or instrumental) conditioning the
animal acts upon the environment (i.e. operates) and
this behaviour (i.e. operant responses) causes
consequences. If the consequence is desired by the
psychologist, the animal receives a reward, so that
its response to the stimulus is instrumental in
creating its reinforcement. For example, in a
famous experiment, hungry rats in a box discovered
by accident that pressing a lever released food
pellets, so they soon changed their behaviour to
press the lever regularly. Skinner's focus is on
the modification of response behaviour in a certain
way. (He has been able to teach pigeons to play a
kind of table tennis by this method.) For Skinner,
learning occurs after a desired response appears -
organisms change their behaviour as a consequence of
their own actions. He believes that human learning
happens in basically the same way as that of
animals. Although it is more complex, it is still
based on operant conditioning.

The approach of behaviourists to learning has
been influential on educational practices. In their

view, teaching is conceived as the manipulation of the environment in order to produce the desired behaviour in students. (The precise nature of this manipulation depends on the particular concept of the stimulus-response relationship of a given theorist.) Skinner has perhaps been most influential because he has specifically presented his learning theory as a means of making education more efficient. In a major article in 1954 - 'The science of learning and the art of teaching' - he described first his work on shaping behaviour by reinforcement and then wrote:

> From this exciting prospect of an advancing science of learning, it is a great shock to turn to that branch of technology which is most directly concerned with the learning process - education.[9]

He then went on to criticise education for its shortcomings, such as poor techniques like the use of aversion and the relative infrequency of reinforcement by the teacher:

> Eventually weakness of technique emerges in the disguise of a reformulation of the aims of education. Skills are minimised in favour of vague achievements - educating for democracy, educating the whole child, educating for life and so on.[10]

Having portrayed this bleak situation, he proposed operant conditioning as a solution and suggested the adoption of the following learning principles:

> a) Knowledge of results and the use of positive reinforcement.
>
> b) The elaboration of complex behaviour by dividing up learning into a series of small steps.
>
> c) Minimum delays in reinforcement.

Skinner proposed that these principles could best be put into practice by replacing much of the teacher's activity with teaching machines.

In the thirty years that have passed since this article, the general approach of behaviourism has had a significant effect on education. The most specifically Skinnerian application has been in the area of programmed learning, educational technology and computer-assisted instruction. One wider consequence has been the concern with increasing the specificity of learning and with defining 'behavioural objectives' for education. Mager's standard text, which first appeared in 1962, Preparing Instructional Objectives, actually uses the format of a programmed text.[11] It stresses the need for stating objectives in terms of overt behaviour that can be measured after learners have completed a unit of instruction in specified conditions. The role of teachers is to decide what behaviours they want their students to show as outcomes of the learning process and to teach in such a way that these behaviours become fixed in the students. This is also the general theme of Bloom's model of a 'taxonomy of educational objectives' which has been developed since 1956 and has greatly influenced curriculum development practices.[12] Current suggestions in Britain for 'criteria referenced' exams in schools reflect a behavourist theory of education. Other examples of the behaviourist approach include various systems of individualised learning, such as the Keller Plan, a personalised system of instruction based on reinforcement theory which has been used in higher education in a number of countries.[13]

Behaviourism has inevitably had a great impact on adult education as well as other sectors of education. In the USA, for instance, competency-based education has been widely used in professional and vocational training programmes, and in adult basic education.[14] In a world perspective, the behaviourist approach has been most widely disseminated in distance education, one of the fastest-growing forms of adult education.

Distance education has developed from correspondence education, which emerged in northern Europe and the USA in the nineteenth century and has long been an element of adult education provision in many countries. A massive expansion has taken place since the mid-1960s in both the advanced industrialised countries and the Third World.[15] This growth has been accompanied by an increasing sophistication of methods, with correspondence study being supplemented by a range of educational technology (including radio, television and computers) and face-to-face teaching. The rationale for this expansion has been made in terms of democratising education (increasing 'access' and the 'openness' of opportunities) and of achieving greater cost-effectiveness. Courses for adults have been developed at every level from basic education to university degrees. Central to distance education systems, even when they are multi-media and include face-to-face teaching, are pre-packaged correspondence texts. These are frequently based on learning principles derived from behaviourism and comprise stated objectives, units in sequenced steps, and reinforcement schedules including self-correction tests and feedback from tutor-marked assignments. The ideas of behaviourism can be seen to underlie courses as disparate as the Ministry of Education's training programme for literacy teachers in Kenya and the Open University's degree courses in Britain.

A close look at adult education in many contexts will show how widespread the behaviourist view of learning is. Yet there seems to have been no sustained critique. Occasionally, critical analysis has been made. For example, Harris and Holmes have produced a brief article on the distance teaching system at the British Open University. They show how behaviourism underlies the stress on educational technology and objectives-based curriculum planning which contributes to the controlled transmission of knowledge at the centre to the dispersed students. They argue that the method becomes a constraint on the teachers, and that it embodies a hidden curriculum of social control and a view of education as depositing information in students:

> Course team academics can choose to teach whatever content they wish but they are severely constrained in their choice of an educationally effective means to convey this content, unless they embrace the 'banking view'.[16]

But such critical analysis is rare and most accounts of adult education practice and of the learning theory behind it present behaviourism unquestioningly.

Marxism however provides a critique of behaviourism. There are elements within behaviourism which may suggest compatibility with a Marxist approach. For example, behaviourism emphasises the 'plasticity' of the adult learner.

Also behaviourism is based on a materialist philosophy which includes the 'realist' position shared by Marxism that reality has an existence independent of people. But in fact there are profound differences, and these originate in the nature of behaviourism's materialism. It will be clear that behaviourism's theory of psychology is actually an example of the 'vulgar' materialism that I discussed in Chapter Two. Behaviourism is basically 'mechanistic', dismissing subjective experience and regarding people as similar to machines (albeit complex machines). It is also 'reductionist', reducing human psychological processes to the level of animal behaviour. The enormous reliance of behaviourist learning theory on animal experiments in the laboratory is a result of the belief in a fundamental continuity of kind between animal and human learning. It is an essentially positivist psychology, attempting to apply the principles of natural science to social phenomena.

As we have seen, while Marxism accepts there are certain similarities in the physiological functioning of animals and humans, it also stresses the social and historical dimension of people's behaviour. It thus sharply distinguishes human learning from that of animals. The deficiency of behaviourism is therefore its failure to account for the complexity of human behaviour.[17] Human learning is not an unmediated succession of stimuli and responses but is elaborated through consciousness, thought and language. People conceptualise, form hypotheses, develop interpretations, use speech and so on in a way that the study of animals cannot illuminate.

The materialism of behaviourism is thus crude and simplistic. It reduces human behaviour, which is social and meaningful, to biological activity (a position which has been well criticised by Rose and Rose[18]). It is precisely this kind of materialism that Marx and Engels attacked in their writings of the mid-1840s.[19] Behaviourism explicitly rejects the concept of consciousness and of human beings having purposiveness and intention. It portrays people as essentially passive, the subject of forces acting upon them. Hence it sees the task of psychology as being the prediction and control of behaviour. The Marxian concept of praxis challenges this view. It emphasises that people are agents acting with purpose and awareness within historically determined circumstances to achieve certain goals. It also stresses the social nature of people, whereas the behaviourist account of learning is very individualistic and neglectful of the interactive nature of human development.

The basic determinism of behaviourism is reflected in its view of education as a process of shaping behaviour by the manipulation of the environment. In this process the teacher aims to develop the 'desired' behaviour in the students through reinforcement procedures. This view of education tends to abstract it from its political and economic context. The issues of class and power, ideology and hegemony, which are fundamental to a Marxist approach to adult learning are entirely missing from the behaviourist approach. Indeed, this is the central flaw of behaviourism when its ideas are transferred to the societal level in proposals for 'social engineering', of which education is an aspect. Who will define 'desired' behaviour and who will control the learning processes?

This kind of environmentalist theory of creating a better society was analysed by Marx and Engels in their discussion of previous forms of materialism. In The Holy Family they showed how eighteenth century French materialism had developed the view (expressed by Condillac) that 'The whole development of man therefore depends on education and external circumstances.'[20] They then demonstrated how this perspective became connected with the politics of communism and socialism, giving as an example Robert Owen, who saw education and the construction of a correct environment as the means of establishing socialism. It is no surprise that Skinner has produced a utopian vision in his novel Walden Two which describes an ideal society (characterised by co-operation, egalitarianism, and so forth) based on principles of operant conditioning.[21]

Marx and Engels criticised such utopian approaches to building a better society. They believed them inherently fallacious because they were based on an appeal to reason that failed to take into account the class struggle necessary to overthrow the entrenched interests of the capitalist status quo. Such approaches fail to see that the environment itself is a product of people's activity and to transform it requires mass involvement. The majority cannot be conceived as inert material to be moulded by an enlightened few. Who will establish the new environment? For Owen, it was a philanthropic person like himself and he actually built experimental communities in Britain and the USA. For Skinner in Walden Two, it was Frazier the man of vision and his selected committee of planners. For Marx, in the third of his Theses on Feuerbach, the changing of the environment and of the people has to involve the people themselves:

> The materialist doctrine that men are products of circumstances and upbringing, and that, therefore, changed men are the products of other circumstances and changed upbringing, forgets that it is men that change circumstances and that the educator himself needs educating. Hence, this doctrine necessarily arrives at dividing society into two parts, of which one is superior to society (in Robert Owen, for example). The co-incidence of the changing of circumstances and of human activity can be conceived and rationally understood only as revolutionising practice.[22]

It is not possible for a group of people to be 'above' society and somehow outside the class structure of the social formation. The viewpoint of environmental determinism cannot explain logically how the enlightened few avoided being determined themselves. It allows no place for the processes by which critical thinking arises and develops into critical action. It therefore cannot see that the transformation of society can only take place by a struggle between the classes within society, by 'revolutionising practice'.

It is for this reason that Holland in his article 'Are behavioral principles for revolutionaries?' is profoundly mistaken. Holland praises the achievements of operant conditioning and advocates 'deliberate design in the control of human affairs'[23] based on the principles of behaviour modification. He argues that it is necessary for the transition to a revolutionary socialist society. He shows how behaviourism is currently being used as a tool to advance the interests of capitalism and gives examples of 'our science in the service of the power structure'.[24] He cites the interesting case of a 1967 research proposal in the USA for using behaviour modification for counter-insurgency in Thailand. The proposal suggested that food could be used as a positive reinforcer to get popular support in the countryside and crop-burning as a punishment. (It also said that the potential applicability of the findings to the USA itself would receive attention.) Holland argues that this is an example of behaviourism being used for the wrong ends and proposes that behaviour modification can in fact be used 'in the changing of man toward a new revolutionary value system'.[25] The basic error here is the one Marx identified in his critique of environmental determinism. Although Holland may have laudable socialist ends in sight, he advocates the wrong means. The methodology of behaviourism embodies a philosophy antagonistic to a concept of social transformation being undertaken through the conscious action of the working class and its allies. Herein lies the lesson for socialist adult educators - an approach to adult education for socialism based on behaviourism is not possible because it is philosophically and politically contradictory.

THE HUMANISTIC APPROACH

The humanistic approach developed in the USA during the 1950s, its main protagonists being Abraham Maslow and Carl Rogers. By the early 1960s it was beginning to be seen as an alternative psychology to behaviourism (and to Freudian psychoanalysis). The approach put people and their experience at the centre of its concern, in conscious opposition to behaviourism and its reliance on animal studies - 'For most of the past thirty years, psychologists have allowed the rat to pre-empt the human.'[26] Rogers in an important paper entitled 'Towards a science of the person' expressed his view of the need to go beyond behaviourism because the observation of external behaviour leads to a very restricted form of knowledge, neglecting the knowledge to be derived from the individual's subjective experience and from inter-personal experience. This inter-personal knowledge derived from empathy towards others he called 'phenomenological knowledge' and it is central to the humanistic approach:

In this world of inner meanings it [i.e. the humanistic approach] can investigate all the

> issues which are meaningless for the
> behaviourist - purpose, goals, values, choice,
> perceptions of others, the personal constructs
> with which we build our world, the
> responsibilities we accept or reject, the whole
> phenomenal world of the individual with its
> connective tissue of meaning. Not one aspect
> of this world is open to the strict
> behaviourist.[27]

This concern with consciousness and issues of
perception, meaning and choice has its roots in the
existentialist philosophy of writers such as
Kierkegaard and Buber. This philosophical
background is to be found also in the great stress
placed on the individual's subjective freedom and
capacity for responsible choice. The humanistic
approach believes that a psychology which is able to
describe inner phenomenological events will have
greater explanatory power than behaviourism. In
contrast to the behaviourist view of a determining
environment, it asserts the significance of
motivations, meanings and choices, and people's
ability to create themselves:

> The inner world of the individual appears to
> have more significant influence upon his
> behaviour than does the external environmental
> stimulus.[28]

Thus Rogers opposes the idea that the causes of
behaviour are simply in the environment and that
people are unfree, the products of their
conditioning. He sees people as able to choose
their own behaviour and change their self-
perception, their attitudes and their personality.
They have an inner freedom and can act voluntarily
and responsibly in 'a different dimension than the
determined sequence of cause and effect.'[29]

The assertion of human autonomy is accompanied
by a belief in the essential goodness of human
nature (in contrast to the neutral view
of behaviourism and the negative view of
Freudianism). From this perspective modern society
is seen as de-humanising. Modern American culture
is therefore depicted in terms of impersonality, of
alienated personal relationships, and of individual
isolation. It is argued that this is reflected at
the intellectual level in logical positivism in
philosophy and behaviourism in psychology.

Ultimately, the threat of nuclear annihilation represents the cataclysmic fate of this society. Humanistic psychology is presented as a significant force for getting beyond this culture and for developing authentic and fulfilled individuals who can create a better, person-centred society.

The focus is therefore very much on the individual and personal relationships. A concern with the concept of the self and with inter-personal communication is characteristic. The idea of personal growth, for example, is central to Maslow's writing. He stressed the creativity and potentiality of the individual and the goal of 'self-actualisation'. Those who achieve self-actualisation are authentic and in touch with their inner selves because they have managed to go beyond the distortions created by socialisation:

> Healthy people seem to have clear impulse voices about matters of ethics and values, as well. Self-actualising people have to a large extent transcended the values of their culture. They are not so much merely Americans as they are world citizens, members of the human species first and foremost.[30]

Maslow envisaged the possibility of people being able to 'overcome their enculturation' and thus being able to find their true, individual identity which social influences have concealed: 'You learn to be authentic, to be honest in the sense of allowing your behaviour and your speech to be the true and spontaneous expression of your inner feelings.'[31]

The reference to learning here is important. Obviously the humanistic approach has a definite view of human learning, in terms of its goals and processes. Many standard texts on the psychology of learning ignore this approach. (See, for example, Theories of Learning by Bower and Hilgard.[32]) This reflects the current nature of academic psychology with its positivist stress on the experimental and empirical and its antagonism to the phenomenological.[33] However, humanistic psychology is actually part of a wider reaction to positivism in the social sciences and its approach does in fact constitute a significant view of learning.

The main element of the humanistic approach is to regard learning basically in terms of personal growth and development. Indeed, it tends to conceive personal change as a process of maturation rather than as new behaviour deriving from the acquisition of external knowledge and values. The approach to learning is one which conceptualises it as a process by which the true nature of the individual is 'unfolded' from within. One learns by following one's own interests, not by the prescriptions of another person. These interests reflect an innate set of needs which are the source of motivation. Genuine learning is motivated by an intrinsic desire to meet these needs, the most significant of which is self-actualisation. The ideal learning environment is therefore one which provides individuals with the freedom to develop their inner potential and become a 'whole person'.

This produces a characteristic stance towards education: 'the schools should be helping children to look within themselves, and from this self derive a set of values.'[34] In other words, the role of education is to release inner human potential and facilitate learning which will lead to self-actualisation. The emphasis is therefore on learning rather than teaching, and conventional education is regarded as an imposition. In Rogers' bold statements 'Teaching, in my estimation, is a vastly over-rated function' and 'the outcomes of teaching are either unimportant or hurtful.'[35] He makes these statements in his book <u>Freedom to Learn</u> which constitutes the most articulate presentation of the humanistic approach to education. The book is deservedly regarded as a classic by adult educators because it is remarkable for its commitment, philosophical coherence and practicality.

It is impossible to do justice to the book in a short space. In it Rogers intertwines descriptions and prescriptions about educational practice with clear expositions of the philosophical and psychological assumptions on which they are based. He focusses on the importance of learning in the education process. Thus he stresses student-centred learning based on personal involvement through goal-setting, self-initiated activities, and self-evaluation. Concomitantly, the role of the teacher is to be non-directive and to be a source of the resources the students need to carry out their own learning. The teacher's purpose is to 'facilitate' learning, to provide freedom for growth. Rogers' main injunction to the teacher is 'trust the student' and he regards the personal relationship between teacher and student as of paramount importance. His concern is with the processes of learning rather than with its content, as he believes the modern world to be characterised by change so that learning static knowledge is futile. Hence he argues 'We would do away with the exposition of conclusions, for we would realise that no one learns significantly from conclusions.'[36] He seeks to encourage processes of inquiry rather than fact acquisition, so that the individual can become an autonomous learner. At the centre of his approach is the use of small groups and learning based on intensive group experience.

His argument is backed up by detailed examples of actual courses for children and adults run by himself and others. These fully illustrate the approach and methods used, and it is underpinned by presentations of the philosophical rationale and psychological principles behind these methods. It is a totally consistent book which, taken in sum, represents an attack on current forms of education at all levels from primary to tertiary. But it also provides practical alternatives, 'a practical plan for educational revolution'.[37]

Freedom to Learn is the most complete expression of the humanistic approach to education and has had a significant influence on adult education. Humanistic psychology takes a positive view towards adults as learners and certainly embraces a view of lifelong learning. In Maslow's memorable words on his educational ideal:

> The college would be lifelong, for learning can take place all through life. Even dying can be a philosophically illuminating, highly educative experience.[38]

The humanistic approach has had an important impact on adult education. This has taken place partly through the writings of Rogers and his work with encounter groups, which have been used in many educational and training situations (particularly in the USA). It has also come about through the work of Malcolm Knowles, whose book The Modern Practice of Adult Education has been extensively used as a handbook by adult educators.[39] Knowles' concept of 'andragogy' and its application to adult education programmes which he elaborated in the book are based on the assumptions of humanistic psychology.

127

A Critique of Orthodox Approaches

Because of Rogers and Knowles we find the ideas of the humanistic approach arising in many different adult education contexts. The language of meeting needs, student-centred learning, self-evaluation and the teacher as facilitator is very pervasive in the field. Also, the dominant mode of adult education is group learning and much of this activity has been influenced by the ideas of humanistic psychology, even if the actual practice is often at variance, as Jenny Rogers suggests in a discussion of adult learning in Britain.[40] The humanistic approach has come to have a significant place in adult education during the last fifteen years. It has exercised such a seductive charm (partly by synchronising with more long-standing concerns for democracy, participation and equality in the classroom) that it has been accepted very uncritically. However, seen from a Marxist perspective, it has serious shortcomings.

On the surface, there seem to be some similarities between the humanistic approach and Marxism. For example, they share a concern with social issues of alienation and values, and with psychological issues of consciousness and cognition. But in fact there are deep divergences. These begin at the philosophical level because humanistic psychology represents a form of idealism. It is part of the attack on positivism and empiricism by existentialist-phenomenological philosophers and social scientists whose work is in the tradition of German idealist philosophy that includes Hegel.[41] As we saw in Chapter Two, philosophical idealism tends to question the independent existence of external reality, suggesting that reality is dependent on minds and ideas. The phenomenological position reduces reality to the meaning given to our experience - to our interpretations - and rejects the notion of an objectively existing and autonomous reality whose true nature we can come to know. This leads to a view of consciousness which tends to disconnect it from historically produced social conditions. It also leads to a voluntarism which asserts personal freedom and diminishes the constraints of the material conditions of existence - in Rogers' words, the individual is 'able in his inner life to transcend the material universe'.[42] The humanistic psychologists place great emphasis on the unique individual whose 'basic nature' or self is somehow independent of the context of the particular mode of production.

Marxist materialism on the other hand regards reality as having an independent existence. It does not minimise the role of ideas but denies that they are pre-existent or autonomous of social being. Hence processes of cognition are fundamentally reflections of external reality and not abstract, asocial processes. Thus values, for example, are seen to reflect different class interests in society, in contradistinction to Rogers' position that values are inherent in the organism. Marxism stresses that the individual has to be seen in a social context. As Marx put it in the sixth of the Theses on Feuerbach: 'the human essence is no abstraction inherent in each single individual. In its reality it is the ensemble of social relations'[43]. One must therefore conclude that whilst humanistic psychology represents an important reaction to the reductive materialism of behaviourism, its idealism makes it theoretically inadequate from a Marxist perspective.

This philosophical idealism means that there are many differences between the humanistic viewpoint and the Marxist approach to education. For example, the humanistic view is that education is basically an imposition. Educational situations should only provide the freedom for the mind to unfold. This view of allowing innate intellectual talent to be released contrasts with the Marxist view of the need to develop intellectual abilities through education. Also, the humanistic view fails to grasp the social context of consciousness, as we have seen. Thus it has no concept of ideology and its key idea of self-actualisation is based on making contact with an inner self (hearing 'inner-feeling-voices' in Maslow's words) which is innate rather than socially produced. Hence it minimises the role of theory in the learning process, because understanding is about stripping away the social distortions which hide the 'true self' and not a question of exposing the mystifications of the kind of society which produces alienated people.

It is this kind of approach which Mao Tse Tung attacked in his characteristically blunt fashion:

Where do correct ideas come from? Do they drop from the skies? No. Are they innate in the mind? No. They come from social practice, and from it alone...It is man's social being that determines his thinking.[44]

129

Mao pinpoints the significance of social practice (i.e. praxis) and this idea is also missing in the humanistic approach. So although humanistic psychology stresses purpose and intentionality, and in education its proponents advocate active learning, this is essentially abstract (- a tendency in idealism that Marx had noted in the first of his Theses on Feuerbach). It does not situate the individual's activity in a social and historical context - thus, motivation, for example, is seen as intrinsic.

The humanistic approach is therefore quite inadequate for understanding the processes of capitalist hegemony, in which education participates. Although it expresses a reaction to the alienation of capitalist society, it in fact fails to make the correct relationship between the individual's consciousness and the social structure. It under-estimates how the dominant values permeate the individual's thinking and behaviour through social institutions and routines. Its essential dualism leads to the idea that if individuals can change themselves then society will improve. The separation of the individual and society, of the personal and the political, allows a conclusion that individuals can re-arrange their ideas and values independently of changes in society. Social change is conceptualised as a matter of individual change and improved communication rather than the results of conflicting class interests. Conflict is reduced to inter-personal problems solvable by encounter groups - as Rogers argued:

> In a culture torn by racial explosions, student violence, insoluble international tensions and all types of conflict, such an instrument [i.e. encounter groups] for the improvement of gut-level communication is of the utmost importance.[45]

Such perspectives are clearly a modern version of the idealism of Hegel who wrote 'when the empire of the mind is revolutionised, then reality must follow.'[46] It was precisely such views which Marx opposed in his early works, for example in the Introduction to a Contribution to the Critique Hegel's 'Philosophy of Right'. Here he attacked the idealist notion that social criticism could remain at the level of ideas rather than involve a praxis which seeks to change the conditions which produce

produce the ideas. For Marx, as O'Malley points out in his editorial introduction to this work, social criticism has three aspects - self-clarification, the clarification of others, and political action - and therefore the critic should be a social scientist, a teacher and a political organiser.[47] This highlights the political dimension of adult education which is absent from the humanistic approach.

The challenge to capitalist hegemony requires theory and practice. It has to confront questions of power in society, and involve both education to unmask reality and political struggle to change reality. It cannot accept all viewpoints (all 'interpretations') as valid but must question the internalised ideological positions which block people from understanding the operation of class interests. The failure of the humanistic approach in this respect can be profoundly disabling in political terms, as Sarup reveals in discussing a student-teacher who used a phenomenological approach in the classroom:

> All her lessons seemed to me to consist only of 'chats', and I suggested to her that she was not 'teaching'. Does not teaching imply a difference between pupil and [teacher], a difference between what is known and what can be known? Teaching seems inevitably to involve intervention - but how can we prevent it from being seen as impositional?...I think I would want to say that because of her (misguided) respect for pupil's ways of constructing reality, the student-teacher actually prevented them from gaining the knowledge that might give them the power to create a less oppressive world.[48]

Educational activity is indeed an intervention, and the abdication of the teacher and the avoidance of theory in the humanistic approach are inimical to socialist adult education. Adult educators committed to socialism introduce explicit theoretical views and connect critical analysis to forms of action for social change. They do this in a classroom situation characterised by a democracy which recognises rather than avoids the difference between teacher and learner. This is a measure of the gulf which separates the humanistic and Marxist practice to adult education. Conventional adult

education based on humanistic psychology is
incapable of creating the counter-hegemony necessary
for socialism.


THE COGNITIVE APPROACH

     'Cognitive psychology' has become an important
school in the psychology of learning over the last
twenty years, and it also poses a major challenge to
behaviourism.  It has put on the agenda again the
nature of complex mental processes, and experimental
investigation has been  undertaken into activities
such as perception, concept formation, language use,
thinking, understanding, problem-solving, attention
and memory.  It is a 'mentalistic' approach
concerned with the individual's inner psychological
functioning in a way that contrasts strongly with
behaviourism and its stress on the analysis of overt
behaviour.  Although as a school of learning theory
it contains many internal variations, for this brief
account I will regard it as an approach which shares
a number of characteristics that have certain
implications for educational practices.
     The origins of contemporary cognitive
psychology are to be found in the work of the
German 'Gestalt' psychologists in the early part of
this century.  Their theories were first published
by Wertheimer in 1912 and were spread to the USA by
Kohler and Koffka in the 1920s. Here they came into
direct conflict with the emergent theories of
behaviourism.  Indeed, the Gestalt theorists
consciously opposed the behaviourist view of
psychological activity.  Kohler, for example,
undertook famous experiments with apes which he
interpreted as indicating the problem-solving
capabilities of apes.  He argued that this was in
direct contradiction to Thorndike's idea of learning
as trial and error.  Koffka in his book The Growth
of Mind included a section entitled 'A Denial of the
Behaviourist's Point of View' and contended that
psychology must be concerned with  human
consciousness.[49]
     The Gestalt psychologists were interested
firstly in processes of perception.  They suggested
that human beings are confronted by a field of
chaotic stimuli and therefore need to impose
organisation and meaning.  Wertheimer, for example,
proposed a number of laws of perceptual organisation
in 1923.  The main one was the 'law of pragnanz'

132

which stated that perception has a tendency to form 'good figures' (i.e. a pattern or configuration, for which 'Gestalt' is the German word) from stimuli. For instance, confronted by random sounds or shapes people tend to group similar items together (hence the 'law of similarity'). Thus people impose order on perceptual information in a predictable way. A second major interest was in the memory and processes of remembering and forgetting. Their 'trace theory' sought to explain how a current stimulus can lead to the recall of past memories that will help in the formulation of a response. Thirdly, they were concerned with problem-solving. They believed that people use higher mental processes in solving problems. The intelligent activity of hypothesising and testing leads to a sudden moment in which the solution is found - a flash of 'insight'. Thinking is a process to resolve the stress arising from the interaction of perception and memory when facing a problem.

These concerns led the Gestalt psychologists to a particular view of learning, which they saw as being derived from these cognitive processes. For example, they argued that people learn by seeing meaning and comprehending principles, that is, by 'understanding'. Such understanding of patterns and rules is transferable to the solving of new problems. They thought that people need to grasp things as a whole and therefore opposed behaviourist approaches to teaching which employed drills to memorise elements of information. They believed learning to be a question of 'insight' and successful problem-solving and not a mechanistic sequence of stimulus and response. Hence teaching should encourage understanding based on problem-solving.

For a number of reasons, including the rise of Nazism in Germany, Gestalt psychology failed to develop and from the 1930s to the 1960s the dominant paradigm of the psychology of learning was behaviourism. However, a re-emergence of concern with mental processes took place in the USA in the mid-1950s and by the 1970s 'cognitive psychology' had become an important influence on learning theory. This contemporary approach also considers areas such as perception and memory and analyses how thinking mediates between stimulus and response. It looks at how people gain knowledge and use it to direct their behaviour. Cognition is used in the sense of 'gain knowledge about' and includes everything that people know - that is, information, skills, and beliefs.[50] A significant component of this school of psychology has been the analogy made between human mental activity and the operation of computers, leading to the conceptualisation of the human being as an 'information-processing system'.

The information-processing model portrays psychological activity in terms of information being received by the senses and then items being selected and passed to the short-term memory where encoding processes transfer them to the long-term memory. This provides a store from which information can be retrieved in order to be used for making a response. The model has been represented diagramatically by Mayer[51]:

INFORMATION PROCESSING MODEL

| Stimulus | Short term Sensory store (STSS) | Short term memory (STM) : Working memory (WM) | Response |
| --- | --- | --- | --- |
|  |  | Long term memory (LTM) |  |

| STSS | STM-WM | LTM |
| --- | --- | --- |
| Capacity: Large or unlimited | Capacity: Limited to about seven chunks | Capacity: Unlimited |
| Mode: Exact and sensory | Mode: Echo | Mode: Organised and meaningful |
| Duration: Brief (Half a second for visual information) | Duration: Temporary (18 seconds without rehearsal) | Duration: Permanent |
| Loss: Time decay | Loss: Displacement or failure to rehearse | Loss: Retrieval failure or interference |

Such models seek to describe thinking processes and abilities. For example, they attempt to explain the cognitive tasks involved in matching sensory stimuli to known patterns (or rules), the structures used to encode and store knowledge, and the strategies of reasoning used to control information in order to solve problems.

Whether or not particular cognitive psychologists adhere to such a model, they do share a concern with the processes of mediation in human behaviour:

> According to the cognitive approach, a person does not acquire behaviour directly but rather acquires a higher-order procedure or rule system that can be used to generate behaviour in many situations.[52]

Cognitive psychology therefore focusses on human intellectual activity and its investigations are with people rather than animals. It attempts to explain processes of thinking and it looks at activities such as memorising, attention, language-use and so forth. These concerns lead to a distinctive approach to the question of how people learn.

There are a number of central elements to a cognitive theory of learning. To begin with, the individual is seen as being in an active relationship with the environment. People have intentions and goals so that thinking is an essentially purposive activity. Learning is therefore an intelligent and active process. Within this process, issues of perception are important because perceptual activity is the first relationship of the person to the situation. Individuals bring experience and expectations to a situation and this leads to selectivity in perception as they organise the stimuli into a meaningful pattern. Learning always involves the organisation and structuring of acquired knowledge because this affects the activities of storing and recalling information for use in new situations. The characteristic way in which people consistently organise and use information from the environment are know as 'cognitive styles'. Squires has listed twelve different styles, defined in terms of tendencies on a continuum, such as convergence-divergence which refers to 'the tendency to look for single outcomes against the tendency to entertain multiple possibilities.'[53]

These styles become apparent in the way people approach problems, and for cognitive psychology learning is fundamentally a question of problem-solving. The process of learning cannot be reduced to the formation of habits, rather it involves the development of the ability to solve problems. Learning is conceived not as the accumulation of facts but as the changing of cognitive structures so that the individual develops understanding, a sense of principles and relationships, in short 'insight'. Thus learning is not achieved simply by doing but by grasping the meaning of things in a way that can be transferred for the solution of new problems. A final element of this approach is therefore the notion of feedback. The learning situation is seen as one in which individuals confront a problem, develop a hypothesis based on the knowledge in their memory, and then test it out. The consequences of action then provide feedback so that correct solutions are confirmed and incorrect ones revealed.

What is the relationship of this theory of learning to educational practice? A recent symposium Cognitive Psychology and Instruction suggested that as yet the influence has been small:

> Modern cognitive psychology is today's dominant theoretical force in behavioral science. More than ever before, complex mental behaviors are being investigated in rigorous scientific ways. However, while cognitive psychology is becoming increasingly mature in its attempts to model the complexity of human performance, it is a fledgling in the domain of applications to education and instruction.[54]

However, I think it is in fact possible to discern influences in the field of education generally and on the practice of adult education in particular. The impact has been most evident in the USA with the influence of cognitive psychology on the development of 'instructional psychology'.[55]

This development has involved the attempt to move from descriptions of how people learn to prescriptions of how to design educational activities. Central to this development has been the work of Bruner whose extensive writings have sought to evolve, in the title of one of his books, 'toward a theory of instruction'. His wide-ranging work has concentrated on the nature of the mediation of human behaviour, including the symbolic activity of language and other systems, the role of culture, and many other aspects of people's activity in the processing of sensory data. He has applied these theoretical explorations directly to questions of pedagogy. His prescriptions include suggestions that schools should teach learning in ways that take account of perceptual processes and knowledge structures.

In general the educational ideas derived from cognitive theory stress problem-centred learning and Bigge, for example, in the final chapter of Learning Theories for Teachers gives an interesting and detailed description of how to teach in a 'reflective' way by problem-raising and problem-solving, using examples from social studies classes.[56] The prescriptions of cognitive psychology focus on the nature of the learner and deduce from that a necessary role for the teacher in expanding the quantity and quality of a student's insights. This approach is seen by the British psychologist Broadbent as a way out of the extremes he perceives in current educational practices:

> One could caricature the position at one extreme as that of the teacher as behaviour modifier, manipulating each shade of the pupil's behaviour with appropriate schedules of reinforcement; while the opposite extreme, and perhaps the most popular nowadays, would be the teacher who does not so much instil knowledge as make it available. If his pupils should choose to want it they can find it.[57]

He believes that cognitive psychology provides the rationale for the rejection of these extremes (which, as we have seen, derive from the behaviourist and humanistic approaches).

These ideas have certainly begun to influence adult education. Knox's compendious work Adult Development and Learning is rapidly becoming a standard text on adult psychology and its chapter on adult learning presents a thoroughly cognitive approach (indeed without acknowledging that there are alternative theories).[58] Also, cognitive research has been extended to problems in adult education. Sticht, for example, has reported on its application to remedial literacy training in the US armed services.[59] His analysis of the services' short literacy programmes from a cognitive viewpoint led to the design of a curriculum for a comprehensive literacy and job skills system.

The approach is now becoming apparent in adult education practice. This is evident in the 'learning to learn' programmes for adults such as those developed in Britain by the Further Education

Curriculum Review and Development Unit[60] and by Squires[61] at the University of Hull. These programmes which teach students how to learn reflect cognitive psychology's concern with the procedures of learning (rather than the content) and its belief in learning strategies and their applicability to different contexts. The increase in post-school opportunities for adults means that programmes such as these are likely to expand.

The assumptions of cognitive psychology can be seen to underpin a number of adult education practices. Sometimes this is explicit, as in the examples above; perhaps more often it is implicit, as in the widespread use of project work. It is reasonable to think that as cognitive theory evolves and research findings in relation to adults are disseminated, it will come to have a significant impact on adult education.

A Marxist analysis of this approach to learning must begin by acknowledging important areas of complementarity derived from a shared concern with the processes of mediation in human learning. For example, cognitive psychology's interest in the role of perception, language, thought and activity in learning and its belief in the positive part of education in psychological development are shared by Marxism. The cognitive approach is certainly much closer to a Marxist approach than either the behaviourist or humanistic one. It is therefore not surprising that Bruner quite often cites Vygotsky and Luria in his writings. It is also an intriguing historical fact that Koffka accompanied Luria on his second trip to Central Asia for the research described in Chapter Two. (He had to leave the expedition early because of illness.) However, the fact that Luria intended this research to disprove Gestalt theories draws attention to significant dissimilarities.

The language of computers that pervades contemporary cognitive psychology suggests the possibility of a mechanistic viewpoint. There is a likelihood that some proponents do see psychological processes not in terms of an analogy (i.e. they are similar to the operation of a computer) but in a reductionist way (i.e. they are the same as a computer). However, the more usual tendency in the cognitive approach is to philosophical idealism rather than mechanical materialism. Indeed, this was the crux of the Soviet critique of Gestalt psychology in the 1920s and 1930s. The Gestalt theorists had their roots in German idealism and one of their late nineteenth century forerunners was Ernst Mach, who was the central target of Lenin's attack in <u>Materialism and Empirio-Criticism</u>. This idealist position sees sense data as 'undifferentiated chaos' that can only be interpreted 'according to certain classes of innate perceptual assumptions with which the mind begins'.[62] The belief in innate ideas that characterised Gestalt psychology is the focus of Marxist criticism. Luria's Central Asian research was designed to show that:

> ...Gestalt perceptual principles were the results not of enduring characteristics of the brain but of ways of perceiving intimately bound up with culturally transmitted meanings of objects. One of their first experiments demonstrated the virtual absence of classical visual illusions, which caused [Luria] to wire excitedly to his friend and teacher Vygotsky 'The Uzbekis have no illusions!'[63]

Marxist analysis regards the Gestalt approach as misrepresenting the relationship between thought and reality. The undialectical view of cognition as a product of a priori, inborn structures also surfaces in contemporary cognitive psychology. For example, Squires in discussing the range of different cognitive styles notes that 'one can detect the urge in a few researchers to reduce all of them to one "deep" style, perhaps with some basis in the structure of the brain.'[64] Also, Bigge's discussion of the underlying philosophy of present-day 'cognitive-field' psychology describes it as essentially relativistic, its position being to 'neither assert nor deny an absolute existent reality'.[65] Such positions are clearly different to that of the Marxist materialism explained in Chapter Two.

This tendency to idealism means that the shared concerns of the cognitive and Marxist theories of learning are not necessarily approached in the same way. For example, cognitive psychology tends to discuss the 'information processing model' abstractly and does not relate the content and form of thought to labour and the mode of production. Similarly, its concern with the structure of knowledge is not informed by a view of knowledge as a social product which considers its class dimension and the role of ideology in concept formation, for instance. Even the stress on activity in learning often seems to have a passive side. The portrayal of insight as a re-arrangement of cognitive structures to understand the environment diminishes processes of activity which re-arrange the environment. Thus, although there are areas of complementarity, the dialectical and historical materialism of Marxism means that these areas are approached in a different way, which puts it at a distance from cognitive learning theory.

## ECLECTICISM

The preceding sections have outlined three markedly different approaches to how adults learn and have suggested a Marxist critique. I have not attempted to be fully comprehensive but rather I have sought to illuminate the relation of Marxist theory to the three major theories of learning that inform conventional adult education practice. In actual fact, it is seldom the case that an adult educator adheres solely to one of the three theories and the practices which derive from it. The most prevalent approach to learning in adult education is an eclecticism which borrows elements from different theories. This eclecticism has two forms, which I call 'sophisticated' and 'naive'. The first represents a conscious attempt to combine different theories in a coherent way. The second regards psychological principles pragmatically and employs different teaching methods without concern for the different theoretical assumptions which underlie them.

The 'sophisticated' form of eclecticism deliberately tries to develop a generalised theory of adult learning by combining different elements. It is typified by Roby Kidd who argues in How Adults Learn that it is necessary to develop a synthesis of learning theories:

> This may sound like a search for El Dorado, and no such magical or scientific theory is likely to arise or be formulated soon. Nevertheless, the need for generalised theory is real and it may be that improved generalisations are already possible.[66]

Kidd takes the view that the concept of learning is used to refer to a very wide variety of experiences (such as memorising a poem, learning to type, and changing one's attitude to others) and because of the differences between these activities it is unlikely that a single approach will explain them all. Hence a generalised theory will necessarily be eclectic. This is the characteristic position of 'sophisticated' eclecticism and it appears in some adult education handbooks, such as Bown and Okedara's book for developing countries An Introduction to the Study of Adult Education.[67]

This position has been most coherently developed in educational psychology by Gagne, whose work The Conditions of Learning has been very influential.[68] He has combined a basic behaviourist position with elements of cognitive theory into a hierarchical model of different types of learning:

| Type | Brief description |
|------|-------------------|
| 1 Signal learning | The classical conditioned response of Pavlov, in which the individual learns to make a diffuse response to a signal. |
| 2 Stimulus-response learning | The connection of Thorndike, discriminated operant of Skinner; sometimes called an instrumental response. |
| 3 Chaining | Two or more stimulus-response connections are joined together. |
| 4 Verbal association | Chains that are verbal. |
| 5 Multiple discrimination | Identifying responses to stimuli that resemble each other, such that some interferences occur. |
| 6 Concept learning | A common response to a class of stimuli. |
| 7 Rule learning | A chain of two or more concepts, reflected in a |

|                    |                                                                                                                                                  |
| ------------------ | ------------------------------------------------------------------------------------------------------------------------------------------------ |
| 8 Problem-solving  | rule as 'If A, then B', where A and B are concepts. Thinking is involved; principles are combined according to a 'higher-order' rule.             |

GAGNE'S EIGHT TYPES OF LEARNING[69]

Lovell in his recent psychology textbook for adult educators, Adults Learning, uses Gagne to show the way in which a unifying theory may be able to explain how different kinds of learning relate to each other.[70] 'Sophisticated' eclecticism is therefore characterised by the explicit desire to synthesise existing learning theories into a new position which provides a consistent explanation of adult learning. However, most writers feel that at this stage a comprehensive theory is not yet available.

'Naive' eclecticism on the other hand does not exhibit this self-consciously theoretical stance. This form of eclecticism has been described by Hilgard and Bower in discussing the relationship between educational practice and learning theory:

> The naive view is that the basic researcher stocks a kind of medicine cabinet with aids to solve the problems of the teacher. When a problem arises, the teacher can take a psychological principle from the cabinet and apply it like a bandage or an ointment to solve the educational problem.[71]

In other words, such educators adopt a learning principle in a pragmatic way and simply use the corresponding teaching method in the classroom. They are not concerned with the question of theoretical consistency or philosophical acceptability but with effectiveness in practice. Indeed, the underlying assumptions behind principles and methods may never come to the surface.

This is clearly exemplified in some of the popular handbooks written for adult education practitioners. A handbook which is well known in Africa is the Adult Education Handbook produced by the Institute of Adult Education in Tanzania in 1973. Its chapter on 'The Adult Learner' presents a set of conditions under which adults learn best with no reference at all to the theories of learning from which they are derived. It simply puts forward psychological principles such as 'adults learn best when information is given to them in logical order consisting of short units within a clear framework'[72] and suggests how the teacher can put the principles into practice. Similarly, Jenny Rogers' book for British adult educators, Adults Learning, has a chapter 'How Adults Learn' which avoids differentiating learning theories and presents ideas such as 'learning to learn' without relating them to the various schools of theory.[73] Such advice to practitioners encourages the 'naive' form of eclecticism and, based on my own experience and on anecdotal evidence, I would say that a significant number of adult educators adopt this position and use teaching approaches pragmatically without concern for theoretical coherence.

The central problem of 'naive' eclecticism is that it brings together incompatible theories unknowingly. As Bigge has said:

> Probably most teachers, from time to time, have adopted conflicting features from a variety of learning theories without ever realizing that they were basically contradictory in nature and could not be brought into harmony with each other.[74]

On the other hand, the problem of 'sophisticated' eclecticism is that it is engaged in an attempt to reconcile the irreconcilable. The three theories outlined earlier in the chapter cannot be harmonised. Behaviourism and humanistic psychology are poles apart philosophically, as their major proponents recognise. Skinner and Carl Rogers have at least twice participated in published symposia[75] in which they presented theories so opposed that Rogers in Freedom to Learn calls them 'two sharply divergent and irreconcilable points of view.'[76] The totally different activities of setting behavioural objectives and of self-initiated/self-evaluated learning are a reflection in educational practice of this difference. Similarly, behaviourism and cognitive psychology are in direct contradiction, so that in education the one conceptualises the learning task in terms of a series of small steps while the other emphasises the understanding of wholes. These two pairs of opposites are underlain by the philosophical divergence between materialism and idealism. But even the two theories which share philosophical idealism differ fundamentally in their interpretation of the learning process so that the contrasting view of the role of the teacher in the humanistic and cognitive approaches provides an indication of the differences between them.

In practice both forms of eclecticism converge and lead to a patchwork of principles and methods. This in my view is the most typical approach of conventional adult education and it reflects a tendency to atheoretical pragmatism (which, in turn, conceals an ideology of liberalism). The criteria for the choice of teaching methods are primarily functional - do they seem to work in practice? However, for the socialist adult educator this approach is problematical. Not only is an eclecticism of orthodox approaches internally contradictory and incompatible with Marxism, so too is an eclecticism which tries to single out one of the major schools of learning theory to combine it with Marxism. Once a political commitment has been made to socialism and to the process of achieving it, then the criteria for choosing adult education practices have to be political. The issue is not simply whether students are helped to learn particular ideas, skills or values but whether the forms of learning they undertake help them to participate in the struggle for ideological hegemony. Form and content must be fused. It is therefore imperative for the socialist adult educator to develop politically consistent educational practices approaches and in so doing go beyond eclecticism.

To achieve this a coherent theoretical position is very necessary. In my view, Marxism provides an appropriate theoretical framework on which to base the critique of other approaches to learning and on which to develop the principles of a socialist pedagogy. What is clearly missing in the English-language literature is a Marxist psychology of adult learning which can validate these principles by reference to empirical evidence. This is an urgent requirement but it need not prevent the development of socialist adult education practices. Such a psychology will be derived from a systematic theory in a similar fashion to the principles I formulated in Chapter Three. (This is in contrast to bourgeois psychology which presumes to develop theory inductively from experimental data.[77]) Hence adult education activities based on my nine principles will be compatible at a general level with a developed Marxist psychology of adult learning, though they will be in need of detailed improvements. The conclusion to be reached at this stage is that eclecticism poses a particular danger to socialist adult education because it drives a wedge between political theory and educational practice.

Having proposed Marxism as an alternative to orthodox approaches to adult learning, one turns to the proliferation of books on adult education that has appeared in English in the last ten years to find Marxism noticeable by its absence. The major developments taking place in the social sciences and educational theory as a result of the renaissance of Marxist scholarship are, with only a few exceptions, passing adult education by untouched. The only context in which a reference to Marxism regularly arises in adult education is in discussions of the work of Paulo Freire. It is therefore essential at this point to ask whether Freire's pedagogy does in fact represent a Marxist practice of adult education and this is the question which I consider in detail in the next chapter.

NOTES

1. P.V. Delker, 'Governmental roles in lifelong learning', Journal of Research and Development in Education 7(4)(1974):24.
2. M.L. Bigge, Learning Theories for Teachers (New York: Harper and Rowe, 1982), p. 13.
3. J.L. Elias and S. Merriam, Philosophical Foundations of Adult Education (New York: Kneger, 1980), p. 206.
4. Quoted in M.L. Bigge, Ibid., p. 18.
5. M. Osborne, A. Charnley and A. Withnall, The Psychology of Adult Learning and Development (Leicester: National Institute for Adult Education, 1982), p. 69.
6. J.B. Watson, Behaviourism (London: Kegan Paul, Trench and Trubner, 1925), p. 3.
7. E.L. Thorndike et al, Adult Learning (New York: Macmillan, 1928), p. 1.
8. Ibid., p. 179.
9. B.F. Skinner, 'The science of learning and the art of teaching', Harvard Educational Review 24 (1954): 29.
10. Ibid., p. 33.

11. R.F. Mager, Preparing Instructional Objectives. (Belmont: Pitman, 1975)

12. B.S. Bloom et al, Taxonomy of Educational Objectives: Handbook 1: Cognitive Domain (New York: McKay, 1956).

B.S. Bloom et al, Taxonomy of Educational Objectives: Handbook 2: Affective Domain (New York: McKay, 1964).

13. F.S. Keller and J.G. Sherman, The Keller Plan Handbook: Essays on a Personalised System of Instruction (Menlo Park: W.A. Benjamin, 1974).

14. J.L. Elias and S. Merriam, Ibid.

15. A. Kaye and G. Rumble, Distance Teaching for Higher and Adult Education (London: Croom Helm, 1981).

16. D. Harris and J. Holmes, 'Open-ness and control in higher education' in Schooling and Capitalism, Eds., R. Dale, G. Esland and M. Macdonald (London: Routledge and Kegan Paul, 1976), p. 83.

17. A.R. Luria, Language and Cognition, (New York: Wiley, 1981), p. 24.

18. H. Rose and S. Rose, The Political Economy of Science (New York: Holmes and Meier, 1976).

19. See particularly The Holy Family (1844), Theses on Feuerbach (1845), and The German Ideology (1846).

20. K. Marx and F. Engels, The Holy Family (London: Lawrence and Wishart, 1976), p. 160.

21. B.F. Skinner, Walden Two (New York: Macmillan, 1948).

22. K. Marx, 'Theses on Feuerbach', in K. Marx and F. Engels, The German Ideology, Ed., C.J. Arthur (London: Lawrence and Wishart, 1970), p. 121.

23. J.G. Holland, 'Are behavioral principles for revolutionaries?' in Behavior Modification. Applications to Education, Eds., F.S. Keller and E. Ribes-Inesta (New York: Academic Press, 1974), p. 196.

24. Ibid., p. 199.

25. Ibid., p. 206.

26. S. Koch, 'Psychology and emerging conceptions of knowledge as unitary', in Behaviorism and Phenomenology, Ed., T.W. Wann (Chicago: Chicago University Press, 1964), p. 31.

27. C.R. Rogers, 'Towards a science of the person', in T.W. Wann, Ibid., p. 119.

28. Ibid., p. 125.

29. C.R. Rogers, Freedom to Learn (Columbus: Merrill, 1969), p. 269.

30. A. Maslow, The Farther Reaches of Human Nature (New York: The Viking Press, 1971), p. 184.
31. Ibid., p. 183.
32. G.H. Bower and E.R. Hilgard, Theories of Learning (Englewood Cliffs: Prentice Hall, 1981).
33. N. Heather, Radical Perspectives in Psychology (London: Methuen, 1976), pp. 11-38.
34. A. Maslow, Ibid., p. 185.
35. C.R. Rogers, Ibid., p. 103 and 153.
36. Ibid., p. 155.
37. Ibid., p. 303.
38. A. Maslow, Ibid., p. 183.
39. M. Knowles, The Modern Practice of Adult Education (Chicago: Association Press, 1970).
40. J. Rogers, Adults Learning (Milton Keynes: Open University Press, 1977), pp. 87-101.
41. It is worth noting that these trends in philosophy and sociology have been paralleled in Marxist theory. For example, the 'humanist' Marxism developed by Korsch and Lukacs in the 1920s which I mentioned in Chapter Two constituted a reaction to a perceived positivism within Marxism and was influenced by Hegel. Also, the work of writers like Sartre and Merleau-Ponty includes attempts to combine existentialism, phenomenology and Marxism. It is this intellectual trend which has significantly influenced Freire, as we shall see in Chapter Five.
42. C.R. Rogers, 'Towards a science of the person', Ibid., p. 129.
43. K. Marx, Ibid., p. 122.
44. Mao Tse Tung, 'Where do correct ideas come from?' in Mao Tse Tung, Selected Readings (Peking: Foreign Languages Press, 1971), p. 502.
45. C.R. Rogers, Encounter Groups (Harmondsworth: Penguin, 1973), p. 166.
46. Quoted in M. Sarup, Marxism and Education (London: Routledge and Kegan Paul, 1978), p. 102.
47. J. O'Malley, Ed., K. Marx, Critique of Hegel's 'Philosophy of Right'(Cambridge: Cambridge University Press, 1970), p. xiv.
48. M. Sarup, Ibid., p. 99.
49. K. Koffka, The Growth of the Mind (London: Kegan Paul, Trench and Trubner, 1928).
50. G.H. Bower and E.R. Hilgard, Ibid., pp. 421-423.
51. R.E. Mayer, The Promise of Cognitive Psychology (San Francisco: Freeman, 1981), p. 25.
52. Ibid., p. 43.
53. G. Squires, Cognitive Styles and Adult

A Critique of Orthodox Approaches

Learning (Nottingham: Department of Adult Education, University of Nottingham, 1981), p. 5.

54. R. Glaser, J.W. Pellegrino, and A.M. Lesgold, 'Some directions for a cognitive psychology of instruction', in Cognitive Psychology and Instruction, Eds., A.M. Lesgold et al (New York: Plenum Press, 1978), p. 495.

55. R. Glaser, Ed., Instructional Psychology. Vol 1. (Hillsdale: Lawrence Erlbaum, 1978).

56. M.L. Bigge, Ibid., pp. 311-341.

57. D.E. Broadbent, 'Cognitive psychology and education', British Journal of Educational Psychology 45 (1975):162.

58. A.B. Knox, Adult Development and Learning. (London: Jossey Bass, 1977).

59. T.G. Sticht, 'Cognitive research applied to literacy training', in Cognitive Psychology and Instruction, Eds., A.M. Lesgold et al (New York: Plenum Press, 1978).

60. Further Education Curriculum Review and Development Unit, How do I Learn? (London: Further Education Curriculum Review and Development Unit, 1981).

61. G.T.C. Squires, Learning to Learn (Hull: Department of Adult Education, University of Hull, 1982).

62. G.H. Bower and E.R. Hilgard, Ibid., p. 4.

63. A.R. Luria, The Making of Mind (Cambridge: Harvard University Press, 1979), p. 213.

64. G. Squires, Cognitive Styles and Adult Learning (Nottingham: Department of Adult Education, University of Nottingham, 1981), p. 4.

65. M.L. Bigge, Ibid., p. 64.

66. J.R. Kidd, How Adults Learn (New York: Association Press, 1973), p. 188.

67. L. Bown and J.T. Okedara, Eds., An Introduction to the Study of Adult Education (Ibadan: University Press, 1981), p. 94.

68. R.M. Gagne, The Conditions of Learning (London: Holt, Rinehart and Winston, 1970).

69. Modified from Gagne, Ibid., by G.H. Bower and E.R. Hilgard, Ibid., p. 552.

70. R.B. Lovell, Adult Learning (London: Croom Helm, 1980), pp. 45-49.

71. G.H. Bower and E.R. Hilgard, Ibid., p. 537.

72. Institute of Adult Education, Adult Education Handbook (Dar Es Salaam: Tanzania Publishing House, 1973), p. 124.

73. J. Rogers, Adults Learning (Milton

Keynes: Open University Press, 1977).
    74.   M.L. Bigge, Ibid., p. 4.
    75.   C.R. Rogers  and B.F. Skinner, 'Some issues concerning the control of human behavior', Science 124(1956): 1057-1066.
    R.W. Wann, Ed., Behaviorism and Phenomenology (Chicago: Chicago University Press, 1964).
    76.   C.R. Rogers, Freedom to Learn (Columbus: Merrill, 1969), p. 274.
    77.   J. Macleish, Soviet Psychology (London: Methuen, 1975), p. 64.

CHAPTER FIVE

**AN ASSESSMENT OF FREIRE'S PEDAGOGY**

There is no doubt at all that Freire has been a
highly significant figure in adult education over
the last fifteen years. His work has had a
particular appeal for radical adult educators and
his emphasis on the political nature of education
has contributed to the renewed connection between
adult education and socialism. However, the
widespread expression of interest in his ideas
within adult education circles provokes questions.
Why are people happy to consider Freire when all
other reference to Marxism is shunned? Why have his
ideas often been co-opted and shorn of political
impact? Is his approach in fact as radical as has
been claimed? It is questions such as these which
make it important for Freire's pedagogy to be
examined closely from a Marxist perspective. The
significance of Freire and of the need to assess his
approach has been neatly caught by Torres:
'...there are good reasons why, in pedagogy today,
we can stay with Freire or against Freire, but not
without Freire.'[1] The central task of this chapter
is to consider whether a Marxist approach is with
Freire or against Freire. Prior to undertaking
this, some brief background information will be
helpful in order to put his work in context.
    Paulo Freire emerged as a national figure in
Brazil in the early 1960s. During the period of the
reformist government of Goulart he participated in
the debate about the nature of national development
and he was associated with the radicals within the
Catholic church who, for example, organised the
Basic Education Movement. His own involvement at
the University of Recife in adult literacy led to
his appointment as Co-ordinator of the National
Literacy Programme in 1963. He developed plans to

150

include twenty thousand groups in the programme during 1964 but in April of 1964 the military overthrew President Goulart. Freire was imprisoned for seventy five days because his literacy programme was seen by the military as politically subversive. He then went into exile and for a period of five years worked in adult education in Chile.

He finally left Latin America in 1969 and went briefly to the Centre for Studies in Education and Development at Harvard University in the USA. It is here that his international prominence began, particularly with the publication in English in 1970 of his books Pedagogy of the Oppressed and Cultural Action for Freedom. The ideas in these books co-incided with (and indeed reflected) a number of international developments, such as the growth of Catholic radicalism in the period around the Second Vatican Council of 1965 and the rise of the New Left in Europe and North America during the 1960s. Freire's Third World origins and political-religious radicalism synchronised perfectly with the zeitgeist of the late 1960s in the West, which was characterised by support for anti-imperialism, the growth of movements of blacks, women and students, and the revitalisation of the Marxist intellectual tradition. The English-language publication of his work in 1970 took place at a moment of crisis in bourgeois hegemony in which many aspects of capitalist society were being brought into question, including education.

During the 1970s, from his position as consultant in the Department of Education of the World Council of Churches in Geneva, Freire achieved striking eminence as a radical educationalist. He travelled worldwide to expound his ideas and to argue for their relevance in both advanced and underdeveloped countries. His influence can be seen on writers about child education but it has been felt most strongly in adult education because of Freire's central concern with the processes of adult literacy. His impact has been widespread, almost cultish at times. This impact can be found in the literature on adult education, where some reference to Freire is now inescapable, and in important international policy statements, such as the 1975 Declaration of Persepolis on the eradication of illiteracy.[2] He has also been of direct help to some specific national literacy programmes, such as those in Guinea-Bissau and Nicaragua.

In 1980 he returned to work in Brazil at the

151

An Assessment of Freire's Pedagogy

Catholic University of Sao Paulo. As yet, he has not produced a significant new work in English on his present thinking and practice. At this time, Freire's ideas are accessible in English in five books and numerous articles, interviews, audio cassettes and video tapes. There is an ever-increasing amount of literature in English commenting on and interpreting his ideas, and of course a substantial body of comment in Portuguese and Spanish. There is also a growing number of accounts of the application of Freire's approach in a variety of educational programmes in both the Third World and the advanced capitalist countries. Some of these have been documented by the Institute of Cultural Action, which Freire founded in Geneva, whilst others appear in articles and books.[3]

As far as adult education is concerned, Freire is seen by many to be the key exemplar of contemporary radical adult education in the socialist tradition. This is the position taken, for example, by Elias and Merriam:

> Freire's philosophy of adult education is an example of a radical philosophy of adult education. The theory is radical in the political sense of utilising education to bring about social, political and economic changes in society.[4]

A surprisingly wide range of writers on adult education have commented approvingly on Freire, expressing only occasional reservations about the complexity of his writing style or the political implications of his approach. Yet it is not always apparent that these political implications have been fully grasped and confronted, or whether for those who do espouse Freire it is in fact simply a form of 'radical chic'. Certainly the political thrust of his work is often blunted. Mackie's comment on Grabowski's collection <u>Paulo Freire: A Revolutionary Dilemma for the Adult Educator</u>[5] is very pertinent:

> The writers consider the political questions posed by Freire, and wrestle with ways to denude, domesticate, absorb and eventually nullify the challenge he makes to their functionalism. Not only do they collectively fail to understand Freire's politics, some even question whether education is a political event at all.[6]

An Assessment of Freire's Pedagogy

The liberal ideology of mainstream adult education
is able to absorb Freire in a number of ways which
weaken the political implications of his work.
However, some writers do understand the full
significance of Freire's politics and clearly
disagree. These writers are the main sources of
critical comment on Freire and they are usually from
outside adult education. Two notable attacks from
conservatives are those of Berger[7], who criticises
Freire for elitism, and of Norman, who regards
Freire's approach as 'totalitarianism in the
making'[8]. Criticism from the left is rare but
Walker does provide a sustained critique, arguing
that Freire's politics are liberal and populist
rather than socialist because they lack a
historical materialist theory of revolution.[9]
   It is evident that the theory and practice of
Freire need to be subjected to a politically-
informed analysis from within adult education. In
undertaking this analysis it is not my intention to
provide a review of the expanding secondary
literature on Freire. Rather I wish to judge his
educational approach from the perspective which I
established in the first three chapters. I believe
that the nine principles formulated in Chapter Three
provide a coherent and distinctive Marxist theory of
adult learning and therefore they can be used to
measure to what extent Freire presents a Marxist
approach to adult education.
   It is important to note at this point the
nature of Freire's corpus in English. He has
published five books in English translation, but the
chronology of their original publication dates is
important for analysing the development of his
thought:

   - Education as the Practice of Freedom
   (comprised of two essays 'Education as the
   practice of freedom' originally published in
   1967 and 'Extension and communication'
   originally published in 1969)

   - Pedagogy of the Oppressed (1968)

   - Cultural Action for Freedom (1970)

   - Pedagogy in Process (1978)

   - The Politics of Education
   (comprised of articles published between 1965

and 1975, the two essays previously published in <u>Cultural Action for Freedom</u>, and an interview from circa 1984)

The British editions of these books are dated 1976, 1972, 1972, 1978 and 1985 respectively and hence obscure this important chronology.[10]
The first three books and half of the fifth book relate to Freire's experience in Latin America during the 1960s. It was the appearance of <u>Pedagogy of the Oppressed</u> and <u>Cultural Action for Freedom</u> in the USA which brought Freire to international attention in the English-speaking world. After 1970 he published a number of articles, papers and interviews in English (some of which are collected in <u>The Politics of Education</u>) and at this time a considerable amount of commentary began to appear. His works written in Europe show continuities with his previous writing but there are also some self-criticisms and from about 1973 there are signs of shifts in his thinking. In 1978 he published <u>Pedagogy in Process</u> based on his experience in helping the national literacy programme in the African country of Guinea-Bissau in 1975-76. The book provides evidence of a significant development in his thinking which is reflected in his mode of analysis and expression. However, most of the secondary literature focusses on his earlier work (Elias and Merriam[11], for example, make no reference to <u>Pedagogy in Process</u>) or accords a minor place to the book on Guinea-Bissau, ignoring the changes that it embodies.
Freire has published no major new work in English since 1978 and only a few articles and interviews ( - the interview in the recently published <u>The Politics of Education</u> is the only item in the book produced after 1975). In presenting my analysis of his pedagogy from a Marxist position I will concentrate primarily on his books (which represent his most considered and elaborated positions). I will differentiate between his early writings and those produced from around 1973 onwards, particularly <u>Pedagogy in Process</u>. It is my contention that some of the weaknesses that I identify in the early writings are corrected to some extent later, so that <u>Pedagogy in Process</u> is much closer to a Marxist aproach to adult education than the previous books (which are the ones that figure most prominently in the majority of interpretations). Before making this argument in

detail, it is necessary to describe the adult education method which Freire has developed to put into practice his theoretical position.

THE PAULO FREIRE METHOD

One of the most important things about Freire is that he not only presents an educational theory but he also describes its practical implications. This is the logical corollary of one of his central ideas, namely that the practices of adult education reflect political and philosophical assumptions:

> All educational practice implies a theoretical stance on the educator's part. This stance in turn implies - sometimes more, sometimes less explicitly - an interpretation of man and the world.[12]

His own approach represents a conscious and explicit effort to ensure a unity of form and content - 'we searched for a method...which, in the lucid observation of a young Brazilian sociologist, would identify learning content with the learning process.'[13] This enterprise of Freire is of the greatest significance for socialist adult educators, who must also aim for a fusion of form and content in their educational practice.

Freire's approach to adult literacy education was known in Brazil in the early 1960s as 'metodo Paulo Freire'. Its methodology underwent minor variations in Chile in the late 1960s and a more major adaptation in Guinea-Bissau in the mid-1970s. The essence of his pedagogy cannot be reduced to methods and techniques precisely because it was developed to meet certain political-philosophical aims. The central aim can be summed up in the idea of 'conscientisation' (conscientizacao), that is, the development in the learners of a critical understanding of society and an awareness of their capacity to change society. The development of this consciousness opens up the possibility of people liberating themselves by changing the social structures which de-humanise them and by building a new society. Thus the Freirean approach conceives education as a process of 'conscientisation' and seeks practices consonant with this aim.

Freire sums up these practices as a 'problem-solving' approach to education, which he contrasts with the 'banking' approach of an education designed to prevent critical thinking and perpetuate the status quo. In the 'banking' approach the teacher deposits ready-made bits of knowledge in the students which they have to memorise and repeat. The students are reduced to passivity and encouraged to adapt to the world as it is rather than question it. Hence it is a process of 'domestication', an exercise in domination. In opposition to this, Freire proposes 'problem-solving' education in which the teacher and learners undertake an act of knowing together, a process of 'dialogue' in which they investigate the problems in the world together. This approach abolishes authoritarianism in the classroom, ends irrelevance and arid intellectualisation, and encourages critical thinking about society. Hence it is a process of 'liberation', a practice of freedom.

Freire has described in detail in <u>Education as the Practice of Freedom</u>[14] and <u>Pedagogy of the Oppressed</u>[15] the method by which a 'problem-solving' approach to adult literacy and post-literacy education was undertaken in Latin America. It took place in a new institution, the 'culture circle':

> ...we launched a new institution...a 'culture circle' since among us a school was a traditionally passive concept. Instead of a teacher, we had a co-ordinator; instead of lectures, dialogue; instead of pupils, group participants; instead of alienating syllabi, compact programs that were 'broken down' and 'codified' into learning units.[16]

Thus the language used to describe the educational organisation was designed to set it apart from banking approaches. In the 'culture circles', learning to read and write took place in the context of developing a critical understanding of society.

The content of the educational programmes was developed in conjunction with the inhabitants of an area. Phase One involved an investigation by the educational team and volunteers from the area into the 'present, existential, concrete situation'[17] to discover the people's 'thematic universe', that is, the main issues in their social situation (such as domination, underdevelopment and so forth). This included linguistic research to find significant words, typical sayings, and expressions linked to people's existence. For example, the language of peasants was different to that of workers in an urban slum. This phase enabled the identification of how learners viewed the world and expressed themselves linguistically. Phase Two involved the selection of certain themes for discussion or words for analysis that would generate critical debate and language development. 'Generative words', for example, were selected according to linguistic criteria (such as phonemic richness) and to their socio-political significance. Not all the themes were from the locality and Freire argued that the team itself had the right to include themes not suggested by the people. The theme he believed to be indispensable for conscientisation was that of the anthropological concept of culture, which helped people to see the difference between nature and human culture and thus realise their role in creating society.

In Phase Three 'codifications' were made of these generative themes or words. These were visual representations (in drawings, posters, or slides) of typical existential situations in the area which could pose problems for discussion:

> Discussion of these codifications will lead the groups towards a more critical consciousness at the same time that they begin to learn to read and write. The codifications represent familiar local situations - which, however, open perspectives for the analysis of regional and national problems.[18]

Preparing these codifications was a subtle task as they had to avoid being 'too explicit or too enigmatic'.[19]  In Phase Four agendas were developed as guidelines for the co-ordinators. These became part of their training programme, which was one of the most difficult parts of the overall programme because it required creating new attitudes in the co-ordinators so that they adopted the dialogue approach. Finally, in Phase Five various kinds of educational material were produced. For literacy, this included cards with the breakdown of the phonemic families which corresponded to each generative word. Once these preparatory stages had been undertaken the programme could begin:

> ...the team of educators is ready to re-present to the people their own thematics, in systematised and amplified form. The thematics

> which have come from the people return to them
> - not as contents to be deposited, but as
> problems to be solved.[20]

In the culture circle the codified situation was presented and discussed. This analysis was known as 'decoding'. In literacy education, the generative word was then introduced and the semantic link between the word and object established. Then the word was broken into syllables and once these were recognised the card presenting the phonemic families was shown.[21] Using this 'discovery card', group members discovered the way of forming words through combining syllables. By means of this method, the members of a culture circle (approximately twenty-five in number) were enabled in six to eight weeks to write simple letters, read newspapers, and discuss important local and national problems. It was therefore highly effective compared to other forms of literacy education (hence attracting attention on technical grounds as well as political grounds).

This in outline is the Paulo Freire method and its rationale. It has been applied in varying ways by others in a number of different contexts in both advanced capitalist countries and underdeveloped countries. Freire himself has reported at length on its application in Guinea-Bissau, stressing that 'experiments cannot be transplanted; they must be reinvented.'[22] Notable developments there were the making of a closer link between education and the productive work of the area (so that the thematic universe of production became more important) and the priority given to other educational content before literacy.

The Paulo Freire method is obviously a very systematic and sophisticated approach to adult education, involving a deliberate intervention in learning processes for explicitly political purposes. In undertaking an assessment of its theoretical stance I am following the injunction of Freire himself, who has written:

> In my conversations with educators, I have
> stressed the need for political
> clarity...rather than techniques or methods.[23]

The section which follows presents a critical analysis of Freire's theoretical position from a Marxist perspective in an effort to achieve the political clarity that will enable us to see the usefulness of his pedagogy for adult education for socialism.


## THE PHILOSOPHICAL FOUNDATIONS

The first principle of the Marxist approach to adult education which was formulated in Chapter Three specifies its philosophical basis. This comprises dialectical and historical materialism and involves a certain ontology and a viewpoint that distinguishes the cultural from the biological. It is this theoretical position that I wish to use as a criterion for considering the philosophical stance which emerges from Freire's writings.

Freire is one of the few writers on adult education who have attempted to present a coherent philosophical foundation for their educational practice. His position is most fully elaborated in the first three books and particularly in Pedagogy of the Oppressed. It is a position which very much reflects the intellectual milieu of Brazil in the early 1960s, which has been described at length by De Kadt in his book Catholic Radicals in Brazil.[24] It is an explicitly eclectic position which draws upon three closely related intellectual currents of the twentieth century - radical Christian theology, existentialism-phenomenology, and humanist Marxism.

Freire's Christianity is influenced by writers such as de Chardin, Mounier and Neibuhr and he has adopted the view that Christian faith entails a commitment to social action against exploitation and oppression and for a humanised world - as he put it in an interview in 1970, 'the role of the church must be the role of liberation, of the humanisation of mankind.'[25] His philosophical position also incorporates existential-phenomenological ideas from writers such as Buber, Sartre and Jaspers. His stress on inter-personal relations and dialogue derive from this perspective, as does his concern with consciousness and the way people construe the world: 'Reality is never just simply the objective datum, the concrete fact, but it is also man's perception of it.'[26] Finally, his position also includes the thinking of humanist Marxists like Petrovic and Kolakowski, for example in its emphasis on praxis and on the need for a utopian vision to negate existing capitalist society.

The conceptual framework and terminology of

An Assessment of Freire's Pedagogy

Freire's early writings very much reflect the three
intellectual currents he has borrowed from in
attempting to provide a philosophical basis for his
educational approach.  Concepts such as witness,
rebirth and the Easter experience derive from
Christianity; inter-subjectivity, intentionality,
and authenticity from existentialism-phenomenology;
praxis, alienation and dialectics from Marxism.  The
question to be considered is, what is the
relationship between this eclectic philosophical
stance and the Marxist position I established in
Chapter Two?  To answer this I will focus first on
the issue of materialism and idealism, and secondly
on Freire's view of humanity and nature.

    To understand his position on the issue of
materialism it is necessary to discuss his
Christianity.  Freire stands in a tradition of
twentieth century Christian thought which has
considered the relationship between Christianity,
capitalism and socialism.  This tradition developed
into a dialogue with Marxism in the late 1950s with
the renewal of Marxism following the Stalin era.
This dialogue has been based on a shared humanism,
expressed in a concern with how capitalism alienates
people and prevents the full development of their
human potential.  Of course, many individual
Christians and many official church positions
remain adamantly anti-communist, seeing atheist
Marxism as the embodiment of evil.  For a long time
this was particularly true of the Catholic church -
as Kee put it 'The papacy which acted so ambiguously
on Fascism had no qualms about excommunicating
members of the Communist Party.'[27]  However, Pope
John XXIII signified a shift away from this view in
his 1963 Encyclical Peace On Earth when he declared
that movements originating in 'false philosophical
teachings regarding the nature, origin and destiny
of the universe and of man' may 'contain elements
that are positive and deserving of approval'.[28]

    In fact some radical theologians have entered
into a far-reaching encounter with Marxism.  They
have accepted the Marxist critique of
institutionalised religion as an ideology that
advances class interests.  This historical
materialist analysis reveals that Christianity has
sometimes been the ideology of a revolutionary class
(as with Protestantism and the bourgeois revolution
against feudalism) but that more often it has played
a reactionary and oppressive role (as with the
Protestant fundamentalists in Central America

today). These radical theologians also accept the Marxist analysis of the nature of class society under capitalism and consequently see a need for social transformation in order to achieve such goals as the social justice and equality which Jesus advocated in the Sermon on the Mount.

This convergence of Christian thinking with elements of Marxism was most notable amongst Catholics in Latin America in the 1960s. It led to various forms of political radicalism and was articulated by Guttierez as a 'theology of liberation':

> A spirituality of liberation will centre on a conversion to the neighbour, the oppressed person, the exploited social class, the despised race, the dominated country. Our conversion to the Lord implies this conversion to the neighbour...it means thinking, feeling and living as Christ - present in exploited and alienated man. To be converted is to commit oneself to the process of the liberation of the poor and oppressed...[29]

In practical terms it was exemplified by the action of Father Camillo Torres, who was killed in 1966 when fighting as a guerilla with revolutionary forces in Colombia. This is the background to the Christianity of Freire. Although Christianity is seldom mentioned directly in his books, it is a highly important part of their underlying philosophy. (It figures more explicitly in his articles and interviews, a number of which attempt to clarify the relationship between his religion and his politics - for example, the essay 'Education, Liberation and the Church' in The Politics of Education).

However, although Christians like Freire have sought to synthesise their faith with Marxism, it seems to me that there is a crucial point of divergence between Christianity and Marxism over the question of god. The concept of god has developed in Christian theology beyond the emphasis on transcendence (god as a supernatural being 'out there') which was characteristic of the traditional theology which Marx attacked. Modern theology now emphasises immanence (the presence of god in the world) and the dialectical relation of the two - in Bonnhoeffer's phrase 'God is the "beyond" in the midst of our life'. But despite this development it is inescapable that the religious view of the nature of being is a theist one and therefore in the final analysis not a materialist philosophy. Thus whatever compatibility may be reached with Marxism in terms of shared social and political goals, in the end the ontological positions are distinct. As Engels put it - 'not with "god" immanent in or opposed to the world is the truth to be found, but much nearer in man's own breast.'[30] A coherent synthesis of Marxism and Christian doctrine at the philosophical level is not possible.

The theism of Christianity is a form of philosophical idealism and it is not surprising that Christians tend to identify with the idealist trends in Marxism, typically finding themselves most in sympathy with the humanist Marxists and with the early writings of Marx such as the Economic and Philosophic Manuscripts of 1844. This tendency in Marxism, as we have seen, emphasises individual freedom and autonomy and the problem of alienation rather than the determining role of socio-economic structures in setting the parameters of historical possibility within which human actions take place. It is this trend within Marxism that Freire refers to in his early works when citing such writers as Fromm, Marcuse, Kolakowski, Lukacs and Petrovic.

The phenomenological influence on his thinking is also a pressure towards idealism. For example, there is an ambivalence in his stance towards the existence of an independent reality. Sometimes, he takes a clearly realist position:

> To be human is to engage in relationships with others and the world. It is to experience that world as an objective reality, independent of oneself, capable of being known.[31]

But at other times he takes a phenomenological position which propounds an objective-subjective dialectic without adhering to the primacy of pre-existent reality:

> Education as the practice of freedom...denies that there exists a reality apart from men. Authentic reflection considers neither man nor the world without men, but men in their relations with the world. In these relations consciousness and world are simultaneous: consciousness neither precedes the world nor follows it.[32]

An Assessment of Freire's Pedagogy

Just after this passage he quotes approvingly a
Chilean peasant who in reply to the educator's
question 'Let's say...that all men on earth were to
die, but that the earth itself remained, together
with trees, birds, animals, rivers...wouldn't all
this be a world?' said 'Oh no,..there would be no
one to say: 'This is a world.'[33] Here Freire veers
towards a view of reality as a social construction,
over-emphasising subjective human consciousness
against objective material reality.

   To my mind, the early writings of Freire evince
a philosophical idealism, although he is careful,
for example, not to suggest that people can liberate
themselves in their consciousness without changing
social conditions. This aura of idealism arises
from his focus on subjectivity and the cultural
plane at the expense of analysis of the political
economy of the objective structures of society. It
is a problem which is remedied to some extent in
Pedagogy in Process which shows a greater concern
with the social relations of production and for
which Marx's Capital. Volume 1 is a more important
point of reference. However, this later book does
not contain any philosophical statement, so that the
most elaborated philosophical position is still that
of the earlier works. Here there is a tendency to
idealism, and the theism of Christianity and the
materialism of Marxism remain an unresolved
philosophical contradiction.

   However, in his view of the relationship
between animals and human beings there is close
compatibility with Marxism. Freire emphasises
throughout his work the difference between animals
and people, between nature and culture. For Freire,
animals are beings of activity who are immersed in
the world and unable to reflect on it. But he
argues that people have the capacity for becoming
aware of the world they inhabit and conscious of
their own activity within it. Hence they are
capable of intentional action and can change both
nature and society. This is a central tenet of his
humanism - the world is humanised when people
realise their ability to change reality and thus
become the active subjects of history rather than
remaining submerged as passive objects.

   This concern with the historical and social
nature of human activity converges with a Marxist
perspective, to the extent that Freire's language
echoes that of Marx's Economic and Philosophic
Manuscripts of 1844. Where Freire is unique in adult

163

education is that he makes the distinction between
nature and culture a key part of the content of his
educational approach. Thus in the 'generative
themes' of his method he introduces the theme of the
'anthropological concept of culture' - 'It clarifies
the role of men in the world and with the world as
transforming rather than adaptive beings.'[34] In
Brazil the first few sessions of the literacy
programme were devoted solely to a discussion of ten
codifications of the theme of nature and culture.
The first picture introduced the theme and
subsequent pictures continued it, with the tenth and
final picture showing a culture circle in action,
enabling the group to reflect directly on its own
activity.[35] For Freire, this is the unique
attribute of human consciousness and self-conscious
existence is what makes it possible for people to
change their situation. It is the philosophical
basis of the very notion of conscientisation. Until
people realise their capacity to make the world,
they are dehumanised. Once they have become
conscious of this, the possibility of humanisation
is opened up:

> The normal role of human beings in and with the
> world is not a passive one. Because they are
> not limited to the natural (biological) sphere
> but participate in the creative dimension as
> well, men can intervene in reality in order to
> change it...men enter into the domain which
> is theirs exclusively - that of History and
> Culture.[36]

Herein lies the significance of his stress on
culture. It is an important point of convergence
with the Marxist principles outlined in Chapter
Three, and it influences other aspects of his
theoretical position, such as the concept of praxis.
It parallels Vygotsky's cultural and historical
approach to human psychology and Freire shares the
Marxist awareness of the significance of the
socially produced sign systems of language and
writing.


THE SIGNIFICANCE OF LANGUAGE AND LITERACY

One of the principles I established in Chapter
Three was that Marxist theory places great
importance on questions of language and literacy for

adult education processes. There is no doubt about Freire's concurrence with this principle. In his early work discussing agricultural extension, Extension or Communication, he made quite clear the significance of the peasants' language and modes of thought for educational efforts to introduce new agricultural techniques. He advocated linguistic investigation to discover the phenomenology of their activity in the sphere of technical methods, arguing that true communication demands a mutually intelligible 'linguistic universe':

> Problem-posing dialogue...diminishes the difference between the sense of an expression as given by a technician, and the grasping of this expression by the peasants in terms of its meaning for them.[37]

Freire is very sensitive to linguistic issues because he regards linguistic and mental processes as virtually identical. The interconnection of thought and language means that words are very much part of people's existential experience, language cannot be isolated from people's social reality:

> Insofar as language is impossible without thought, and language and thought are impossible without the world to which they refer, the human word is more than mere vocabulary - it is word-and-action.[38]

This view accords with the Marxian position expressed in The German Ideology that language has an essentially social character: '...neither thoughts nor language in themselves form a realm of their own...they are only manifestations of actual life.'[39]

Freire's emphasis on the social nature of language is clearly central to his educational method, which takes as its starting-point the language and themes of the participants' experience. Hence he argues that the literacy process is about 'reading the world' as much as 'reading the word' and must involve a critical understanding of the social structures which shape language and thought. For Freire (as for Vygotsky) literacy is a mental tool which has cognitive dimensions that differentiate the literate and the illiterate. In particular, the acquisition of literacy can develop an increased sense of control over one's environment and Freire quotes comments by Chilean peasants to illustrate this.[40]

On the other hand, language can play a role in the processes of oppression and alienation, an aspect of Marxist linguistics being that language use reflects class relations and ideologies. Freire considers this when discussing which language - Creole or Portuguese - should be used for literacy in Guinea-Bissau. He argues that the imposition of a foreign language was part of colonial domination and continues to be an aspect of neo-colonialism. Thus to overcome cultural alienation and colonial dependence it is necessary to assert the national language. Hence Freire regarded the development of Creole as a written language to be a priority in the struggle for reconstruction in Guinea-Bissau. However, the literacy programme in fact used Portuguese, with which people in many areas were not familiar. A subsequent report by the Institute of Cultural Action, entitled Guinea-Bissau '79. Learning by Living and Doing recorded disappointing results from literacy work in Portuguese in such areas and questioned the national linguistic policy.[41]

It is significant that Freire ended Pedagogy in Process with the pledge to return to the issue of language. This would indeed by a valuable contribution. Freire's concern with linguistic issues is fundamental to his educational approach but in fact he does not deal with them systematically. The development of a coherent theory of language and literacy is vital for the development of socialist adult education and Freire is important because he points in the correct direction. The task, however, remains to be done.


THE MODE OF PRODUCTION

The fourth and fifth principles formulated in Chapter Three centre on the concept of the mode of production. They therefore highlight a distinctive element of Marxist theory, namely the important role played by production in shaping the nature of society and the consciousness of individuals. A satisfactory account of adult learning must consider human psychology in the context of the mode of production, and its particular social relations of production and labour process. In the historical development of Marxist thought that I have referred to in earlier chapters, the reaction of 'humanist' Marxism to the positivist and determinist theories of 'official' Marxism led to a one-sided preoccupation with aspects of the superstructure of society. The characteristic concerns of this tendency in Marxism were the subjective areas of culture, ideology and consciousness. While study of these concerns represented a positive achievement historically insofar as it recovered these issues for Marxist analysis, it was attained at the cost of a neglect of the objective structures of society. The importance of the labour process and the need for analysis of the political economy of specific modes of production were overlooked. The historical pendulum of Marxism had swung from materialism to idealism.

Freire in his early writings was influenced by humanist Marxism and one indication of this is his neglect of the role of work in cognitive processes and the absence of concrete analysis of the structural context of adult education. In these writings he does not use the conceptual framework of Marxist political economy and his discussion centres on the psychology of cultural domination rather than the economic mechanisms of exploitation which underlie ideological processes. This is a conscious reaction against mechanistic forms of Marxism which reify social reality and historical processes and which regard social change in a deterministic way:

> Conscientizacao represents the development of the awakening of critical awareness. It will not appear as a natural byproduct of even major economic changes, but must grow out of a critical educational effort, based on favourable historical conditions.[42]

This is a typical criticism of official Marxism's tendency to regard changes in consciousness as entirely dependent on changes in the economic base and exemplifies humanist Marxism's stress on the role of conscious human intervention in history. Of course, Freire is not unaware in these works of the structural determinants of consciousness, rather he chooses to place his emphasis differently. However, the consequence of this is that the labour process is not given the centrality to human psychology that I argued for in Chapter Two. He does occasionally mention work and he recognises that culture is essentially the product of people transforming nature through work. This is clear in the codifications of the theme of the difference between culture and nature, where the human activity of work is the paradigm of the human capacity to transform the world.[43] But production and the labour process are given comparatively little attention and his few attempts at the analysis of the social formation of Brazil are highly unsatisfactory from the perspective of historical materialism. To summarise the early works, then, it can be said that Freire's focus is on forms of consciousness rather than the mode of production. Although he is aware of the structural context of psychological processes, he fails to analyse that context or explicate the connections between the individual and the social structure.

However, there is evidence of a shift in Freire's thinking during the first part of the 1970s. For example, there are signs of this in his paper at the International Symposium on Literacy in Persepolis in 1975 in which he discusses how the class structure of society shapes education and why there is therefore a need to differentiate societies and historical periods when planning educational action for liberation.[44] The shift towards a greater appreciation of the social structure and its material basis is made clear in Pedagogy in Process. The very language of the book with its use of concepts like mode of production, material conditions, class analysis, political economy and so forth indicates a new concern with the structural context of education and consciousness. I will mention three aspects of this concern.

First, Freire pays close attention to the need to analyse the concrete social situation in which the educator is working and to identify the relationship between education and the particular society. In Guinea-Bissau the need to relate educational activity to changes in society became clear, so that decisions were taken to introduce literacy education only in areas where changes in the material conditions were already taking place (for example, in co-operative production) because here it responded to a real need. This involves a subtle change from the idea of education/cultural action as creating social change to one in which it follows or accompanies changes in the social relations of production. This leads him to a re-presentation (even a re-interpretation) of his Brazilian experience which stresses that literacy followed the formation of Peasant Leagues and took root in their criticism of the social relations of capitalist production.[45]

Secondly, he discusses at length the political and economic objective of social reconstruction in Guinea-Bissau which gave priority to developing the forces of production and transforming the relations of production. He feels that this plan for society provides the objectives for education as well. The book is therefore remarkable for its emphasis on the need to establish a strong relation between education and production, study and work. To develop a socialist society:

> ...requires an effort towards massive changes at the level of infrastructures and simultaneous action of an ideological nature. It implies the reorganisation of the means of production and the involvement of workers in a specific form of education, through which they are called to become more than skilled production workers, through an understanding of the process of work itself.[46]

This analysis of the relationship between education and production takes on great significance for 'the very validity of the struggle for literacy.'[47]

Thirdly, Freire moves closer towards a labour theory of knowledge by showing a new interest in work as the source of knowledge. He reports on how in Guinea-Bissau production came to be an important part of the content of literacy and post-literacy education:

> The programmatic content of education emerges from a permanent process of critical reflection. Social practice, especially that related to production, is one of the determining factors. Analysis of practice in production opens the possibility for serious study that can move gradually to a deeper level, the level of the basic reason for things.[48]

He argues that the study of production is the key to understanding the political economy of the country (and gives an extended example from rice production). This is a measure of the development in his thinking towards the incorporation into his educational approach of analysis of the productive

basis of society. Indeed, the analysis of work
('the study of the processes of work and its social
organisation, the study of different modes of
production: precapitalist, capitalist,
socialist.'[49]) becomes central to the thematic
codifications and discussions in the adult education
activities he writes about in <u>Pedagogy in Process</u> so
that this later book begins to show a concern with
the issues raised by my fourth and fifth principles.


PRAXIS AND KNOWLEDGE

In the sixth principle which I formulated in
Chapter Three, I drew attention to the role of human
activity in the process of knowing. I identified
the purposive and intentional nature of such
activity and summed it up in the concept of praxis.
This concept is associated with humanist Marxism,
receiving attention from Lukacs in the 1920s, for
example, and from writers such as Kosik and Petrovic
in the 1960s. The idea refers to the unique
capacity of people to create and change the world
and themselves. As I noted earlier, there is a
controversy within Marxism over the concept. The
debate centres particularly on the extent to which
this creative human activity is free (or limited by
the concrete historical determinants of social
reality) and the extent to which it is the most
important concept of Marxism (or one of less
significance than the concepts of Marx's science of
society). For me it is a very important concept,
especially for the study of education, but I think
it has to be firmly rooted in the context of
political-economic analysis (as we see in the work
of Gramsci).
The sixth principle was based upon an earlier
epistemological discussion that had regarded praxis
as (a) the source of knowledge, (b) the criterion of
the correctness of knowledge, and (c) the objective
of knowledge (whereby learning provides the basis
for new activity). Praxis therefore expresses the
link between thought and action (theory and
practice) and thus conceptualises the relationship
between consciousness and reality. The role of
praxis in knowledge is an important principle on
which to base educational activity. This is a
position with which Freire concurs and he makes
frequent references to writers within the praxis
tradition in Marxism. I think it is true to say

that Freire's discussions of the implications of praxis for adult education constitute the most elaborated statement of my sixth principle that I have encountered.

Freire's starting-point is his emphasis on the fact that educational approaches reflect epistemological positions because education is about knowledge. Hence he writes 'as an act of knowing, learning to read and write presupposes not only a theory of knowing but a method which corresponds to the theory.'[50] This, of course, reflects his fundamental view that educational activities involve philosophical questions.

His own theory of knowledge begins with the idea that people are different from animals because they are able to detach themselves from their natural and social environment, reflect upon it and themselves, and then act to change it. People are therefore in a continual process of activity in the world and reflection upon that activity. Thus the central concept of Freire's epistemology is praxis, that is, conscious action:

> The act of knowing involves a dialectical movement which goes from action to reflection and from reflection upon action to a new action. For the learner to know what he did not know before, he must engage in an authentic process of abstraction by means of which he can reflect on the action-object whole, or, more generally, on forms of orientation in the world.[51]

For Freire, praxis unites thought and action and hence avoids the separation of these which leads either to empty theorising or to mindless activism. It leads him to conclude that education must help people in the process of objectifying the world, critically understanding it, and acting to change it.

His pedagogy is therefore an explicit attempt to embody the theory of knowledge based on praxis. It centres on dialogue, a process in which the educator and educatee search for knowledge together. This search, being founded on praxis, is not simply intellectual but presupposes action as well. Freire conceives learners as active, curious and creative:

> This is why dialogue as a fundamental part of the structure of knowledge needs to be opened

> to other Subjects in the knowing process. Thus
> the class is not a class in the traditional
> sense, but a meeting-place, where knowledge is
> sought and not transmitted.[52]

In contrast, the concept of education as an act of
transmission or transference of knowledge reveals an
incorrect epistemology based on a faulty
understanding of people's relationship to the
natural and social environment. It is this view,
which regards knowledge as static and learners as
passive, that underlies the 'banking education'
which he criticises so often.

It is clear that his own adult education method
derives from his epistemology and the idea of
praxis. The whole process of problem-posing and de-
codification is based on this theory. In
Cultural Action for Freedom he talks about the
culture circle as providing the 'theoretical
context' for analysing the former praxis and
enabling learners to become capable of a new praxis
in the 'concrete context' of social activity. The
use of the same idea in an article written a decade
later which discusses his work in Sao Tome and
Principe indicates the continuity of the role of
praxis in his method.[53]

However, although there is this continuity, it
is noticeable that in Pedagogy in Process Freire
uses the expression 'social practice' more than
praxis and he makes more specific both the content
of that practice (in particular, the struggle for
production and class conflict) and its determining
context: 'knowledge is always a process, and
results from the conscious action (practice) of
human beings on the objective reality which, in
turn, conditions them.'[54] He thus dispels any
doubts arising from his earlier works, in which the
concept of praxis sometimes seems rather abstract
and liable to conceal an idealism that over-
emphasises human freedom to change circumstances. I
therefore conclude that Freire provides a very
helpful consideration of praxis and knowledge for
use by socialist adult educators, pointing the way
to how theory should inform human action. But in
relation to the role and content of theory, serious
problems arise, as we shall see in the next two
sections. To begin with, what is the role of theory
in developing a praxis based on critical
consciousness?

CULTURAL ACTION AND THE UNVEILING OF REALITY

Principles seven and eight in Chapter Three are based on the concepts of ideology and hegemony. The two principles embody the idea that dominated classes internalise the world-view of the ruling class. This happens through the lived experience of the social relations of production and through active theoretical propagation by the ruling class. It leads to a situation in which the dominated classes consent to their own subordination and accept this status quo as natural. However, achieving a critical distance from hegemonic subordination is possible, despite the social weight of ruling class ideology. A central task of socialist adult education, as contained in these two principles, is to help the working class and its allies to challenge ideological domination and develop an alternative set of ideas and values, a counter-hegemony. It therefore aims at a change of consciousness. This is its main educational objective and the starting-point is to reveal the reality hidden by surface appearances and thus unmask ruling ideas. The theoretical tools for this task are provided by Marxism.

Although Freire does not use the conceptual language of hegemony but rather the language of cultural domination, the essential concerns of his approach are very similar to those encapsulated in my seventh and eight principles. His own approach is based upon an analysis of different levels of consciousness which leads him to develop a particular educational method. The aims and processes he advocates are very close in form to a Marxist approach but less close in content. Freire's analysis has certain weaknesses from a Marxist perspective which results from blurring a crucial issue of theory, as I will explain.

Freire develops his theory of cultural domination and cultural action for freedom from his analysis of consciousness, 'these historically and culturally conditioned levels of understanding.'[55] This analysis is presented in a fragmentary rather than systematic fashion and is rather opaque in its expression. I think it is also unsatisfactory in many ways when seen from a Marxist perspective but its importance lies in its having been attempted, so that a specific link is established between the idea of modes of consciousness and forms of education.

He begins from the point that it is people's

relation to reality which results in knowledge (and which is expressed in language). The content of consciousness is therefore the understanding of the relationship between phenomena, the perception of the causal links between data. He distinguishes three main levels of consciousness in terms of this understanding.[56] The first he calls 'magic consciousness' which 'simply apprehends facts and attributes to them a superior power by which it is controlled and to which it must therefore submit'. This level of consciousness is characterised by fatalism and fails to understand causality. The next level he calls 'naive consciousness' which 'sees causality as a static, established fact' and may perhaps be regarded as a kind of empiricism. Thirdly, there is 'critical consciousness' which submits causality to analysis and therefore looks for the underlying relationship between things.

While the psychology of consciousness is important to educational action, it must of course be related to specific political and economic conditions. Freire is aware of this:

> To understand the levels of consciousness, we must understand cultural-historical reality as a superstructure in relation to an infrastructure. Therefore, we will try to discern, in relative rather than absolute terms, the fundamental characteristics of the historical-cultural configurations to which such levels correspond.[57]

However, I do not think he is successful in this endeavour and he remains at the level of generalities such as the 'Third World' and the 'dependent society' because he does not use the concepts of historical materialist analysis to identify more precisely the context of different levels of consciousness. Thus he presents 'magical consciousness', for example, primarily as a characteristic of peasant communities. A pertinent question is whether such a consciousness is a remnant of pre-capitalist modes of production and, if so, what is its relationship to the 'alienated' and 'fetishised' form of consciousness that Marx identified as typical of capitalism and which also attributes to facts a 'superior power'. Freire starts an important line of inquiry which, from my view-point, he does not satisfactorily resolve. In this Freire is a victim of his tradition - it is one of the strengths of humanist Marxism to have focussed on the cultural plane and one of its weaknesses to have neglected its economic basis.

However, his consideration of consciousness leads him to deal with the key issue of mythologised reality via his conception of 'cultural invasion', the process whereby one group in society imposes its own view of the world on another. He discusses how this leads to the oppressed internalising the model of society presented by the dominating class. He looks at this both in terms of colonial domination (drawing on the ideas of Fanon and Memmi) and in terms of the national ruling class. He argues that a whole variety of myths serve to constitute a psychology of oppression leading to what he calls a 'culture of silence', a phrase which catches the idea that the oppressed accept the situation without raising their voice in question. These myths include those at the level of the individual (the poor are lazy, ignorant and unproductive) and at the level of society (there is freedom, equality, opportunity, and rebellion is a sin against god).

The result is that the oppressed accept the notion that they are naturally inferior and that exploitation is a natural state of affairs, 'the oppressed cannot perceive clearly the "order" which serves the interests of the oppressor whose image they have internalised.'[58] Obviously this is the ideological situation which, using Gramsci's language, I referred to in Chapter Two as hegemonic subordination. Freire can therefore be seen to be discussing issues of central importance for socialist adult education. Nevertheless, it should be noted that he discusses the processes of theoretical propagation (through institutions such as education, religion, and the media) rather than the way ideology also arises from the social relations of production. For example, he does not clarify which myths are the result specifically of the capitalist mode of production. Similarly, he only rarely specifies in terms of class analysis the significance of cultural invasion and the resistance to it embodied in cultural action for freedom. But when he does, we become fully aware that his pedagogy is potentially about helping the oppressed develop from a class-in-itself to a class-for-itself:

> ...when the people have reached a relatively clear picture of oppression which leads them to

> localise the oppressor outside themselves, they
> take up the struggle to surmount the
> contradiction [i.e. of opposing classes] in
> which they are caught. At this moment they
> overcome the distance between 'class necessity'
> and 'class consciousness'.[59]

It is on the basis of these understandings of the
processes of ideology and hegemony that Freire's
educational approach is founded - 'we wanted to
offer the means by which people could supersede
their magic or naive perception of reality by one
that was predominantly critical'.[60] This indeed is
the kernel of conscientisation, which I identified
above as the central objective of Freire's method:

> Conscientizacao is a permanent critical
> approach to reality in order to discover it and
> discover the myths that deceive us and help to
> maintain the oppressing dehumanising
> structures.[61]

This is a goal which is entirely compatible with the
Marxist educational aim of unmasking ruling ideas.
Hence the outer form of the Freirean method has a
lot to commend it. However, it has a key
theoretical flaw arising from an issue over which
Freire shows considerable ambivalence and
evasiveness.

The issue centres on the position of the
teacher (co-ordinator) in his method. Problem-
posing education aims to get people to see beyond
the surface appearances of reality, in contrast with
banking education which mystifies reality. It does
this by presenting codifications for discussion by
the learning group (culture circle). It is hoped
that through this discussion the learners will come
to question taken-for-granted explanations and
develop a critical consciousness. The process is
based on a dialogue between the teacher and the
learner which Freire insists must be genuine and
avoid imposition and manipulation. The task of the
teacher is to 'challenge' the learners 'to penetrate
the significance of the thematic content with which
they are confronted'[62] in the codifications. Now,
the question arises as to what is the basis of the
teacher's challenge and, at an earlier stage, what
is the basis of the choice of themes for
codification. Obviously, the basis must be a theory
of society which has concluded that people's

everyday assumptions are very much influenced by the
dominant ideology and which has an accompanying set
of values which gives priority to revealing this
ideology.

It is over the role of this theoretical stance
in the educational process that Freire shows a
profound ambivalence. His dilemma lies in how to
relate the authority the teacher derives from a
correct theory to his humanist antagonism to
imposition:

> While it is normal for investigators to come to
> the area with values which influence their
> perceptions, this does not mean that they may
> transform the thematic investigation into a
> means of imposing these values. The only
> dimension of these values which it is hoped the
> men whose thematics are being investigated will
> come to share (it is presumed that the
> investigators possess this quality) is a
> critical perception of the world, which
> implies a correct method of approaching reality
> in order to unveil it. And critical perception
> cannot be imposed.[63]

The ambivalence which this quotation expresses is
located in the evasiveness about the role of theory
in his educational approach. His entire method is
obviously dependent on a theoretical position (as he
often states in general terms). The identification
of generative themes requires not only an analysis
of a local situation but also a social theory which
includes a conceptual framework of people/nature,
liberation/domination, development/underdevelopment
and so forth and thus enables the educational team
to situate local problems in a national and
international totality. This is revealed in the
'aspects for discussion' suggested to teachers in
Brazil when using the generative word 'plow'. These
are listed as: 'The value of human labour. Men and
techniques: the process of transforming nature.
Labour and capital. Agrarian reform.'[64] It is by
no means predictable that a discussion of a plough
should raise the question of labour and capital, for
example, unless the teacher was committed to
considering the prevailing relations of production
as problematic. The whole process of 'challenging'
the learner's perception of reality only becomes
possible when the educators consistently question
the dominant ideology as expressed by the learners.

Hence the development of 'critical consciousness' cannot be considered abstractly but only in relation to a theory which is critical of the dominant ideology. An account of education for critical consciousness must therefore accept head-on the superiority in terms of theoretical understanding of the teacher and must also specify the content of this theoretical understanding.

I would argue that Freire is usually reluctant to posit the teacher's theoretical superiority because he identifies this necessarily with imposition. Nevertheless, at one point in <u>Pedagogy of the Oppressed</u> he does indicate a solution to his dilemma when talking about revolutionary leaders (who in fact he regards as educators):

> Although they may legitimately recognise themselves as having, due to their revolutionary consciousness, a level of revolutionary knowledge different from the level of empirical knowledge held by the people, they cannot impose themselves and their knowledge on the people. They cannot sloganise the people, but they must enter into dialogue with them, so that the people's empirical knowledge of reality, nourished by the leaders' critical knowledge, gradually becomes transformed into knowledge of the causes of reality.[65]

Here he suggests the possibility of dialogue conceived as an encounter between people who, at the level of consciousness and knowledge, are unequal.

But it is only in <u>Pedagogy in Process</u> where the dilemma is faced squarely and he distinguishes between valuing and idealising popular wisdom.[66] In doing so he refers to Amilcar Cabral's identification of 'weaknesses of culture', revealed for example in unscientific explanations of thunder, belief in the efficacy of amulets to deflect bullets, and belief in the inferiority of women. Here Freire makes clear that the people's views have to be judged as incorrect in this instance. Relativism is untenable.

One of his most recent comments on the issue is in his discussion of his work in Sao Tome and Principe:

> The opposite of being directive is not being non-directive - that is likewise an illusion.

> The opposite both of manipulation and
> spontaneity is critical and democratic
> participation by the learners...[67]

This of course is the only solution - the educators
must share their theoretical knowledge with learners
(who apply it to their concrete situation) in a
process which does not deny inequality of knowledge
but which is based on co-operative and democratic
principles of equal power.

My argument is that there is a populist and
liberal element in Freire's thinking that pulls him
towards an uncritical faith in 'the people' and
makes him ambivalent about saying outright that
educators can have a theoretical understanding
superior to that of the learners and which is, in
fact, the indispensable condition of the development
of critical consciousness. This ambivalence has
perhaps been remedied in his later writings.
However, he remains evasive about specifying what
the content of that theory should be. The
eclecticism of his own theoretical stance stops him
from singling out the theory which is most useful in
unveiling the mystifications of bourgeois ideology.

Let me summarise at this point. The emphasis
on the cultural plane is at the centre of Freire's
educational approach, quite rightly as education is
a site of cultural reproduction and resistance. His
objective is conscientisation and he proposes his
method as a means of developing this critical
consciousness. But in his early works particularly
he shows a deep ambivalence about the theoretical
position of the educators that is necessary if they
are going to help learners to 'unveil reality'. So
although he quotes approvingly Lenin's maxim that
'without a revolutionary theory there can be no
revolutionary movement'[68] he never spells out the
content of this theory. His own eclecticism
prevents him from identifying Marxism as the theory
which can most comprehensively expose the ideology
of capitalism and therefore provide the basis of
critical education. Thus, in the final analysis, it
is the weakness of Freire's political theory that
disables his approach as a vehicle for socialist
adult education. His emphasis on the cultural plane
is revealed as inadequate because it is not
synchronised with an explanation of the political
economy of revolution. Cultural action for freedom
is empty if it is not theoretically and practically
connected to political and economic action for

socialist revolution.

THE POLITICS OF REVOLUTION

The ninth and last principle that I put forward in Chapter Three locates adult education in the context of the practical struggle for revolutionary socialism. It emphasises that education is part of the process of cultural and ideological struggle for counter-hegemony and must be linked to organisations seeking economic and political power. It is derived in general from the theory of revolution proposed in Chapter One and in particular from Gramsci's theory of hegemony discussed in Chapter Two. It concludes that adult education for socialism must be connected with activities to change the political and economic structure of capitalist society.

Freire shares the concern that education should contribute to revolution - 'problem-solving education...posits as fundamental that men subjected to domination must fight for their emancipation.'[69] And he discusses education's role both in preparing the ground for revolution ('cultural action') and in continuing to develop people's attitudes and capabilities after the revolution ('cultural revolution'). He also puts forward the view that revolution is itself an educative process, drawing parallels between revolutionary leaders and educators. Thus there are broad similarities between his approach and one committed to developing socialist hegemony. However, there are problems when we consider his position on the politics of revolution. In discussing this I will note again the difference between Pedagogy in Process and the early works because I think that the later book remedies to some extent their political weaknesses. These weaknesses originate in the vagueness and errors of Freire's theory of revolution.

We saw in Chapter One that a revolution involves a transformation in society whereby political and economic power changes hands from one class to another. In a bourgeois revolution, the capitalist class takes power from the feudal ruling class; in a nationalist revolution, a national ruling class takes power from foreign rule. For a socialist revolution, the working class and its allies must take over power from the capitalist class. This means taking political control of the state and economic control of the means of

180

production. It is only on this basis that the majority of society can end their economic exploitation (based on the capitalist extraction of surplus value) and its accompanying forms of political control. Such a revolution occurs in a situation in which the necessary objective conditions (like increased proletarianisation and exploitation) and subjective conditions (like heightened class consciousness) converge to make the existing status quo unstable. In this kind of situation, the energy of the exploited classes can be organised as a social force to overthrow capitalism and establish a new social order. This theory of revolution provides an explanation of how socialism can be achieved in certain conditions. It centres on such concepts as the mode of production, the class structure, class conflict, the state, power, political organisation and class consciousness.

It is this kind of theoretical perspective on revolution that Freire fails to provide. He presents no analysis of the social structure of the capitalist mode of production. The 'oppressed', for example, is a very vague term in Freirean usage. He seldom clarifies what he means (though he does once suggest they are 'cheated in the sale of their labour'[70]). He never provides a thoroughgoing class analysis which could, for instance, consider crucial class differences within the countryside (say between landless rural workers and landholding peasants). Similarly, he uses a concept the 'epoch' which has none of the analytical power of the concept of mode of production. Thus, for example, he fails to analyse the situation in Brazil in the early 1960s in terms of the increased penetration of capitalist social relations of production with the industrial development that had taken place in the 1940s and 1950s. So he gives no account of the economic basis of the social context in which his early literacy work took place.

Of course, insofar as he has borrowed from Marxism this reflects the tendency of humanist Marxism to be concerned with the subjective (attitudes, consciousness, and so on) in a way that neglects the structural. This admittedly is part of a deliberate reaction against mechanistic forms of Marxism which assume that economic contradictions will of themselves inevitably lead to revolution, over-emphasising objective conditions and neglecting the subjective. Freire often criticises this mechanistic view, particularly in Pedagogy of the Oppressed. However, it leads him to stress the cultural at the expense of the political and economic. He is aware of the danger of his own position, as he shows when explaining the notion of conscientizacao:

> Conscientizacao implies that in discovering myself oppressed I know that I will be liberated only if I try to transform the oppressing situation in which I find myself. And I cannot transform that situation just in my head - that would be idealism, a way of thinking which believes that conscience [consciousness] can transform reality just by thinking. In this instance the structures would go on the same and my freedom would not begin to grow.[71]

But Freire provides no theoretical analysis of the nature of these structures and how they can be transformed, so that by not showing the way out of the idealist cul-de-sac he leaves himself open to the charge of idealism.

Thus he presents what is, in the end, a romantic view of revolution which gives no indication of how and in what objective circumstances revolution can be achieved. For example, he has no conception of the role of the working class as an agency of emancipation. Indeed, he has a tendency to portray revolution in subjective, individual terms and not in terms of the objective realities of class struggle. He often uses strong Christian overtones in showing revolution as an act of love, a product of faith in humanity. By so doing he places consideration of revolution on a moral plane rather than in the context of a theory of society and historical development. This is the source of the very abstract nature of his early writing when it refers to revolution.

Another indication of the weakness of Freire's writing about revolution in his early works is that there is a total absence of a clear specification of the goal of revolution. We know in general terms what Freire is against - alienation, dehumanisation, oppression - but we do not know what he is advocating. For this reason, his talk about revolution often appears rhetorical. The goal of freedom and human liberation is an empty one because he gives no guide to the forms of political and economic institutions through which it would become possible. He talks vaguely about the revolution being undertaken by the 'authentic left' and he warns about the dangers of bureaucracy after a revolution. But he avoids saying his goal is a socialist revolution and he gives no account of the changes in the social relations of production, in the role of state power and so on that would make concrete the nature of society in which people can achieve their human potential. Thus whilst he shares the Marxian vision of a society 'guaranteeing to all the free development and exercise of their physical and mental faculties'[72] he does so as a Christian humanist not as a socialist.

However, in <u>Pedagogy in Process</u> we do see a shift in this position when he discusses Guinea-Bissau, where the nationalist government after independence in 1975 adopted a socialist programme. Freire was then in a practical situation in which there was a 'model of society' and in which adult education was to be organised according to its role in constructing this society.[73] It is interesting to note that Freire, in discussing how this model is derived from the theoretical work of Amilcar Cabral, states that 'This model is, first of all, a political model'[74] which involves a cultural project within it and also economic goals. The practical primacy given here to politics situates more properly the role of educational activity. Also, Freire refers frequently to the new society trying to move towards socialism. In this context, he specifies the kinds of changes in production, political forms, social services and so forth which characterise socialist development (including as a comparative example the Tachai commune in China). He can therefore be seen in this book to begin to commit himself to adult education for socialism, a much clearer position than his earlier radical humanism.

These contrasting positions can also be found in his views on the role of political organisation. In his first three books, for example, his views are very much influenced by his antagonism to official Marxism and bureaucratic socialism. This antagonism expressed itself practically during his work in Brazil - De Kadt suggests that in 1962 Freire transferred his work with the culture circles of the municipality of Recife to the university's extension service in order to avoid the influence of the

Brazilian Communist Party.[75] This action was characteristic of the position of many of the radical Catholics in Brazil prior to the 1964 coup. De Kadt describes this radical position as 'populist', defining populist movements like this:

> 1. They are made up of intellectuals (and students), concerned with the life-situation of the down-trodden masses in society, the 'people', who apparently cannot by themselves assert their interests;
>
> 2. These intellectuals have a deep-seated horror of the manipulation of the people; their central credo is that solutions to the problems lived by the people must ultimately come from the people themselves, that their own ideas and visions, developed in a wholly different milieu, may at most serve as a sounding board for, but never as signposts to the people.[76]

This definition catches very well the political position displayed by Freire in his early writings (although he himself attacks there 'populismo', which in Brazilian usage refers to a leader manipulating the masses for his own interests). This kind of populism led the Catholic radicals to oppose that concept of political organisation which stresses the role of the party in mobilising dominated classes to undertake their own emancipation, based on clear ideological leadership. It is exemplified by the section on 'organisation' in Pedagogy of the Oppressed which criticises attitudes of manipulation but makes no practical alternative suggestions for forms of political organisation.[77]

Freire's antagonism to the politics of official Marxism is revealed in theoretical terms in his early writings by the avoidance of 'class' and 'party' and the concentration on 'the people' and 'the revolutionary leader'. In this he aligns himself with the anti-Bolshevik tendency of humanist Marxism. This is a political position akin to what Lukacs, in a criticism of his own earlier views, calls 'messianic utopianism'.[78] It is an exceedingly apt phrase for Freire's concept of revolutionary politics with its emphasis on the middle-class leader who has undergone an 'Easter experience' of class suicide in order to be with the people:

> ...Guevara incarnated the authentic
> revolutionary utopia as did few others. He was
> one of the great prophets of the silent ones of
> the Third World.[79]

On this issue I am in substantial agreement with the
comments of Walker. The section of his chapter
which is entitled 'Educators and Revolutionary
Leaders' provides a devastating critique of Freire's
over-emphasis on petty-bourgeois political
leadership.[80] Walker identifies this as 'populist,
rather than socialist' politics and argues that it
reflects an idealism and voluntarism stemming from
Freire's Christianity. However, while Walker
extends his critique to all periods of Freire's
work, I personally note some changes during the
1970s. For example, the 1973 interview 'A
Conversation with Paulo Freire' gives greater
emphasis to the role of the revolutionary party in
helping the dominated class become a 'class-for-
itself' and to linking conscientisation to political
action.[82] Similarly, in Pedagogy in Process there is
more concern with the party and its role in
mobilising and organising the people and providing
ideological leadership. Freire refers approvingly
to Guinea-Bissau's ruling party (PAIGC) as 'the
vanguard of the people'[82] and he is much more
specific about political organisation. He also
expresses some scepticism about the commitment of
petty-bourgeois intellectuals, concluding that 'it is
easier to create a new type of intellectual - forged
in the unity between practice and theory, manual and
intellectual work - than to re-educate an elitist
intellectual.'[83]

However, I remain uneasy about Freire's
analysis of the politics of revolution. He has
given no systematic account of the conditions of
revolution, the form of political organisation or
the programme of action. The evidence that he has
committed himself to the politics of revolutionary
socialism is fragmentary. My conclusion, then, is
that to talk as Freire does of revolution and theory
without specifying precisely the contents of those
terms, is to court misinterpretation and encourage
confusion. To provide a clear basis for relating
adult education to the politics of socialist
revolution, it is necessary to rephrase Lenin in a
totally unambiguous way - there can be no
revolutionary socialist movement without Marxist
theory. This is not a position with which Freire

has identified himself and this constitutes the most important limitation on his usefulness to the development of a socialist approach to adult education.


THE CONSEQUENCES OF ECLECTICISM

In the foregoing analysis I have considered Freire's approach in terms of the principles I regard as embodying a coherent Marxist approach to adult learning. The analysis discussed eight of these nine principles in detail. (I took for granted that Freire agrees with the belief in adult developmental potential contained in my second principle.) It will be apparent that my overall assessment of Freire's pedagogy from this Marxist perspective is a mixed one. This is a conclusion he himself predicted in his Preface to Pedagogy of the Oppressed when he wrote 'I am certain that Christians and Marxists, though they may disagree with me in part or in whole, will continue reading to the end.'[84] There are definitely enough points of convergence to make his work of compelling interest to socialist adult educators. But there are also enough points of divergence to provoke significant disagreement. The mixed verdict that is therefore inevitable arises from a single source - Freire's eclecticism.

I noted earlier in the chapter that Freire's theoretical position derives from three main traditions - Christianity, existentialism-phenomenology, and humanist Marxism. The common denominator of these traditions is a form of philosophical idealism, found in the theism of Christianity and the Hegelian roots of both existentialism-phenomenology and humanist Marxism. Thus it is an eclecticism which brings together elements which have a certain complementarity. In fact, it should perhaps be described as syncretism (i.e. the adding of other elements to a religious belief) because Freire is first and foremost a Christian. Other theoretical elements are additions to this primary position, they do not coexist as equals.

Freire's eclecticism has been mentioned by numerous commentators - Leach, for example, writes of his 'jackdaw-like' borrowing of concepts.[85] The most extended analysis is to be found in Mackie's chapter 'Contributions to the thought of Paulo

Freire' which attempts to detect the origins of
these borrowings. Although I do not fully agree
with Mackie's analysis (for example of Freire's
socialism), I think his conclusion is important:

> ...the very diversity of his thought is both a
> strength and a weakness: a strength in that it
> creatively draws together many strands of
> contemporary thinking into a dynamic and
> challenging theory; a weakness, in that such a
> procedure makes it all too easy for one aspect
> of Freire's writing to be spotlighted at the
> expense of others.[86]

This conclusion identifies clearly the problem of
multiple interpretations of Freire. In fact the
diversity of his thought is not a strength as Mackie
suggests, it is only a weakness. Freire's
theoretical position is ambiguous, contradictory,
evasive and incoherent. For me, eclecticism is a
pejorative description. However, I recognise that
for others it is a positive word - Retamal, for
example, writes of Freire's work as 'one of the most
important contemporary eclectical efforts to set up
a dialogue between Christians and Marxists.'[87]
Indeed, the combining of different elements together
is the reason why there has been such widespread
interest in his work by adult educators of very
different persuasions.
    It is possible that this general interest may
diminish - Giroux when reviewing <u>Pedagogy in Process</u>
suggested that:

> Freire's most recent work might cost him his
> liberal supporters...with the publication of
> <u>Pedagogy in Process</u>, it will be difficult to
> mis-interpret the political assumptions behind
> Freire's theory and practice.[88]

Certainly I agree that this book does represent a
shift in position and comes closer to a Marxist
approach which integrates the analysis of the
ideological plane with that of the political
economy. But Freire, while acknowledging the
evolution of his own ideas, has not provided an
extended critique of his earlier positions nor has
he himself identified a major development in his own
thought. (In this respect, <u>The Politics of
Education</u>, which contains hardly any new material,
does not signify an intellectual advance.) Thus his

whole corpus remains the point of reference for adult educators. His writings, taken as a whole, represent a thoroughgoing eclecticism which provides a kind of Rorschach test into which adult educators project their own viewpoint. This leads, not surprisingly, to two contradictory positions. On one side, Freire is adopted by liberal (and not-so-liberal) educators for essentially conservative purposes. On the other side, Freire becomes an inspiration for socialist educators. Let me consider these positions more closely.

Reference to Freire and his method is made in contexts in which it is clear that those using his ideas do not have socialist political goals. For example, Smith's book exploring the meaning of conscientizacao in practice was based on a non-formal education project in Ecuador run by the Ministry of Education and the University of Massachusetts, funded by the US Agency for International Development. One aim of the project was 'to utilise modified forms of Freire's methodology to demonstrate that such a method of literacy was more effective than the literacy system being used.'[89] Now it is of course inconceivable that the US government would sponsor education designed to promote socialism in Ecuador. Indeed, the Central American policy of the USA has for years been designed to prevent socialism. So obviously Freire's approach had been sanitised of any potentially subversive implications.

This phenomenon has been called 'co-option' by Kidd and Kumar, who discuss it at length in their article 'Co-opting Freire. A critical analysis of pseudo-Freirean adult education'. In this article they argue that Freire's ideas have been diluted and misused in many Third World adult education projects, particularly those aiming to incorporate peasants into capitalist agriculture. They identify such adaptations of Freire as 'pseudo-Freirean' and present a case study of World Education, Inc. This is a private US organisation (supported by bodies like the World Bank and USAID) which sponsors non-formal education in fifty Third World countries in the US sphere of influence. World Education has used Freirean approaches and the article gives concrete examples from its literacy projects in Thailand, India and Turkey. Kidd and Kumar attack:

> ...the use of Freirean terminology and method without its substance as a smokescreen for the

continued domestication of Third World peasants
and workers in the interests of foreign
capital.[90]

But while the article provides an extended
description of how Freire is used for conservative
ends, it does not give an explanation of why this
happens.   In my opinion, this is because they
themselves have misread Freire, seeing more in his
work than is actually there.  (It is noticeable that
they do not refer to Pedagogy in Process.)  Freire's
terminology and method can be used like this
precisely because the substance of theory on which
it is based is so ambiguous.   In fact, they are
wrong to regard the phenomenon as 'co-option'.   It
is a result which Freire's eclecticism encourages.
Indeed, it should never be forgotten that Freire's
own work in Brazil and Chile in the 1960s was with
modernising capitalist governments.
    It is my impression that  the majority of
commentaries on Freire and the majority of
programmes which claim to use his approach are
politically conservative.   It is not surprising that
the Consolidated Edison Company in New York used his
approach to teach uneducated and unskilled people so
that they might become 'employable and promotable'[91]
or that even the national literacy programme of the
military government in Brazil itself (MOBRAL) used
some Freirean techniques.   These seem to me not to
be 'misuses' of Freire but rather the logical
consequences of his own eclecticism.
    However, it is also true that a number of
socialist adult education programmes have
derived benefit from the Freirean approach.   For
example, adult literacy programmes in Portugal in
1974-1976 and in Nicaragua in 1980 both made
reference to Freire's ideas.   One of the most
detailed accounts of a socialist use of Freire's
ideas is to be found in Shor's Critical Teaching and
Everyday Life.[92]   In this book Shor describes his
work as an English teacher on the City University of
New York Open Admissions programme to develop
literacy and critical thought with his working class
students.   He situates his work in the classroom
within the political economy of expanded higher
education in the USA in the 1970s  He discusses  in
very practical terms exactly what implementing a
Freirean approach in this kind of situation means.
He makes very clear what developing a 'critical
classroom' involves and how it can challenge the

everyday ideological domination expressed in racism,
sexism and class mystification. Significantly, Shor
recognises the importance of <u>Pedagogy in Process</u>.
The only weakness in the book is that he does not
suggest how the new critical awareness of his
students - their 'structural perception' - can lead
to political action outside the classroom. But as a
statement of the theory and practice of socialist
teaching influenced by Freire his account is
unsurpassed. Nevertheless, it is necessary to add
that a number of people involved in working class
adult education have started with a great interest
in Freire's work but have become disillusioned about
its usefulness (as in the case of the Community
Action Research and Education Project in Northern
Ireland).[93]
    The political distance between the
geographically proximate training programme of the
Consolidated Edison company and the classroom of
Shor in New York is starkly symbolic of the
consequences of Freire's eclecticism. If a
capitalist corporation and a socialist teacher can
both refer to the same source of ideas, then
obviously that source is deeply equivocal. From a
Marxist viewpoint, this is why an assessment of
Freire has to be so rigorous. Freire's potential to
be helpful to socialist adult educators is only as
strong as their own ability to discern what is
useful and what is politically disabling.
    This is the task which I have attempted to
undertake in this chapter. I have tried to weigh up
Freire's work and indicate what is positive and what
is not only unhelpful but actually obstructive. In
this balance sheet, I have suggested that there is
a lot to be learnt from Freire's stress on the
political nature of adult education, from his
anthropological concept of culture, his sensitivity
to linguistic issues, and his concern with
consciousness and cultural domination. On the other
hand, I have identified philosophical weaknesses, a
neglect of the mode of production and political-
economic analysis, and a lack of commitment to
Marxist theory and socialist revolution. I have
also singled out <u>Pedagogy in Process</u> for particular
attention. I would like to note here that two of the
letters in the book - Letter 11 and Letter 15 - do
in fact provide a very significant insight into the
nature of socialist adult education and the approach
to adult learning that it should incorporate. But
my final verdict is that, from a Marxist

perspective, Freire's work as a whole does not provide a satisfactory basis for adult education for socialism. His work is eclectic and lacks the 'imperious coherence'[94] that he himself demands of revolutionaries. The question that now arises is what constitutes a socialist pedagogy for adult education?


NOTES

1. C.A. Torres, 'From the "Pedagogy of the Oppressed" to "A Luta Continua". An essay on the political pedagogy of Paulo Freire', Education with Production, Vol. 1 No. 2 (1982): 94.

2. L. Bataille, Ed., A Turning Point for Literacy (Oxford: Pergamon, 1976), pp. 273-276.

3. See, for example, I. Shor, Critical Teaching and Everyday Life (Boston: South End Press, 1980).

4. J.L. Elias and S. Merriam, Philosophical Foundations of Adult Education (New York: Kneger, 1980), p. 139.

5. S.M. Grabowski, Ed., Paulo Freire: A Revolutionary Dilemma for the Adult Educator (Syracuse: ERIC Clearing House on Adult Education, 1972).

6. R. Mackie, Ed., Literacy and Revolution: The Pedagogy of Paulo Freire (London: Pluto Press, 1980), p. 9.

7. P.L. Berger, Pyramids of Sacrifice (New York: Basic Books, 1974), Chap. 4.

8. E. Norman, 'Totalitarianism in the making', Times Educational Supplement, 2/11/78: 2.

9. J. Walker, 'The end of dialogue: Paulo Freire on politics and education', in Literacy and Revolution: The Pedagogy of Paulo Freire, Ed., R. Mackie (London: Pluto Press, 1980).

10. P. Freire, Cultural Action for Freedom (Harmondsworth: Penguin, 1972).
P. Freire, Pedagogy of the Oppressed (Harmondsworth: Penguin, 1972).
P.Freire, Education: The Practice of Freedom (London: Writer and Readers Publishing Co-operative, 1976).
P. Freire, Pedagogy in Process (London: Writers and Readers Publishing Co-operative, 1978).
P. Freire, The Politics of Education (London: Macmillan, 1985)

11.   J.L. Elias and S. Merriam, Ibid.
12. P. Freire,   Cultural Action for Freedom (Harmondsworth: Penguin, 1972), p. 21.
13.  P.  Freire,  Education:  The Practice of Freedom (London: Writers and Readers Publishing Co-operative), p. 49
14.   Ibid., pp. 41-58.
15. P.Freire, Pedagogy   of   the   Oppressed (Harmondsworth: Penguin, 1972), pp. 60-95.
16. P. Freire,  Education:  The  Practice of Freedom (London: Writers and Readers Publishing Co-operative), p. 42.
17. P. Freire, Pedagogy  of  the  Oppressed (Harmondsworth: Penguin, 1972), p. 68.
18. P. Freire  Education:  The  Practice  of Freedom (Harmondsworth: Penguin, 1972), p. 51.
19. P. Freire, Pedagogy  of  the  Oppressed (Harmondsworth: Penguin, 1972), p. 86.
20.   Ibid., p. 94.
21.   Freire gives the example of the Portuguese word for brick, tijolo. He shows how it is broken into its constituent syllables - ti, jo, lo, - and then the phonemic family of each syllable is presented (e.g. ta-te-ti-to-tu).  The most important point is when the three families are presented together:

ta-te-ti-to-tu
ja-je-ji-jo-ju
la-le-li-lo-lu

This 'discovery card' enables the learners to synthesise new words from vertical and horizontal combinations of syllables eg. luta (struggle), jato (jet), tela (screen).  From P. Freire, Education: The Practice of Freedom (London: Writers and Readers Publishing Co-operative, 1976), p. 54.
22. P. Freire, Pedagogy in Process, (London: Writers and Readers Publishing Co-operative, 1978), p. 9.
23.  Ibid., p. 47.
24. E. De Kadt, Catholic Radicals in Brazil (London: Oxford University Press, 1970).
25. R. Davis, 'Education  for  awareness: a talk  with  Paulo  Freire',  in  Literacy and Revolution: The Pedagogy of Paulo Freire, Ed., R. Mackie (London: Pluto, 1980), p. 68.
26. P. Freire, Cultural  Action  for Freedom (Harmondsworth: Penguin, 1972), p. 31.
27. A. Kee, A  Reader  in Political Theology

(London: SCM Press, 1974), p. 2.

28. Quoted in R. Pierce, Contemporary French Political Thought (London: Oxford University Press, 1966), p. 84.

29. G. Guttierrez, A Theology of Liberation (London: SCM Press), pp. 204-205.

30. F. Engels, 'The condition of England', in K. Marx and F. Engels, Collected Works Vol. 3 (London: Lawrence and Wishart, 1975), p. 465.

31. P. Freire, Education: The Practice of Freedom (London: Writers and Readers Publishing Co-operative, 1976), p.3

32. P. Freire, Pedagogy of the Oppressed (Harmondsworth: Penguin, 1972), p. 54.

33. Ibid., p. 55.

34. Ibid., p. 92.

35. P. Freire, Education: The Practice of Freedom (London: Writers and Readers Publishing Co-operative, 1976), pp. 62-81.

36. Ibid., p.4.

37. Ibid., p. 137.

38. P. Freire, Cultural Action for Freedom (Harmondsworth: Penguin, 1972), p. 29.

39. K. Marx and F. Engels, The German Ideology. Ed., C.J. Arthur (London: Lawrence and Wishart, 1970), p. 118.

40. P. Freire, Ibid., pp. 43-44.

41. IDAC, Guinea-Bissau '79. Learning by Living and Doing (Geneva: IDAC, 1979). See also Freire's remarks on Creole in the interview in The Politics of Education (London: Macmillan, 1985), pp. 183-185.

42. P. Freire, Education: The Practice of Freedom (London: Writers and Readers Publishing Co-operative, 1976), p.19.

43. Ibid., pp. 62-81.

44. P. Freire, 'Are literacy programmes neutral?', in A Turning Point for Literacy Ed., L. Bataille (Oxford: Pergamon, 1976).

45. P. Freire, Pedagogy in Process (London: Writers and Readers Publishing Co-operative, 1978), pp. 110-111.

46. Ibid., p. 15.

47. Ibid., p. 112.

48. Ibid., p. 144.

49. Ibid., p. 115.

50. P. Freire, Cultural Action for Freedom (Harmondsworth: Penguin, 1972), p. 31.

51. Ibid.

52. P. Freire, Education: The Practice of

_Freedom_ (London: Writers and Readers Publishing Co-operative, 1976), p. 148.

53.    P. Freire, 'The  people speak their word: learning to read and write in Sao Tome and Principe', _Harvard Educational Review_, Vol. 51, No 1 (1981): 27-30.

54.    P. Freire, _Pedagogy in Process_ (London: Writers and Readers Publishing Co-operative, 1978), p. 89.

55.    P. Freire, _Education: The Practice of Freedom_ (London: Writers and Readers Publishing Co-operative, 1976), p. 17.

56.    Ibid., p. 44.

57.    P. Freire, _Cultural Action for Freedom_ (Harmondsworth: Penguin, 1972), p. 57.

58.    P. Freire, _Pedagogy of the Oppressed_ (Harmondsworth: Penguin, 1972), p. 38.

59.    Ibid., p. 132.

60.    P. Freire, _Education: The Practice of Freedom_ (London: Writers and Readers Publishing Co-operative, 1976), p. 44.

61.    P. Freire, 'A few notions about the word conscientisation', in _Schooling and Capitalism_, Eds., R. Dale, G. Esland and M. Macdonald (London: Routledge and Kegan Paul, 1976), p. 225.

62.    P. Freire, _Education: The Practice of Freedom_ (London: Writers and Readers Publishing Co-operative), p. 159.

63.    P. Freire, _Pedagogy of the Oppressed_ (Harmondsworth: Penguin, 1972), p. 83.

64.    P. Freire, _Education: The Practice of Freedom_ (London: Writers and Readers Publishing Co-operative), p. 83.

65.    P. Freire, _Pedagogy of the Oppressed_ (Harmondsworth: Penguin, 1972), p. 104.

66.    P. Freire, _Pedagogy in Process_ (London: Readers and Writers Publishing Co-operative, 1978), p. 24.

67.    P. Freire, 'The people speak their word: learning to read and write in Sao Tome and Principe', _Harvard Educational Review_, Vol. 51. No. 1. (1981): 28.

68    P. Freire, _Pedagogy of the Oppressed_ (Harmondsworth: Penguin, 1972), p. 96.

69.    Ibid., p. 58.

70.    Ibid., p. 26.

71.    P. Freire, 'A few notions about the word 'conscientisation'', in _Schooling and Capitalism_, Eds., R. Dale, G. Esland and M. Macdonald (London: Routledge and Kegan Paul, 1976), p. 225.

72. F. Engels, 'Socialism: Utopian and scientific', in K. Marx and F. Engels, Selected Works Vol. 2. (London: Lawrence and Wishart, 1950), p. 140.

73. It is not my concern here to analyse to what extent the actual course of history in Guinea-Bissau from 1975 to the present exhibits socialist development or socialist adult education. Rather I am concerned to analyse Freire's position as he expressed it in his book. A critical analysis of the Guinea-Bissau literacy campaign has recently been completed: L. Harasim, Literacy and National Reconstruction in Guinea-Bissau: A Critique of the Freirean Literacy Campaign. Unpublished Ph.D thesis. (Toronto: Ontario Institute for Studies in Education, 1983.)

74. P. Freire, Pedagogy in Process (London: Writers and Readers Publishing Co-operative), p. 77.

75. E. De Kadt, Ibid., p. 104.

76. Ibid., p. 98.

77. P. Freire, Pedagogy Of the Oppressed (Harmondsworth: Penguin, 1972), pp. 143-146.

78. G. Lukacs, History and Class Consciousness, (London: Merlin Press, 1971), p. XXV.

79. P. Freire, Cultural Action for Freedom (Harmondsworth: Penguin, 1972), p. 75.

80. J. Walker, Ibid., pp. 134-144.

81. P. Freire, The Politics of Education (London: Macmillan, 1985), pp. 151-164.

82. P. Freire, Pedagogy in Process (London: Writers and Readers Publishing Co-operative, 1978), p. 34.

83. Ibid., p. 104.

84. P. Freire, Pedagogy of the Oppressed (Harmondsworth: Penguin, 1972), p. 17.

85. T. Leach, 'Paulo Freire: dialogue, politics and relevance', International Journal of Lifelong Education, Vol. 1. No. 3 (1982): 187.

86. R. Mackie, 'Contributions to the thought of Paulo Freire' in Literacy and Revolution: The Pedagogy of Paulo Freire, Ed., R. Mackie (London: Pluto, 1980), p. 118.

87. G. Retamal, Paulo Freire, Christian Ideology and Adult Education in Latin America (Hull: Department of Adult Education, University of Hull, 1981), p. 11.

88. H.A. Giroux, Ideology, Culture and the Process of Schooling (Sussex: Falmer Press, 1981), p. 135.

89. W.A. Smith, The Meaning of Conscientizacao

- The Goal of Paulo Freire's Pedagogy (Amherst:
University of Massachusetts, 1976), p. 4.

90. R. Kidd and K. Kumar, 'Co-opting Freire.
A critical analysis of pseudo-Freirean adult
education', Economy and Political Weekly, Vol XVI.
Nos. 1 and 2, January 3-10 (1981): 27-36.

91. S. De Leon, 'Radical approach to
literacy', New York Times, May 1 (1977):p. 36.

92. I. Shor, Ibid.

93. T.Lovett, C. Clarke and A. Kilmurray
Adult Education and Community Action (London: Croom
Helm, 1983), pp. 141-144.

94. P. Freire, Cultural Action for Freedom
(Harmondsworth: Penguin, 1972), p. 74.

CHAPTER SIX

## ADULT EDUCATION AND SOCIALIST PEDAGOGY

In this chapter I will begin by summarising the purpose and curriculum content of socialist adult education as these have emerged from my earlier discussions. I will then discuss the concept of a socialist pedagogy and provide concrete illustrations in a number of case studies. Finally I will consider the development of a socialist pedagogy for adult education.

I have argued in earlier chapters that capitalist adult education in general serves to reinforce and legitimate the division of labour and relationships of power of the capitalist mode of production. Its purposes are therefore two-fold. First, to develop the differentiated intellectual capabilities, attitudes and skills required by the hierarchical structure of the capitalist labour market. Secondly, to engender the ideology and social practices which legitimate and perpetuate the capitalist social order. The nature of the organisation, contents and methods of adult education in capitalist social formations reflects these purposes. It thus presents the kind of adult education which socialists must negate and to which they must provide alternatives.

The aims of socialist adult education are therefore directly opposite to those of capitalism. These aims are as follows:

a) to challenge the ideology and culture of capitalism and create a counter-hegemony;

b) to develop the general knowledge and technical expertise necessary to reorganise production and society in a fully democratic way.

Socialist adult education seeks to meet these aims on as large a scale as possible, reaching not only leadership cadres but also the masses on whom a successful revolution depends. Thus although the development of 'organic intellectuals' and cadres (party workers, trade union officials, community organisers and so forth) has a high priority, equally important are mass adult education programmes to reach the majority of the adult population. Socialist adult education can be conceptualised in terms of three dimensions - political, general, and technical education. (These should be considered as dimensions of a single activity and not as separate entities.)

One dimension is political education, whose focus is the development of socialist political awareness and behaviour. Class consciousness is a significant factor in the struggle for socialism and a primary task for socialist adult education is to create such a consciousness. This means engendering an understanding of capitalist society by unmasking the dominant ideology. It also means developing an understanding of how to change capitalism and a personal commitment to this goal. This dimension is encompassed by the concept of creating a counter-hegemony that I discussed in Chapter Two. It requires the evolution of new ideas (for which Marxism is the indispensable theoretical basis) and new social practices (of co-operation, solidarity and so on). In the broadest sense, this implies the creation of an anti-capitalist culture, opposed to class oppression, sexism, racism, and ethnic discrimination. In the Third World, especially, it means opposing the manifold forms of cultural imperialism.

The development of socialist political awareness involves an understanding of what needs to be done through participation in collective action. Hence it is particularly important to link adult education to participation in struggles in the work-place and the community. The personal involvement in struggles against capitalism and the analysis of this activity is a significant combination of theory and practice, as Engels noted:

> Marx...entirely trusted to the intellectual development of the working class, which was sure to result from combined [i.e. collective] action and mutual discussion.[1]

The dimension of political education therefore regards involvement in anti-capitalist struggles as educative in itself, especially when connected with theoretical analysis. It is the provision of opportunities for analysis that is the task of socialist adult education and its contribution to the development of class consciousness. The main content of this political education is the study of society from the perspective of Marxism.

Another dimension of socialist adult education is general education, which seeks to develop general intellectual capabilities and knowledge. The foremost task here is to develop literacy and numeracy. The capacity to read and write is absolutely fundamental for a well-informed participation in the social and political affairs of modern society - in Lenin's phrase 'An illiterate person stands outside politics.'[2] Also, literacy, as Vygotsky suggested, is important for complex mental processes. It provides an aid to the planning and organising of mental activity and contributes to a sense of personal control of one's environment. Literacy and numeracy are the basic mental tools for use in further intellectual development and are therefore essential to the individual's general education.

The development of other cognitive skills is important, providing the basis for other educational advance, including the development of political awareness and technical expertise. Shor has expressed this well:

> Critical education can be an empowering support for social emergence. Reading closely, writing clearly, thinking critically, conceptualising and verbalising are some means to penetrate the maze of reality. These are foundations for becoming a conscious re-maker of social life.[3]

The aim embodied here is that of developing such capabilities as creativity, critical analysis, independent judgement and articulate expression. Such capabilities can obviously be formed by the rigorous and critical study of a wide variety of subjects, through which a broad general knowledge can simultaneously be acquired.

The final dimension is that of technical education, conceived broadly in terms of developing the skills necessary both for operating and managing production processes, and for running organisations such as trade unions, neighbourhood committees and political parties. This dimension therefore embraces scientific knowledge, technical skills and management expertise on the one hand, and organisational skills such as book-keeping, committee procedures and legal advocacy on the other.

It is a singular characteristic of capitalism that the development of its division of labour separated the direct producers from the scientific knowledge and technical skills which they had possessed in pre-capitalist craft and agricultural production. The process of separation was described in detail by Marx in Chapter 14 of Capital. Volume 1 on 'The division of labour and manufacture', which shows how the working class became intellectually impoverished by the development of capitalism:

> The knowledge, judgement and will which, even though to a small extent, are exercised by the independent peasant or handicraftsman...are faculties now required only for the workshop as a whole. The possibility of an intelligent direction of production expands in one direction, because it vanishes in many others. What is lost by the specialised workers is concentrated in the capital which confronts them. It is a result of the division of labour in manufacture that the worker is brought face to face with the intellectual potentialities of the material processes of production as the property of another and as a power which rules over him.[4]

Science and technical expertise became separated from the workers and became part of the means of their exploitation and oppression. Education under capitalism plays a key role in reproducing this separation, so that the working class is denied the knowledge and skills it requires to take control of production.[5] The expansion of opportunities for continuing education and for paid educational leave which is taking place rapidly in the industrialised capitalist countries contributes to this reproduction, its goal being only the adaptation of the work-force to the new conditions of capitalist production. Developing the capacity of the working class and its allies to understand the processes of production and to manage them remains crucial for the overthrow of the social relations of capitalist production. Thus a close connection between adult education and production (for example, in socialist co-operatives) is important, and scientific knowledge, technical skills, and management expertise are significant subject areas for socialist adult education.

There is also the need to develop another set of practical skills, namely those required for running socialist organisations. These include such skills as those used in trade union negotiations, in committee roles, and in producing a community newspaper. The organisation of the working class and its allies is an important subjective factor of socialist revolution and it requires a range of skills and attitudes (such as those necessary for democratic decision-making) which adult education can develop.

These three dimensions of socialist adult education within capitalist social formations represent the first steps towards developing the 'new person', the all-round person willing and able to work for a new society. The 'new person' combines socialist political awareness, a high level of intellectual capability and general knowledge, and technical expertise. Socialist adult education is thus characterised by the wish to achieve Marx's goal of producing 'fully developed human beings'[6], a goal which is obstructed by the fragmentation, specialisation and alienation of the individual that is inherent in the capitalist division of labour. This is the long-term goal which socialist adult education strives to achieve within the confines, pressures and limitations of capitalism. Any particular example of socialist adult education in these circumstances is likely to fall short of this goal. But the goal is clear and provides the rationale for developing a socialist pedagogy.


THE CONCEPT OF A SOCIALIST PEDAGOGY

The preceding section outlined the purpose and curriculum content of socialist adult education. This section considers the nature of a socialist pedagogy, that is, an approach to teaching and learning which is based on principles consonant with socialist theory. In Chapter Three I formulated a set of such principles on which to base a Marxist approach to adult learning. The concept of a

socialist pedagogy is based on translating these
theoretical principles into actual educational
practices. There are six main aspects of pedagogy
which I propose to consider from the Marxist
perspective I have established in the previous
chapters. They are as follows:

- the process of acquiring knowledge;
- the role of language and literacy;
- the social relations of the educational
  situation;
- the methods of teaching;
- the mode of evaluating learning and teaching;
- the relation of learning to production and
  political action.

I will discuss each of these aspects before going on
to present three case studies which illustrate how
they have been dealt with in particular capitalist
social formations.
      The first aspect to be considered is that of
the process of acquiring knowledge (including skills
and attitudes). This process is conceived not as one
in which students passively consume knowledge but as
one in which teachers and students collaborate
together to produce the knowledge that will serve
the students' interests outside the educational
situation. The starting-point of this process is
unambiguously the experience of the students and the
issues and problems of their everyday existence. It
is the critical analysis of this experience which is
at the centre of socialist pedagogy. This
experience becomes the basis of ever-widening areas
of analysis, so that personal experience is located
in its total economic and political context. The
educational situation provides the environment for
making explicit how capitalist hegemony affects all
areas of personal life (through social practices,
the media, work relations and so forth). In Shor's
illuminating phrase, it provides the opportunity for
'extraordinarily re-experiencing the ordinary.'[7]
Thus it is a distancing process which, from a
specific beginning, opens up the widest possible
areas of study. It is based on the development of
conceptual skills and Marxist theoretical knowledge
which are amongst the areas of special expertise
that the adult educator brings to the educational
situation.
      It is fundamental to socialist pedagogy that
the learners' interests influence the direction of

the learning process and that their experience is its starting point. The development of a course of study then involves a process which Reed has aptly called 'negotiation', that is, 'a collective process of determining the purpose, defining the content and structuring the study programme'[8] in which both the students and the adult educator have responsibility for reaching an agreed programme. This being the case, it is necessary to emphasise that both within the process of negotiation and within the learning process itself, the adult educator does not accept the students' view of their interests and experience uncritically.

Socialist adult educators lay claim to a theoretical understanding which is able to penetrate the dominant ideology of capitalism. Many aspects of this ideology have been internalised by students so that it is reproduced in their ideas, values and social practice. Student experience therefore has to be analysed critically in the light of Marxist theory which the adult educator introduces. Elshtain has expressed this clearly:

> If life experience, unmediated through a critical conceptual medium, is given a privileged epistemological status, and the 'feelings' which attach to this experience are embraced without challenge or criticism, the analysis of conclusions which emerge will be riddled with the fatal flaws of a false, because uncritical, consciousness...

> The 'life experiences' of students must and should be taken seriously as one dimension within the creation of radical and critical consciousness. But this experience must be mediated through conceptual categories if it is to support, to sustain and to provide the prelude for critical theory.[9]

The process of knowledge acquisition within a socialist pedagogy thus accords a significant role to Marxist theory, while acknowledging the importance of student experience. The phrase 'the theorisation of experience' perhaps catches the essence of socialist pedagogy on this point.

This of course implies the constant effort to unify theory and practice. Socialist pedagogy opposes purely abstract study and sees learning as a process which includes the application of what has been learned. The concept of praxis and the view of learning as involving purposeful interaction with the environment provides the basis for pedagogical approaches which encourage activity and application in the process of knowledge acquisition.

Additionally, socialist pedagogy regards the rigidified subject divisions characteristic of capitalist education as barriers to understanding society because they create fragmentation, whereas the task of socialist adult education is to engender the comprehension of totalities and of the place of the particular in the general. The compartmentalisation of knowledge is an obstacle to the coherent analysis of capitalism, a product of that very division of labour which socialism seeks to end. Specialisation, subject disciplines, and institutional departments are all obstacles to the holistic viewpoints needed to understand capitalism and how to change it. The basic pedagogical principle here is therefore an emphasis on issue-centred study rather than subject-centred study. Thus the characteristic approach to the acquisition of knowledge is through the inter-disciplinary (or rather, trans-disciplinary) investigation of the themes, issues and problems raised by the students' social existence.

The general stance of a socialist pedagogy to the aspect of the process of acquiring knowledge has been well summarised by Castles and Wustenberg:

> Education for transformation means that [students] become the subjects of the learning process and not its passive objects. Learning takes on the character of a collectively determined research process...[10]

The second aspect of pedagogy to consider is the role of language and literacy in teaching and learning. Language is at the centre of the educational processes of talking and listening, writing and reading, so that linguistic issues are necessarily an important concern. The basic Marxist assumption here is that language is not simply a relationship between the individuals concerned in an educational situation. Language is a social product and reflects the relations of power in society (including those of gender and race as well as class). It is thus itself part of the process of capitalist hegemony.[11]

The hierarchical stratification of society is

reflected in the different status awarded in capitalist education to different forms of language. For example, forms of speech associated with certain classes, regions or ethnic group s are often discriminated against in favour of a 'standard' form of the language. In some countries, entire languages are excluded from use in education, and in the Third World the use of foreign languages as a medium of education reflects the continuing power of imperialism. The key point for socialist adult education is that the forms of language used in the educational situation cannot be divorced from the wider context of domination and subordination. Just as language serves to reproduce relations of power, so it can participate in the challenge to these relations.[12] Hence the importance in adult education, for example, of opposing sexist language, resisting the denigration of 'non-standard' English, or promoting indigenous languages in the Third World. Language involves both the content of thought and the process by which people think and is therefore of great concern to socialist pedagogy.

The graphic representation of language, that is literacy, is also an important aspect of the educational situation. Illiteracy is related to the social conditions of capitalism and very much influences adult education activities. In advanced capitalism, it is often perceived as an individual problem, and 'explained' in terms of deficient intelligence or learning disability, a process of explanation which separates the individual's psyche from their life and activity.[13] In underdeveloped capitalism it is more widespread amongst adults and is an obvious symptom of low levels of educational provision. The significance of literacy as both a cognitive tool and as the means of political participation makes its development one of the main goals of socialist adult education, as we have seen. Literacy's role in cognition means that the psychology of the non-literate, who is often a student in adult education, is of special account. It is for these reasons that the related issues of language, literacy, cognition and hegemony are very significant to socialist pedagogy.

The third aspect of pedagogy concerns the social relations of the educational situation. The social relations include those between the adult educator and the students, and between the students themselves. The most characteristic relationships within capitalist education are authoritarian teacher-student relations and competitive student-student relations. As Bowles and Gintis suggested in Schooling in Capitalist America, many aspects of the social relations of education under capitalism correspond to those of the social relations of the work-place. The role of socialist pedagogy in this respect is to establish relationships and social practices in the educational situation which will undermine this correspondence and prefigure socialist culture. The relationships sought are ones of co-operation, equality, participation and democratic control.

The educational situation therefore requires the active involvement of students in taking the decisions and the responsibility for planning and carrying out the study programme. In terms of the relationships between students, there is a stress on common goals rather than personal ones, and on collective effort rather than individualism and competition. Methods of work such as mutual help, peer teaching, and group activities are designed to foster such relationships (and are also the skills of co-operation that socialist adult education seeks to develop). The social relations of the educational situation promoted by socialist pedagogy are essentially collective. What are the implications of this for the relationship between adult educators and students?

This is an important question because many adult educators who oppose the authoritarianism of traditional capitalist pedagogy have adopted forms of 'student-centred' pedagogy. These pedagogical forms have their origins in the ideas of Carl Rogers and the humanistic approach which I discussed in Chapter Four. Their response to the issues of power, control and authority in the educational situation has been basically libertarian and has involved the abdication of the adult educator to the passive role of 'facilitator' and 'resource person'. However, this is an unsatisfactory response from the Marxist viewpoint:

> Whilst authoritarianism obviously serves the interests of capital, its reverse in libertarianism does not necessarily serve to undermine the social relationships of domination on which capitalism depends. Indeed, a pedagogical ideology of permissiveness and freedom may be particularly appropriate for capital given certain social

conditions, and do little to generate an effective counter-hegemony. It may, rather, help to reinforce the illusion that individual freedom within capitalist societies is possible without any fundamental transformation of the system.[14]

'Student-centred' pedagogy does not tackle the problem that students have internalised capitalist hegemony which thereby affects their capacity to act in their own interests. It does not solve the tension of freedom and control dialectically, failing to recognise that democratisation seeks to achieve an equality of power between participants who may in other ways be unequal. Socialist pedagogy acknowledges the authority of adult educators, an authority derived from their expertise (based on a body of knowledge, a Marxist theoretical framework, and skills of organising educational processes) which students, at the beginning of a programme, lack to varying degrees. It seeks forms of social relationships in the educational situation which situate this authority in a democratic context that enables leadership to function in a way that is not a form of domination.[15]

Socialist adult educators bring to the educational situation a necessary expertise and they initially assume a position of authority and leadership (a position which is itself the product of the unequal personal development that capitalism generates). They take responsibility for making their expertise available in a way that will further the learners' interests. They participate in a collaborative process which aims to raise the level of awareness and competence of the learners and hence their position is not static. The relationship of the adult educator to the students is a dynamic one which alters as the learners develop their own capacities and reduce the original gap of knowledge and awareness between themselves and the adult educator:

> This ideal eventuality - the full subjective emergence of the students and the withering away of the teacher - means that the initiating/organising [and theoretical] function has become generalised in class, distributed to the group rather than an expertise possessed by one person.[16]

Socialist pedagogy is neither 'teacher-centred' nor student-centred' but transcends this dichotomy by a democratic collaboration between the adult educator and the students. The democratisation of learning is an essential contribution by adult education to the development of a counter-hegemony. The lived experience of alternative kinds of relationships and social practices in the educational situation is an important complement to the intellectual demystification of capitalist ideology, with new forms of behaviour making concrete new ways of thinking.

The fourth aspect of pedagogy to consider is the methods of teaching. The general rationale for the choice of techniques in socialist adult education is clearly provided by the foregoing discussion which suggests that co-operative group activity and the collective investigation of problems are a characteristic mode of learning within socialist pedagogy. From this perspective, the socialist adult educator is seen to be involved in a collaborative programme, pursuing goals agreed upon with the students. To achieve these goals a variety of procedures may prove to be appropriate. Thus teaching techniques are not considered in abstraction but as embedded in the social relations of the educational situation. Hence socialist pedagogy assesses the adequacy of techniques within the context of the purposes and social relations of a particular programme. The lecture, for example, which is often the paradigm of authoritarian pedagogy, may be in certain circumstances an appropriate method (for example, to convey an overview of the issue for investigation in its historical context). Similarly, inappropriate group discussion may prove to be aimless and make no constructive contribution to a counter-hegemony.

Techniques do not, of themselves, provide the means of socialist pedagogy. Indeed, divorced from revolutionary ends, apparently radical methods can become reactionary, as we saw in the case of Freire's method in the previous chapter. Teaching techniques have to be considered as ways in which knowledge is mediated and it is the purpose, nature and social context of that knowledge by which their adequacy must be judged. This is not to deny the importance of teaching methods and indeed one of the special areas of expertise of the adult educator is to provide access to the range of techniques which may be helpful at a given time in a learning programme. (There are a wide range of techniques available - for example Adult Education Procedures is a standard adult education handbook and it lists fourteen techniques, from the colloquy to the group discussion to the symposium.)[17] Nor do I wish to suggest that techniques are value-free. Certain techniques, such as programmed learning, are inseparable from capitalist ideology. My point is that the choice of methods of teaching in socialist adult education is determined by the context in which they are required, that context providing the political criteria by which their adequacy can be judged.

Fifthly, we need to look at the mode of evaluating teaching and learning. Education is an organised intervention in the normal human process of learning for a specific purpose, and educators and students need to assess the effectiveness of such interventions. However, within capitalist education, modes of assessment are clearly part of the process of legitimating domination. The grading of students by teachers is part of the process of differentiation within education which relates to the wider hierarchy of the social division of labour.[18] It makes ranking appear 'objective' and 'natural' and part of the normal social order (whereas in fact that very social order is the historically specific product of capitalism). Obviously such evaluation is not neutral or objective but reflects ideological assumptions and the power of the teacher to enforce them. (Because of the need to ensure the teacher's dominance, the evaluation of teachers by students seldom occurs with any seriousness.) It is this kind of evaluation process which takes place explicitly within those forms of capitalist adult education which are geared to qualifications, and implicitly in other forms, where the adult educator's judgement is revealed informally (for example, by expressions of approval).

Evaluation within socialist adult education constitutes an alternative practice, which has four important characteristics. First, its criteria have to be developed collectively by the adult educator and the students as part of the process of negotiating the purpose and goals of the programme. The measure of learning progress is therefore not an arbitrary external 'standard' but the product of dialogue between the adult educator and the students. Forms of assessment thereby become

essentially diagnostic, rather than the basis for
competition and comparison within the group.  They
form a systematic and on-going means of seeing
whether the group as a whole, as well as its
individual members, are accomplishing the learning
goals that were initially established.  If these
goals are not being met, then evaluation provides
the opportunity to analyse why not.

The second major characteristic is that
evaluation seeks to improve the effectiveness of the
programme collectively, involving discussion based
on the principle of criticism and self-criticism,
not only between the adult educator and the students
but also amongst the students.  This involves
evaluating the combined work of the adult educator
and the learners.  Socialist evaluation is not a
one-sided movement away from judging students to
judging teachers because that, as Harold has pointed
out, breaks down collective responsibility:

> ...the vaguely student-centred evaluation
> questionnaires used to get feedback on teaching
> encourage students to think of the class as
> something outside of themselves. They can rate
> it a failure without feeling implicated.[19]

The important point is that socialist pedagogy
emphasises co-operative work rather than
individualistic competition and combined
teacher/student activity rather than separation, so
that it is based on a collective responsibility for
learning which must be reflected in its mode of
evaluation.

Thirdly, evaluation is seen as part of the
learning process itself. The discussion of the
purposes and criteria of evaluation raises important
ideological questions whose analysis has an
educative function.  Similarly, the consideration of
the problems in achieving goals reveals obstacles to
the learning process which have their origins in the
wider society rather than the deficiencies of the
individuals in the group and hence provides further
opportunities for analysis of capitalist hegemony.

Finally,  the evaluation of teaching and
learning does not restrict itself to an internal
consideration of the educational situation in
isolation from wider social experience. The purpose
of socialist adult education is to contribute to the
overthrow of capitalism and therefore its
effectiveness, in the final analysis, has to be

judged in terms of the learners' praxis. Has the learning that has taken place within the programme helped the learners to be more effective in their struggles to take control of production and society?

The importance of this measure of evaluation derives from the sixth aspect of socialist pedagogy, namely the relation of learning to production and political action. Learning within capitalist adult education is often separated from production (this is especially characteristic of the liberal tradition) or, in forms of occupational training, is tied closely to the labour demands of capitalism. It does not seek to challenge the existing social relations of production, so that even trade union education tends to be restricted by the parameters of capitalism. Similarly, a deliberate separation is made between learning and political action (justified ideologically by ideas like 'knowledge for its own sake').

In a Marxist perspective, learning is conceived as the product of purposeful activity within the environment, an activity through which people change themselves and their surroundings. Thus praxis is the source, the objective and the test of learning. Socialist pedagogy is therefore founded on the learners' study of and participation in the struggle to control production and society. Hence it seeks to couple learning with the experience of the work-place and the community. Forms of study based on this experience are central to socialist adult education and are aimed at enabling the students to understand capitalist society and at equipping them for the struggles to change it through economic and political action. The linking of learning to production and political action is the key to the unity of theory and practice that socialist pedagogy seeks to achieve.

The following case studies, drawn from Asia, Europe and Africa, are intended to provide concrete illustrations of attempts to implement a socialist approach to adult education in a number of different capitalist social formations. Each case study includes a brief sketch of the political economy of the period in question, a description of the adult education activities under consideration, and a commentary on their implications for socialist pedagogy. The case studies have therefore been designed to show how the different aspects of pedagogy have been tackled by socialists in varying circumstances of struggle against capitalism.

## ADULT EDUCATION AND RURAL TRANSFORMATION IN NORTH-WEST CHINA, 1935-1947

Between 1935 and 1947 the Chinese Communist Party (CCP) controlled the regional government in a remote area of North-west China. Here, from the capital Yenan, it evolved a distinctive approach to the problem of rural development. This approach accorded an important role to adult education, both for the training of cadres and for the education of the peasant masses. The kind of adult education associated with the Yenan period provides an example of socialist pedagogy in the context of rural underdevelopment.

China during this period was undergoing a prolonged social, economic and political crisis. Foreign powers had penetrated China during the nineteenth century, introducing capitalist social relations of production particularly to the coastal areas of the east in cities like Shanghai. In 1911 a democratic revolution had overthrown the emperor and established a parliamentary republic. In 1927 the major political party, the Kuomintang, which was dominated by the merchant bourgeoisie and the large landowners, entered into a civil war with the CCP. It achieved military victories over the CCP, which was forced to retreat in the Long March of 1935 to Shensi. Here, under the political leadership of Mao Tse Tung, it took control of the Shensi-Kansu-Ningshia Border Region.

After the invasion by Japan in 1937, the CCP formed a united front with the Kuomintang to fight the War of Resistance. This uneasy alliance finished in effect in 1941 because the Kuomintang feared the CCP's military and political successes behind Japanese lines. However, renewed civil war did not break out until after the defeat of the Japanese in 1945. During this second civil war the CCP was pushed out of the Border Region in 1947 but it finally defeated the US-backed Kuomintang in 1949 and took control of the whole of China.

The Yenan period was therefore overshadowed by the military demands of the civil wars and the anti-colonial struggle, the Border Region providing a base for the CCP's Red Army. The region itself was very isolated, both geographically and economically (being blockaded by the Kuomintang for most of the period). It was also one of extreme rural poverty and economic backwardness, exemplified by regular famine and a 60% infant mortality rate. In 1935 pre-capitalist relations of production were still dominant, accompanied by landlord political oppression and cultural features such as illiteracy and pre-scientific beliefs.

In the region, which had a population of about one and a half million, the CCP over the years followed a number of different policies in relation to rural development. In 1935 and 1936 it carried out agrarian reform in many areas. This distributed land from the landlords and rich peasants to the poor peasants, reducing extremes of wealth and poverty and the worst forms of exploitation. During these years, reliance was placed on mobilising the poorer peasantry in class struggle and in participation in local organs of government. But after the formation of the united front in 1937, emphasis was placed on the war against Japanese imperialism and class conflict within Chinese society was played down. CCP policies stressed nationalism and the war effort, stable government and the development of electoral democracy, and reformist economic programmes. But with the end of the united front in 1941, a re-evaluation of party policies and methods took place, leading to the 'rectification movement' designed to unify the party around common goals and methods. A radical new approach to rural development was promulgated from 1942 with the aim of transforming the rural political economy, through popular mobilisation of the poor and middle peasantry and the decentralisation of power. Selden has identified the six main components of this approach: the simplification and localisation of administration; the 'to the village' campaign which sent cadres to the countryside; the reduction of rent and interest in areas where there had not been land reform; the development of co-operatives; the movement for increased production; and popular education.[20]

During the Yenan period the CCP developed in practice forms of adult education designed to contribute to the overthrow of what it called the 'semi-colonial, semi-feudal' social order. These forms of adult education evolved with experience and came to constitute an explicitly socialist approach to pedagogy in cadre and mass education.

The key institution for cadre education was K'angta, the Anti-Japanese Military and Political

College established in Yenan in 1936. The college
was set up by the CCP in order to train basic and
middle-level political cadres and army officers.
Mao Tse Tung was chairperson of its Education
Committee and significantly influenced its policies
and methods. A Chinese description of the college
in 1939 shows that it was run on socialist adult
education principles guided by a clear political
purpose.[21]

The college operated in conditions of scarce
resources and had simple facilities. It took
students for courses lasting one semester of four to
six months. These short, intense courses were
designed to meet the demands made by the armed
struggle and by rural development in the Border
Region. There was a constant emphasis on relating
theory to reality, with practical activities
including military exercises and involvement in
production. The methods and content of each course
were established at the beginning according to the
battle experience, political awareness and
educational level of those enrolled and the type of
cadres required. Thus its 'educational method is
not subject to mechanical or arbitrary
formulation'[22] but related to the particular group -
for example, experienced Red Army soldiers being
different to peasant activists who had emerged
during the agrarian reform. The curriculum covered
the areas of political education, military training,
and general education.

The pedagogical approach that was developed at
K'angta provided the model for the large-scale cadre
education through conferences and local groups that
took place between 1942 and 1944 within the CCP
itself in the 'rectification movement'. It also
provided the model for the mass education programmes
implemented after 1943 within the new approach to
rural development.[23]

Mass adult education was a distinctive feature
of the Border Region Government's policy throughout
the Yenan period, and after 1943 it was explicitly
given a higher priority than school education. The
pressure of war and the need to raise productivity
made the development of adult capacities important.
Also, the emphasis given to popular political
participation throughout the period meant great
stress on raising the political awareness of the
masses, for example in the large-scale educational
programmes for the elections of 1937 and 1941.
Adult education in North-west China under the CCP

was designed to enable the peasant masses to take an active part in the transformation of rural society, engendering the confidence, creativity and skill to implement the general guidelines provided by the party and the government.

Mass adult education was organised in such a way as to allow adults to learn without reducing their involvement in production. Thus there were winter schools (in the agricultural off-season), night schools, literacy classes linked to production units like co-operatives and women's spinning groups, a 'little-teacher' system of literate school-children teaching adults, newspaper discussion groups and so forth. The provision of adult education made a flexible response to local conditions, particularly after the introduction in 1944 of the 'popular management, government assistance' system of village-level education committees.

The content of the courses centred on literacy, political education and practical economic skills. For example, in the winter of 1943-1944, literacy classes and other classes were held on alternate days, the other classes including each month seven on political education, three on production, two on current affairs and three on methods of organisation.[24] But adult education also played a role in programmes such as the development of co-operative production and the mass health and hygiene campaign. Additionally, there was a popular culture movement, which included touring cultural teams visiting the villages to entertain and educate the people with 'Yang-Ko' performances, which combined local songs and dances into dramatic performances exposing the evil of the old order and promoting the new society.[25]

By 1943 both cadre and mass adult education were characterised by a consciously developed socialist pedagogy, which can be analysed along the six dimensions I introduced earlier in the chapter. First, this pedagogy regarded the acquisition of knowledge as a dialectical process of investigation, theory and practical activity. The epistemological basis for this was developed in Mao's essays On Practice[26] and On Contradiction[27] which were originally given as lectures at K'angta in 1937. The integration of theory and practice was regarded as fundamental and was translated into an educational process based on empirical observation of a problem, analysis, the conceptualisation of a

solution, and the practical implementation of the
solution followed by a summing-up of the results.
The reality investigated was that of the actual
political, production and military problems of the
Border Region; the theory was explicitly that of
Marxism-Leninism and Mao's application of it to
Chinese conditions.

Secondly, the CCP placed great emphasis on
basic literacy as a central goal of adult education.
It also attempted language reform. China has a
complex language situation, based on dialectical
differences and numerous minority languages. The
language of education traditionally was a variant of
the Peking dialect, known as official speech or
Mandarin. In order to read it, at least 1,200
characters had to be learned.[28] The CCP attempted
at Yenan to simplify the language and colloquialise
it. To facilitate literacy learning a large-scale
campaign was launched in 1942 to promote a new
romanised, phonetic script. However, this failed
although it did shorten the time taken to learn to
read. It was not popular with the masses, primarily
because of its limited usefulness as the documents
associated with political participation remained in
Chinese characters.[29] The pedagogical principle of
concern with linguistic issues is clearly
demonstrated in the Yenan period, with considerable
success in literacy but failure in language reform.

Thirdly, the social relations of the
educational situation were conceived democratically,
stressing a spirit of co-operation between teacher
and students and amongst students. The teacher's
function was to provide leadership, but within the
context of mutual help, mutual criticism and mutual
learning:

> Education was to be a constant process of
> mutual learning and mutual transformation. The
> teacher was to take the lead but he was not
> just to stuff the student full of facts.
> Rather, he was to provide the student with a
> method for examining and transforming material
> reality. Student and teacher being a part of
> that reality, would themselves be transformed
> in the process.[30]

The democratic style of leadership was particularly
clearly articulated after the 'rectification
movement' because the movement gave great attention
to the relationship of the cadre to the masses and

to styles of work. This concern is exemplified in Mao's 1943 statement on behalf of the CCP's Central Committee entitled <u>Some Questions Concerning Methods of Leadership</u>.[31] This presented an approach to leadership that combined dialectically the ideological authority of the party cadre with the practical experience of the peasant masses. Significantly, political leadership was conceived in educational terms and the methods of the political cadre thus provided a model for the teacher's role which was democratic and not authoritarian or bureaucratic.

Fourthly, certain methods of teaching were advanced, especially to combat the conventional methods based on the lecture, class recitation, and rote learning. Within the general approach of the co-operative investigation of practical problems, the lecture was assigned the minor role of providing introductions and summaries and great emphasis was put on discussion, complemented by small mutual-help study groups and independent individual study.

Fifthly, the mode of evaluating teaching and learning can be seen clearly in the practice at K'angta, where forms of testing served a different function to conventional examinations. Tests were used as a motivating factor and as a way of measuring progress in order to improve educational methods, not as an occasion for individual competition. Thus test questions were discussed in advance and during the tests students could consult references and each other. The students then helped to mark the papers, the emphasis being not on grades but on assessing personal progress.[32] In a broader perspective, it is evident that the concept of knowledge acquisition as a dialectical process in which practice is the key stage meant that the actual performance of practical activities by the student was the central measure of learning. Thus the ultimate criterion of evaluation was the contribution learning made to solving the problems of rural development and of the military situation.

This evaluation criterion was based on the sixth pedagogical principle, which made pre-eminent the need for adult education to render a practical contribution to greater political participation by the masses, to increased and reorganised production, and to the military struggle against the Japanese and the Kuomintang. Taken together, these six principles form a consistent socialist pedagogy.[33] Adult education in Northwest China between 1935 and

1947 therefore provides a good example of adult education for rural transformation which put into practice a socialist pedagogy.


ADULT EDUCATION AND CLASS STRUGGLE
IN PORTUGAL, 1974 - 1976

In April 1974 the dictatorship in Portugal was overthrown. There was a brief period of intense class struggle in which the Marxist proponents of socialism took a prominent role in national life. But capitalism reasserted itself and by July 1976 the crisis was over. The upsurge of mass political activity during these two years was accompanied by a variety of adult education programmes. These programmes provide examples of socialist pedagogy in the context of class struggle in a relatively underdeveloped European country.

Portugal had been under a dictatorship since 1926. After 1932, under Salazar, the regime had been fascist, based on authoritarian rule in all spheres of public life. However, when Caetano succeeded as Prime Minister in 1968 he responded to the social pressures created by the unpopular colonial wars in Africa, industrialisation, and the growing discontent with repression and backwardness, by initiating a period of liberalisation. He introduced minor reforms intended to replace coercion by hegemonic rule which would provide the political flexibility necessary for liberal capitalism and economic modernisation.

This process was interrupted by the military coup of April 1974 led by the Armed Forces Movement (MFA). The coup met with enthusiastic public support and the ensuing months were marked by massive involvement in political activity. The small urban proletariat (centred in Lisbon and Oporto) participated in strikes and demonstrations, and occupied work-places and houses. Grass-roots organisations, such as residents' committees, tenants' associations, workers' committees and consumer co-operatives, sprang up everywhere. Students took over schools and universities. In the countryside, the rural proletariat of the Alentejo region occupied the large estates. By mid-1975 landless labourers had established four hundred and sixty collective production units, having expropriated nearly a quarter of all cultivated land.[34] However, outside the urban areas of the coast and the rural areas of the south, left-wing political activity was resisted.  The northern and central regions have a peasant class structure, with pre-capitalist relations of production persisting in the north-east and a large semi-proletariat in the north-west.  The peasant proprietors provided political support for anti-socialist campaigns led by large land owners and the bourgeoisie and during 1975 the country verged on civil war.

Throughout this time the MFA was at the centre of political developments.  Its officers dominated the provisional governments of 1974 and 1975.  A right-wing coup attempt in March 1975 enabled the radical faction in the MFA to assert itself and undertake nationalisations and the institutionalisation of the MFA as a state body. But the Constituent Assembly elections of April 1975 were won by bourgeois political parties committed to parliamentary democracy and were a defeat for Marxist socialist forces.  A left-wing coup in November failed and the influence of the MFA began to decline.  The possibilities of socialism steadily decreased and the provisions of the April 1976 Constitution for 'securing the transition to socialism' were by that stage essentially rhetorical.

During the 1974-1976 period the Marxist proponents of socialism had been split in two, between the pro-USSR Portuguese Communist Party (PCP) and the so-called 'revolutionary Left'.  The PCP had operated clandestinely under fascism, infiltrating the armed forces and organising the urban and rural proletariat.  After the 1974 coup it emerged as the strongest Marxist body, with an influential position in the MFA.  It regarded the coup as a national democratic revolution which had left capitalism 'predominant but not determinant'.[35] It set its priority as gaining control of the state. Its political strategy was to influence the MFA and the government and to build strong, centralised organisations of workers.  It envisaged spreading the revolution from the centre and encouraged the MFA to originate political activities amongst the people.

The organisations of the revolutionary Left (though divided amongst themselves) may be grouped together in their opposition to the PCP's analysis and strategy.  These organisations had their roots in the international renaissance of Marxism in the 1960s.  They regarded the coup not as a revolution but as the initiator of a pre-revolutionary situation, in which the state was still capitalist. Their political strategy focussed on the creation of decentralised and autonomous popular organisations, directly involved in local struggles and characterised by participatory democracy. They emphasised 'people's power' and building socialism from below. They wanted the MFA to protect and encourage popular organisations.

Both of these Marxist trends were present in the MFA itself (which also contained non-socialist elements). Thus Marxist socialists during the Portuguese crisis were split in two by a dichotomy they were unable to resolve. In 1974 and 1975 there was no united centre of revolutionary politics able to promote an integrated strategy of mass participation and the capture of state power for the overthrow of capitalism. When in July 1976 the social democratic Socialist Party formed the first constitutional government, the process of capitalist liberalisation was back on course.

The events of 1974 and 1975 did not constitute a revolution because there was no fundamental change in class power. There was a period of intense class struggle and the bourgeoisie's control of the repressive and ideological apparatuses of the state was temporarily threatened. But by 1976 bourgeois parliamentary democracy had been established, providing a more stable political form for monopoly capitalism than fascist dictatorship. The possibility of socialism had been blocked by the objective conditions of the class structure and the subjective conditions of the ideological and organisational disunity of the socialists.

During these two years of class struggle adult education was seen by socialists as having an important role in enabling the masses to participate fully in political events after years of repression and educational neglect (29% of adults were illiterate, the highest proportion in Europe). The approaches to adult education exemplified the two-fold division amongst Marxists. The PCP saw adult education as part of a centrally-directed process of mobilising support for the revolution, especially in the rural areas of the north and centre where there was least sympathy for socialist politics.[36] It supported the idea of mass literacy and a programme of political education by the MFA. In the summer of 1974 it encouraged a literacy campaign by university students in the north. The campaign was influenced by the methods of Freire and met considerable resistance. (The peasants in this area, in conjunction with the Catholic church, were also opposing 'red pedagogy' in the schools.) The PCP Congress of October 1974 gave the 'extinction of illiteracy' a high priority and the PCP promoted the bill for a National Literacy Programme in the Assembly in July 1975.

The PCP also supported the MFA's 'Campaign for Cultural Dynamisation'. This was a political education programme influenced by the Cuban literacy campaign which aimed to transform the political culture in the countryside and 'mobilise the most inert and constrained sectors of the population'.[37] Over two thousand cultural sessions (involving revolutionary songs, talks about national politics, and discussion of local issues) were held between October 1974 and March 1975 in the northern and central areas.

The PCP's approach to adult education reflected its directive concept of politics and strategy of using power at the level of the state to consolidate the revolution. On the other hand, the revolutionary Left supported adult education work linked to the self-managing organisations of people's power which were involved in local struggles against capitalism. After April 1974 popular organisations had been established all over the country, but mainly in the urban areas and the Alentejo. They represented people's direct involvement in the political, economic and cultural upheaval of the period and included attempts to exert control over the work-place (for example, through co-operatives and workers' committees) and over community affairs (for example, through residents' committees and tenants' associations). The need for new knowledge and skills created by these collectively-run organisations engendered a demand for adult education and an assertion of popular culture. This led to a variety of local initiatives in adult education linked to the popular organisations.

Two specific examples may be cited as illustrations. The first is a Popular Culture Centre in a small town in the Alentejo established in a royal palace occupied by 'political and cultural militants' in March 1975. The centre organised cultural activities, ran a sports centre and a library, and provided literacy and basic education courses for adults. It had a drama group

which performed in neighbouring villages and
agricultural co-operatives on themes like land
ownership and workers' organisation. It helped to
establish a residents' committee to solve local
housing problems. The centre itself was controlled
by the General Assembly of Friends of the Centre,
composed of

> ...all workers employed by another, or members
> of production or consumer co-operatives, who
> publicly oppose fascism and condemn the
> economic or intellectual exploitation of man by
> man.[38]

The second example is the socio-cultural
section of a federation of agricultural co-
operatives in the Azambuja region near Lisbon. The
first co-operative here was established in May 1975
by a group who occupied a large estate owned by an
aristocratic family, which was seen as a relic of
feudalism. The group developed a co-operative on
principles of collective work, fair wages and
internal democracy. It linked up with other co-
operatives and formed a federation. A socio-
cultural section was developed to handle matters of
social welfare, health and education. The section
gave priority in education to (a) the collection and
study of local history and folklore; (b) literacy
and basic education for adults; and (c) training
programmes in specific skills such as accounting,
marketing and secretarial work. It also took
responsibility for the flow of information within
the federation through the media of festivals,
plays, debates, courses, leaflets and news-sheets.
The period 1974 to 1976 in Portugal was marked
by intense class struggle, in which a wide variety
of adult education experiments played a part.
Although it is difficult to generalise, some
interesting approaches to the concept of a socialist
pedagogy emerged. The first aspect to consider is
the process of acquiring knowledge. The
documentation of those adult education programmes
linked to the popular organisations suggests that
the idea of learners determining the content of
learning based on their own experience and problems
was seen as central. Clearly many activities were
based on the concept of learning as a research
process into local issues - for example, a branch of
the Railway Workers' Union wanted to examine the
history of the railways from the workers' view-

point.[39]   Because such activities were usually part
of attempts to develop a popular culture expressing
working class interests and experience, one can
conjecture that a critical approach to reality was
taken.   It is unclear to what extent Marxist theory
played a role in this critical analysis but it was
certainly widespread in the popular organisations.
The example of the courses developed by an
educational association of emigrant Portuguese
workers in Paris illustrates well an inter-
disciplinary approach to learning based on branching
out from a central theme in  a process informed by
Marxist theory, as we see in the diagram on page
224.[40]
     Secondly, illiteracy received great attention
because of its prevalence amongst workers and
peasants, particularly in the rural áreas. However,
socialists differed in their approach to the
problem.  The PCP saw illiteracy as an obstacle to
political participation and sought to use literacy
programmes to mobilise the masses. (Research into
the literacy work using a Freirean approach which
was resisted in the north would provide a useful
additional perspective on the process of
conscientisation, as Stoer has pointed out.)[41]   The
revolutionary Left for its part saw people's
existing active involvement in popular organisations
as creating the need for literacy skills, so that
literacy work should be a by-product of increased
politicisation.
     Thirdly, the social relations of the education
situation were a major concern of the popular
organisations.   They regarded the democratic
experience of running collective, self-managed
bodies as itself a significant source of learning
and of socialist counter-hegemony.  It was felt

> ...that the experience of association life was
> a vital part of the process of adult education
> and that all participants should master
> democratic procedures for taking decisions and
> organising active groups, by using methods
> which did away with 'teachers' and 'pupils' and
> placed all associates on an equal footing.[42]

The  collective working methods of the organisations
as a whole were seen as educative and they were also
incorporated into the practices of the more closely
defined adult education activities. For example, in
study sessions different group members might take a

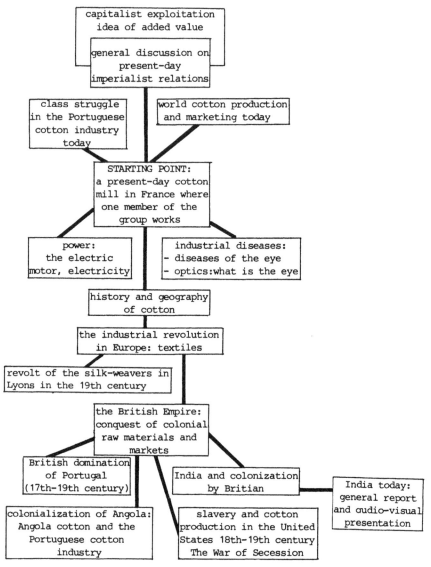

GENERAL OUTLINE OF THE THEME OF COTTON MILLS

"Diagram from EXPERIMENTS IN POPULAR EDUCATION IN PORTUGAL, 1974-1976 (Educational studies and documents, 29) © Unesco 1978. Reproduced by permission of Unesco".

teaching role on particular topics.  However, although a general picture of democratic relationship emerges, it is not clear whether the role of the adult educators was solved in a way that recognised their specialised expertise.

Fourthly, in respect to teaching methods, it is apparent that group discussion and research activities were central to the pedagogical approaches adopted.  One particularly interesting feature is the emphasis given to cultural media such as plays, exhibitions, sound recordings, slides and local newspapers.  A group of miners near Oporto who established a museum to honour their work and struggles even had a film made to bring the museum to life and communicate it to others.[43]  The methods of teaching and learning were conceived in the broadest possible way, techniques being chosen according to their capacity to contribute to the total process of educational development and cultural action that was taking place.

The modes of evaluating this teaching and learning, the fifth aspect of pedagogy, gave high priority to its effect on practice - as the leaders of the Paris educational association put it 'What is the use of knowledge if it is not to promote action?'[44]  Much of the adult education work undertaken was directly concerned with solving the problems of daily existence.  But the formal courses were aimed at securing the certificate of primary education ( - required for official purposes like getting a driver's licence or passport -) which was evaluated within a national system.  The contradiction between methods and contents of learning adapted to the adult's daily realities and the existing school examination system soon became apparent.  This led to the formalisation of a new mode of assessment for adults in 1976 by a Ministerial Decree which represents a very interesting institutionalisation of socialist ideas about evaluation.[45]

Finally,it is clear that adult education was firmly linked to class struggle in the work-place and the community. However, as we have seen, the approach amongst socialists diverged.  The PCP advocated a centrally-directed form of politics, deriving from control of the state, and regarded the revolutionary Left as 'anarcho-populist'.  Its conceptualisation of the role of adult education in the class struggle reflected this political strategy, with its support for centrally-run literacy and political education campaigns. On the other hand, the revolutionary Left regarded the PCP as Stalinist, bureaucratic and reformist, and advocated decentralised, self-managing organisations which would develop people's power in opposition to the capitalist state. It saw adult education's role in the class struggle as emanating from the needs and interests of the popular organisations. Thus whilst the Portuguese experience reaffirms the pedagogical principles of relating adult education to the struggles to take control of production and society, it also indicates different approaches to the implementation of that principle.

## ADULT EDUCATION AND CULTURAL RESISTANCE TO IMPERIALISM IN KAMIRITHU, KENYA, 1976 - 1982

In 1976 the villagers of Kamirithu in Kenya established the Kamirithu Community Education and Cultural Centre. They developed at the centre an adult education and cultural programme based on literacy and dramatic performances. This programme challenged the cultural imperialism that characterises post-colonial Kenya. The experience of the Kamirithu centre provides an example of socialist pedagogy in the context of adult education and cultural resistance to imperialism in the contemporary Third World.

Kenya today epitomises the economic, political and cultural influence of imperialism on underdeveloped capitalist countries. The historical origin of this situation lies in the colonial occupation by Britain in 1895 and the subsequent development of the capitalist mode of production. Central to this process of capitalist penetration was the dispossession of the fertile land of the central highlands and its transfer to European settlers. This drove many peasants off the land, making them reliant on wage labour. Those peasants who retained land began to produce cash crops, their incorporation into the market economy laying the material basis for the development of an indigenous petty bourgeoisie (many of whom came to side with colonial rule).

Colonialism was met at every stage by forms of resistance. Armed resistance in the first twenty years of colonialism was followed by the organised opposition of workers in the 1920s. There was cultural resistance in the 1930s, for example in the

Muthirigu dance and drama movement which expressed the people's opposition to forced labour and colonial oppression. After 1945, organised trade union and political opposition grew steadily and the British attempted to crush it by imposing a State of Emergency in 1952. Resistance then took the form of armed struggle and the Kenya Land and Freedom Army (Mau Mau) undertook a guerilla war to end foreign domination. The colonial government reacted with prison camps and concentration villages. But the escalation of nationalist opposition compelled Britain to find a political solution and in 1963 it conceded independence.

Political independence made little difference to the economic structure, as Britain had intended, and since 1963 Kenya has seen increased capitalist development and integration into the world capitalist economy.[46] Although the Kenyan petty-bourgeoisie has expanded into large-scale agricultural production and into trade and manufacturing, the position of foreign industrial and commercial capital has remained well entrenched. The ruling class has used its control of the state to ensure the conditions required for accumulation by both national and foreign capital, particularly through tight political control and the repression of labour. Thus twenty years after independence, Kenya is in a typical neo-colonial situation, internally racked by intensified class struggle, externally vulnerable to foreign economic, political and cultural interests.

The people of the Kamirithu area had participated actively in the Mau Mau struggle and in 1955 Kamirithu had been created as a concentrated 'emergency village'. It became a permanent settlement and is now a village of about ten thousand people. Its residents include industrial and commercial workers who work in nearby industries or in Nairobi (the capital, twenty miles away). They also include agricultural workers who work on the large plantations in the surrounding highland area formerly occupied by European settlers. There are as well peasants, who mainly hold less than four acres of land, though some rich peasants hold up to ten acres. And there is a lumpenproletariat of the landless unemployed who find occasional work, for example on the plantations during the harvest. It is a poor, badly-housed community, in which perhaps two thousand people are squatters. Its situation has been summarised like this:

The living conditions at Kamirithu are appalling. For instance, there is a squatter community consisting of ten families with a total population of 66 living in the most dehumanising conditions on a three-quarter acre piece of land. There are no sanitation facilities, no street lighting and no medical facilities, in this village of more that ten thousand people.[47]

It was in these conditions of poverty, squalor and hopelessness that a group of workers, peasants and intellectuals came together in 1976 to find a new purpose for the disused community centre. The group formed a management committee and decided to organise activities in the following areas - adult education, cultural development, production skills, and community health. It decided to run the centre on the basis of collective decision-making, with sub-committees responsible for each area of activity.

The first programme was that of the education sub-committee, which decided to develop a literacy project based on the community's needs and problems. It held discussions on immediate local issues such as lack of land, unemployment, low wages and poor facilities, and on the general issue of poverty and its causes. The committee (which included illiterate members) decided to use these problems, coded in posters, songs, stories and role plays, as the content of the teaching materials. After a six month planning period, four literacy classes opened with a total of fifty-five participants. Within six months the majority of participants had learned to read and write and after a year they were writing letters, stories and autobiographies.[48]

Once the literacy project was well-established, it was agreed to develop cultural activities. The peasant and worker members of the centre decided that they wanted to do plays. These plays would provide entertainment and education, form the basis of follow-up reading material for the newly literate, and help to raise money for other activities. Two university intellectuals who were residents of the village and members of the management committee, Ngugi wa Thiongo and Ngugi wa Mirii, were assigned the task of drafting a script, following discussions by the centre's committees and literacy classes. During 1977 a script was written, discussed and revised by the centre's members, and then intensively rehearsed in a democratic process of collective work involving over two hundred people. Meanwhile other community members designed and built an open-air theatre with a seating capacity of more than two thousand, which was financed through the community's own efforts.

The play <u>Ngaahika Ndeenda</u> (I Will Marry When I Want) depicted the lives and history of the people of Kamirithu in their own language, focussing on their current problems in the face of exploitation and oppression. It portrayed the growing political consciousness of a poor young woman (including her resistance to sexism) within the context of the growing opposition to exploitation by the working class and the peasants. The play ended with a strike in a factory and crop destruction on a plantation. It was a clear call for peasant and worker unity against imperialism and its domestic class allies.[49] It was performed ten times to huge crowds, sparking off national interest in community cultural projects. It released talent and creative energy that gave voice to the feelings of the workers and peasants and it thus contained the seeds of a grass-roots movement of opposition to imperialism. In December 1977 it was banned and Ngugi wa Thiongo was put into political detention for a year.[50]

Despite this political repression, the centre continued its activities. The literacy programme increased it enrolment. The orchestra and choir formed for the play continued to meet and made two records. A women's group established a production co-operative.[51] And two years after Ngugi wa Thiongo's release from detention, work began in 1981 on another play, <u>Maitu Njugira</u> (Mother Sing for Me). This play was a musical with the historical theme of workers' resistance to repressive colonial labour conditions in the 1920s and 1930s. At its heart were resistance songs from all over Kenya which the mother sang to her daughter.

The centre decided to perform the play at the National Theatre in Nairobi, a symbol of cultural imperialism with its Broadway musicals and English plays. However, the group was prevented from using the theatre, so it undertook public rehearsals at the university in February 1982, performing to over ten thousand people. The government reacted quickly to this cultural expression of opposition to foreign domination (even though the play was set in the colonial period). In March the centre was deregistered and all drama activities in the Kamirithu area were banned. Armed police destroyed the open-air theatre and took down its signboard proclaiming a 'people's cultural centre'. The government took over the control of the centre, renaming it the Kamirithu Polytechnic and Adult Literacy Centre.[52]

The programme of the Kamirithu centre between 1976 and 1982 provides insight into the use of a socialist pedagogy in the context of cultural resistance to imperialism. The documentary record does not in fact explicitly indicate that Marxist principles underlay the educational and cultural activities of the centre. But both Ngugi wa Thiongo and Ngugi wa Mirii show a clear Marxist perspective in their accounts and can therefore be presumed to have introduced this perspective in their contribution to the activities. Certainly the evidence of the programmes themselves reveals a socialist approach, which can be analysed in terms of the six dimensions of pedagogy I introduced earlier.

The stance towards knowledge adopted within the Kamirithu programmes (including the dramas, conceived as 'collective self education')[53] was clearly one of active knowledge production by all participants. It was one which took as its starting-point the experience of the centre's members and which was designed to serve their interests. In the literacy programme, for example, the students decided on the content of the teaching materials before it started. Ngugi Wa Mirii in discussing this process shows that the problems of everyday existence in Kamirithu were analysed in a way that located them in their wider context (why is there poverty? what is its cause?) and in their historical dimension.[54] Although it is not spelt out, I deduce that a Marxist perspective was introduced into this analysis and into the discussions which produced Ngaahika Ndeenda. The intellectuals involved in the programmes helped to avoid a populist approach to the community's experience and engendered a critical analysis.

The issue of language and literacy raised by the Kamirithu programmes are clearly articulated in terms of class struggle in the reports. The period of colonialism had been characterised by a deliberate attack on the national languages of Kenya and the culture they embodied. The education system, both during and after the colonial period, was the major promoter of English, the language of

domination. Ngugi wa Thiongo, an internationally-
known writer in English, was galvanised by the
experience of working at Kamirithu in 1977 into
giving much higher priority to the need for cultural
expression in Kenyan languages as a challenge to the
hegemony embodied in English. A clear lesson drawn
from Kamirithu is that the use of the language
spoken by the peasant and workers is the only basis
for adult education programmes founded on their
interests. Similarly, Ngugi wa Mirii situates
literacy skills in their class context:

> Literacy is a knowledge of symbols representing
> thought and is thus part of the wider
> communication between human beings in the
> labour process.[55]

He shows how the denial of these skills of coding
and decoding information is part of the mental
suppression of the dominated classes. The
development of these skills was an essential part
of the personal and political development of the
participants in the Kamirithu programmes.

The social relations of the educational
situation are evident at the level of the centre as
a whole, in which a collective and democratic
approach to decision-making had been adopted from
the beginning. This approach was reflected in the
literacy classes, in which the students participated
in planning and managing the programme (including
recruiting their own teachers, setting their own
regulations and raising their own funds). It is
also found in the collective production of the first
play, with its extensive discussions and process of
criticism and self-criticism. The intellectuals
involved in the centre's work were acknowledged as
useful for their particular expertise (as a writer
or adult educator, for example) but were accountable
to collective decision-making. Other members had
other areas of expertise (such as building and
music) which were contributed equally within the
democratic framework of co-operation, participation
and control.

The teaching methods used at the centre can be
considered in terms of the literacy classes and the
cultural activities. The literacy method was
derived from Freire, though there were adaptions,
such as the significant role given to the students
themselves in determining the content. The dramas
can be conceived methodologically both as an

educational process for those involved in their
production (developing a very wide range of
knowledge, skills and attitudes) and as an
educational event for the audiences, an entertaining
way of challenging the dominant ideology and raising
political awareness.

There is no discussion in the reports on
Kamirithu of the role and process of evaluation.
Mention is made of writing and sending letters as
evidence of literacy attainment and obviously the
process of producing the plays included continual
collective assessment of their content and form.
However, it seems reasonable to conclude that the
participants in the centre's programmes judged the
effectiveness of their learning in terms of their
enhanced ability pursue their class interests in the
wider society.

Finally, it is evident that because the purpose
of the Kamirithu programmes was to help the
participants advance their own interests, learning
and cultural expression were part of the broader
struggle to change Kenyan society. There is nothing
to suggest that these programmes were linked to
organised economic or political struggle. In fact,
the political repression in Kenya is such that no
Marxist party can become visible and trade union
activity is severely restricted. This means that in
such circumstances, adult education and cultural
action can become an important form of resistance,
building awareness, developing skills and
organisational capacity, sowing the seeds of
counter-hegemony. The Kamirithu Centre therefore
demonstrates one of the ways in which workers,
peasants and intellectuals can use a socialist
approach to adult education and culture in the fight
against international and domestic capital in the
Third World.


THE DEVELOPMENT OF A SOCIALIST PEDAGOGY
FOR ADULT EDUCATION

The above case studies have provided accounts
of three very different circumstances in which adult
education has been a weapon of struggle within a
capitalist social formation. They constitute
concrete expressions of how socialists have striven
to implement adult education practices that support
their political purposes. The periods and
programmes I have considered are not uncontentious

in terms of Marxist analysis (as the complexities of the Portuguese case indicate) and within a short space I have only been able to present overviews rather than in-depth analyses. However, the case studies do show how different aspects of a socialist pedagogy have been carried out in practice. They therefore illustrate my argument that Marxist principles of adult learning lead to a distinctive approach to questions of knowledge acquisition, the role of language and literacy, the social relations of education, teaching methods, evaluation, and the relation of learning to daily life.

I regard the presentation of these examples as part of a necessary process of recovering historical experience and making available contemporary experience in terms of an analytical perspective which seeks to develop the concept of a socialist pedagogy for adult education. Clearly the analysis of other experiences would also contribute to this development.

A particularly interesting example would be the practical activity of Gramsci in workers' education in Turin, especially during the 'two red years' of 1919-1920.[56] The only extended discussion in English of Gramsci's general approach to education is that of Entwhistle in his book <u>Antonio Gramsci.</u> <u>Conservative Schooling for Radical Politics</u> but this is a seriously misleading interpretation.[57] The bulk of the book focusses on Gramsci's views on the schooling of children, which were largely a criticism of the Dewey-inspired reforms in Italian education in the 1920s. Entwhistle wrongly equates Dewey's child-centred pedagogy (and its modern manifestations) with a socialist approach, thus arriving at the false conclusion that Gramsci's critique constitutes conservatism. In fact, Gramsci's ideas on many pedagogical issues - such as his view of language as a carrier of hegemony, his belief in the need for a high level of literacy and cognitive skills, and his conception of the centrality of work to human experience - reveal a Marxist perspective that Entwhistle fails to grasp.[58] (The section of the book on the education of adults does not deal with pedagogy.)

The significance of Gramsci for adult education is that he was a major Marxist theoretician and politician who regarded adult education as having a key role in the struggle against capitalism. Gramsci put enormous emphasis on the political education of adults[59] and on their general and

technical education. He believed that workers'
organisations could provide both the lived
experience and the organised education to create in
the working class a new consciousness. His 1919
article entitled 'Workers' Democracy' exemplified
his ideas. Here he argued that the institutions of
the workers' movement should form an educational
context which 'should effect a radical
transformation of the workers' mentality (and)
should make the masses better equipped to exercise
power'.[60] A study from a Marxist perspective of his
adult education activities in study circles,
discussion groups, educational clubs and so forth
amongst the workers of Turin, especially during the
revolutionary period of 1919-1920, would be of
enormous value.

Perhaps the example of Italy in 1919-1920, and
the case studies of China and Portugal, might seem
to suggest that a socialist pedagogy is only viable
during periods of extreme capitalist crisis. This
would be misleading, as the example of Shor's book
Critical Teaching and Everyday Life about teaching
in New York in the 1970s indicates. However,
accounts of socialist adult education in periods of
relative capitalist stability are less numerous,
particularly of activity within state-funded
programmes. In this respect it would be very useful
to have accounts of socialist pedagogy during the
1970s within, say, local authority adult education
in an advanced capitalist country like Britain, or
within government programmes in an underdeveloped
capitalist country like India.

Another source of experience is that of the
socialist countries. My focus in this book has been
socialist adult education in the context of
capitalist social formations, but obviously the
practices developed within socialism are also
important. The analysis of historical experience,
such as the polytechnical education for adults in
the USSR in the 1920s, and of contemporary
experience, such as the 1980 National Literacy
Crusade in Nicaragua, would constitute another
contribution to an understanding of the concept of a
socialist pedagogy and the issues involved in its
practical implementation. The more that is known
about what socialists have done in different times
and in different places, the more adult educators
will be able to see the possibilities for action
within their own circumstances.

What I have sought to do in this chapter is to

provide some guidelines for such action. I have applied the Marxist principles of adult learning established in Chapters Two and Three to six aspects of pedagogy, thereby indicating their practical implications for the teaching of adults. Clearly certain areas of consideration require both greater theorisation and more empirical research. For example, the role of language and literacy in the teaching and learning of adults seems to me relatively undeveloped in terms of a Marxist psychology. And to other areas I have given only glancing attention. For example, the specific issues involved in the acquisition of technical skills require greater elaboration (which might fruitfully be based on research in the context of a socialist producers' co-operative). However, although this study is not totally exhaustive, it does represent an attempt to undertake for adult education the task which Sharp identified in 1980:

> I do not think that the analysis has yet been done which can guide us very much in the practice of Marxist pedagogy. The goals are clear but radical teachers lack a theory of pedagogy and are forced to rely on little more than hunches and intuitions. As I shall argue, this is an urgent theoretical and political task for Marxists and for educators.[61]

This chapter, by translating Marxist theoretical principles into adult education practices, has been intended to help adult educators go beyond 'hunches and intuitions' and develop a coherent socialist pedagogy.

NOTES

1. F. Engels, 'Preface to the English Edition 1888 [of the Manifesto of the Communist Party]', in K. Marx and F. Engels, Selected Works Vol. 1 (London: Lawrence and Wishart, 1950), p. 25.
2. V.I. Lenin, 'The New Economic Policy and the tasks of the Political Education Departments', in V.I. Lenin, Collected Works Vol. 33. (Moscow: Progress Publishers, 1964), p. 78.
3. I. Shor, Critical Teaching and Everyday Life (Boston: South End Press, 1980)p. 37.
4. K. Marx, Capital Vol. 1 (Harmondsworth: Penguin, 1976), p. 482.
5. See, for example, A. Gorz, 'Technical

intelligence and the capitalist division of labour', in Society, State and Schooling. Eds., M. Young and G. Whitty (Lewes: The Falmer Press, 1977).

6.    K. Marx, Ibid., p. 614.

7.    I. Shor, Ibid, p. 93.

8.    D. Reed, Education for Building a People's Movement (Boston: South End Press, 1981), p. 181.

9.    J.B. Elshtain, 'The social relations of the classroom: a moral and political perspective', in Studies in Socialist Pedagogy. Eds., T.M. Norton and B. Ollman (London: Monthly Review Press, 1978), pp. 302-303.

10.   S. Castles and W. Wustenberg, The Education of the Future (London: Pluto, 1979), p. 192.

11.   R. Sharp, Knowledge, Ideology and the Politics of Schooling (London: Routledge and Kegan Paul), pp. 141-146.

12.   This issue is discussed at length in C. Searle, Words Unchained (London: Zed, 1984), which is a study of the role of language in the Caribbean, focussing particularly on Grenada during the period of the anti-imperialist revolution, 1979-1983.

13.   See G.S. Coles, 'Adult illiteracy and learning theory: a study of cognition activity', Science and Society Vol XLVII No. 4 (1983-84): 451-482.

14.   R. Sharp, Ibid., p. 165.

15.   D. Reed, Ibid., pp. 195-201.

16.   I. Shor, Ibid., p. 100.

17.   P. Bergevin, D. Morris and R.M. Smith, Adult Education Procedures (New York: Seabury, 1963).

18.   I. Hextall, 'Marking work', in Explorations in the Politics of School Knowledge. Eds., G. Whitty and M. Young (Nafferton: Nafferton Books, 1976).

19.   B. Harold, 'Beyond student-centred teaching', in Studies in Socialist Pedagogy. Eds., T.M. Norton and B. Ollman (London: Monthly Review Press, 1978), p. 319.

20.   M. Selden, The Yenan Way in Revolutionary China (Cambridge: Cambridge University Press, 1971), pp. 210-211.

21.   Mobilisation Society of Wuhan, 'Educational method at K'angta', in Revolutionary Education in China. Ed., P.J. Seybolt (White Plains: International Arts and Sciences Press, 1973).

22.   Ibid., p. 36.

23.   P.J. Seybolt, 'The Yenan revolution in

mass education', China Quarterly No. 48 (1971): 660.

24. M. Lindsay, 'The education system: early communist origins, 1939-1946', in Education and Communism in China. Ed., S.E. Fraser (London: Pall Mall, 1971), p. 39.

25. M. Selden, Ibid., p. 268.

26. Mao Tse Tung, 'On Practice', in Mao Tse Tung, Selected Readings (Peking: Foreign Languages Press, 1971).

27. Mao Tse Tung, 'On Contradiction', in Mao Tse Tung, Selected Readings (Peking: Foreign Lanugages Press, 1971).

28. R.F. Price, Education in Modern China (London: Routledge and Kegan Paul, 1979), pp. 70-76.

29. M. Lindsay, Ibid., pp. 42-46.

30. P.J. Seybolt, Ibid.

32. Mao Tse Tung, 'Some Questions Concerning Methods of Leadership', in Mao Tse Tung, Selected Readings (Peking: Foreign Languages Press).

32. Mobilisation Society for Wuhan, Ibid., pp. 343-344.

33. The character of this pedagogy was well summarised at the time in the following official document - Civil Affairs Office of the Shen-Kan-Ning Border Region Government, 'Yenan University Educational Policy and Temporary Regulations (May 21, 1944)', in Revolutionary Education in China. Eds., P.J. Seybolt (White Plains: International Arts and Sciences Press, 1973).

34. M.V. Cabral, 'Agrarian structures and recent rural movements in Portugal', Journal of Peasant Studies, Vol. 5, No. 4 (1978): 411-445.

35. A. Cunhal, General Secretary of the PCP, quoted in S. Stoer, 'Democracy and socialism in education in Portugal', in Schooling and the National Interest. Vol. 1. Eds., R. Dale et al, (Sussex: Falmer Press, 1981), p. 345.

36. S. Stoer, The April Revolution and the Contribution of Education to Changing 'Portuguese Realities'. Unpublished PhD thesis. (Milton Keynes: Open University , 1983).

37. MFA document quoted by S. Stoer, Ibid., p. 219.

38. A. Melo and A. Benavente, Experiments in Popular Education in Portugal, 1974-6 (Paris: UNESCO, 1978), p. 16.

39. A. Melo, Portugal's experience of reform through popular initiative', Convergence, Vol. XI, No 1 (1978):30.

40.   A. Melo and A. Benavente, Ibid., p. 27.

41.   S. Stoer, Ibid., p. 246.

42.   A. Melo, Adult Education in Portugal (Prague: European Centre for Leisure and Education, 1983), p. 43.

43.   A. Melo, 'Portugal's experience of reform through popular initiative', Convergence Vol XI, No 1 (1978): 29-30.

44.   A. Melo and A. Benavente, Ibid., p. 26.

45.   Ibid., p. 42-44.

46.   B. Beckman, 'Imperialism and capitalist transformation: critique of a Kenyan debate', Review Of African Political Economy, No. 19 (1980): 48-62.

47.   Ngugi wa Mirii, 'On literacy content', in Participatory Research, Eds., Y. Kassam and K. Mustafa (New Delhi: Society for Participatory Research in Asia, 1982), p. 245.

48.   Ibid., pp. 246-248.

49.   Ngugi wa Thiongo, Barrel of a Pen (London: New Beacon Books, 1983), pp. 48-50.

50.   Ngugi wa Thiongo, Detained (London: Heinemann, 1981), pp. 72-80.

51.   R. Kidd, 'Popular theatre and popular struggle in Kenya: the story of the Kamirithu Community Education and cultural Centre', Theatrework, Vol. 2 No. 6 (1982):54.

52.   Ngugi wa Thiongo, Barrel of a Pen (London: New Beacon Books, 1983), pp. 39-51.

53.   Ngugi wa Thiongo, Detained (London: Heinemann, 1981), p.76.

54.   Ngugi wa Mirii, Ibid., pp. 246-247.

55.   Ibid., p. 242.

56.   G.A. Williams, Proletarian Order (London: Pluto, 1975).

57.   H. Entwhistle, Antonio Gramsci. Conservative Schooling for Radical Politics (London: Routledge and Kegan Paul, 1979).

58.   For critical reviews of Entwhistle's book which similarly question his interpretation of Gramsci, see M.W. Apple in Comparative Education Review, Vol. 24. No. 3 (1980): 436-438 and M. Alden in Convergence, Vol. XIV No 3 (1981):91-94.

59.   W.L. Adamson, Hegemony and Revolution (Berkeley: University of California Press, 1980), Chap. 5.

60.   A. Gramsci, 'Workers' Democracy' in A. Gramsci, Selections from Political Writings (1910-1920), Ed. Q. Hoare (London: Lawrence and Wishart, 1977), p. 68.

61.   R. Sharp, Knowledge, Ideology and the

Politics of Schooling (London: Routledge and Kegan Paul, 1980), 140.

Chapter Seven

**CONCLUSION**

From the mid-1960s adult education world-wide experienced an enormous expansion of activity. Its emergence as a more significant part of the provision of education in society led to an increased concern with its political nature, and there arose in the 1970s a renewed interest in the potential of adult education as a part of the struggle against capitalism.

As a result, socialists working in adult education were confronted with the issue of how to unify their political theory and their educational practice. However, sources of ideas and inspiration were few. Despite the growing number of articles and books in English on adult education, hardly any had a socialist perspective. Only Freire seemed to offer an approach aimed at radical social transformation and his work therefore took a central place. And yet, as I found in my own experience, there was something unsatisfactory about the Freirean approach. After all, his name was invoked by many reactionary programmes as well as by radicals. This sense of dissatisfaction with Freire and my awareness of a dearth of alternatives to orthodox adult education prompted me to undertake a study which would articulate a specifically socialist approach.

I have therefore sought in this book to develop from first principles a Marxist approach to adult education. My intention has been to provide the basis for the unity of theory and practice that I have conceptualised as a socialist pedagogy, that is, an approach to the teaching and learning of adults consonant with socialist politics. To do this has necessitated a wide-ranging analysis of Marxist politics, philosophy, social theory and psychology in order to establish the theoretical perspective required for making a critique of orthodox and Freirean approaches and for developing a socialist approach. I have argued that Marxist principles reveal the inadequacies of other approaches and provide a sound foundation for adult education practices which can unmask capitalist ideology and generate a counter-hegemony that will equip the working class and its allies to take power. The study has therefore suggested an approach to adult education which can provide suitable support to the organised economic and political struggle against capitalism.

But the book only represents a starting-point for the further development of a socialist pedagogy for adult education. In order for this approach to be refined and extended, continuing theoretical work and practical activity are needed. What is required is a dialectical process in which theory provides a guide for educational action while practical experience reveals issues and problems for further study.

The necessary theoretical work has three aspects. First, there is need to elaborate further the conceptual basis of socialist pedagogy by developing the relevant areas of Marxist theory. Chapter Two is clearly only a beginning in this respect, providing the ground-work for a more sophisticated discussion which will involve deeper inquiry into selected theoretical fields (such as psychology) and taking into account the most recent developments in Marxism (such as the 'critical theory' of Habermas). Marxism is in a very dynamic phase of its theoretical development and those concerned with socialist adult education must participate in its ferment and contribute especially to its conceptualisation of education.

The second area of theoretical work is that of empirical analysis from a Marxist perspective of all facets of adult education in capitalist society. There is a need to uncover the processes of determination which shape the nature of adult education organisation and practice in specific circumstances. This can only be done by undertaking empirical studies of adult education in particular national contexts, both advanced and underdeveloped, using Marxist tools of analysis (such as the concepts of political economy sketched in Chapter One). There are regrettably few accounts which explicate in detail the relationships between a

241

given national class structure and the form of adult education which obtains. Yet it is only on the basis of such an analysis of their situation that adult educators can develop strategies for counter-hegemonic activity.

Finally, there has to be undertaken critical study of both historical and contemporary experiences of socialist adult education, in capitalist and socialist social formations. As I indicated in the previous chapter, we need to have a much more accessible body of information about what Marxist adult educators have done in the past and what they are doing now in different parts of the world. Such historical and international information can counter tendencies to ignore the past and to be parochial, tendencies which serve to cut off the educational worker from the lessons learned by others in the struggle for socialism.

The purpose of this conceptual, empirical and historical research is to provide a sound foundation for the practical activity of committed adult educators. The principles of socialist pedagogy derived from theoretical work (as in Chapter Three) must be translated into actual educational practices in the day-to-day situations of adult education – the evening class in the secondary school, the lunch-time session in the co-operative workshop, the discussion in the shade of the tree at the village meeting-place. Socialist adult educators need to undertake their own purposeful experiments and reflect critically on these activities in order to develop the working models of socialist pedagogy that are appropriate to their circumstances. Such models can demonstrate clearly the alternatives to those adult education practices which perpetuate capitalist hegemony, and they can make a concrete contribution to the organised struggle against capitalism.

The practice of socialist adult education therefore rests on a combination of critical research and critical action. Its effectiveness depends on a coherence of political theory and educational activity. The development of socialist pedagogy aims to create this coherence and thus help adult education to play its role in building the forces capable of undertaking the revolutionary transformation of society.

**BIBLIOGRAPHY**

Note: The works of Marx, Engels, Lenin and Mao are entered initially by their original date of composition with the date of the specific edition cited following later.

Adamson, W.L. Hegemony and Revolution. (Berkeley: University of California Press, 1980)

Advisory Council For Adult And Continuing Education. Continuing Education: From Policies to Practice. (Leicester: Advisory Council for Adult and Continuing Education, 1982)

Alden, H. Gramsci's theoretical legacy. Convergence Vol. XIV No. 3 (1981): 91-94.

Allman, P. 'The nature and process of adult development', in Education for Adults. Volume 1. Adult Learning and Education. Ed. Tight, M. pp. 107-123. (Beckenham: Croom Helm, 1983)

Althusser, L. 'Ideology and ideological state apparatuses', in Althusser, L. Lenin and Philosophy. (New York: Monthly Review Press, 1971)

Apple, M.W. 'Ivan Illich and Deschooling Society: the politics of slogan systems', in Social Forces and Schooling. Eds., Shimahara, N. and Scrupski, A., pp. 337-360. (New York: McKay, 1975)

Apple, M.W. Ideology and Curriculum. (London: Routledge and Kegan Paul, 1979)

Apple, M.W. Review of Antonio Gramsci. Conservative Schooling for Radical Politics by Harold Entwhistle. Comparative Education Review Vol 24., No. 3 (1980): 436-438.

Apple, M.W. Cultural and Economic Reproduction in Education (London: Routledge and Kegan Paul, 1982)

Apple, M.W. Education and Power. (London: Routledge and Kegan Paul, 1982)

Anderson, P. The antimonies of Antonio Gramsci. New Left Review Vol. 100 (1977): 5-80.

Bataille, L. Ed. A Turning Point for Literacy.

(Oxford: Pergamon, 1976)

Beckman, B. Imperialism and capitalist transformation: critique of a Kenyan debate. Review of African Political Economy No. 19 (1980): 48-62.

Berger, P.L. Pyramids of Sacrifice. (New York: Basic Books, 1974)

Bergevin, P., Morris, D., and Smith, R.M. Adult Education Procedures. (New York: Seabury, 1963)

Berki, R.N. Socialism. (London: Dent, 1975)

Bernstein, B. Class, Codes and Control. Volumes 1-3. (London: Routledge and Kegan Paul, 1971, 1973, 1977)

Bernstein, R.J. Praxis and Action. (Philadelphia: University of Pennsylvania Press, 1971)

Bigge, M.L. Learning Theories for Teachers. (New York: Harper and Rowe, 1982)

Bloom, B.S. et al. Taxonomy of Educational Objectives: Handbook 1: Cognitive Domain. (New York: McKay, 1956)

Bloom, B.S. et al. Taxonomy of Educational Objectives: Handbook 2: Affective Domain. (New York: McKay, 1956)

Boggs, C. Gramsci's Marxism. (London: Pluto, 1976)

Bogoiavlenski, D.N. and Menchinskaia N.A. 'The psychology of learning, 1900-1960', in Educational Psychology in the USSR. Ed. Simon, B. and Simon, J., pp. 101-161. (London: Routledge and Kegan Paul, 1963)

Bower, G.H. and Hilgard, E.R. Theories of Learning. (Englewood Cliffs: Prentice-Hall, 1981)

Bowles, S. and Gintis H. Schooling in Capitalist America. (London: Routledge and Kegan Paul, 1976)

Bown, L. and Okedara J.T. Eds. An Introduction to the Study of Adult Education. (Ibadan: University Press, 1981)

Boydell, T. Experiential Learning. (Manchester:

244

University of Manchester, Department of Adult and Higher Education, 1976)

Braverman, H. Labour and Monopoly Capital. (London: Monthly Review Press, 1974)

Brewer, A. Marxist Theories of Imperialism. A Critical Survey. (London: Routledge and Kegan Paul, 1980)

Broadbent, D.E. Cognitive psychology and education. British Journal of Educational Psychology 45 (1975): 162-176.

Brown, L.B. Psychology in Contemporary China. (Oxford: Pergamon Press, 1981)

Brown P. Ed. Radical Psychology. (London: Tavistock, 1973)

Brown, P. Towards a Marxist Psychology. (New York: Harper Colophon, 1974)

Cabral, M.V. Agrarian structures and recent rural movements in Portugal. Journal of Peasant Studies Vol. 5, No. 4 (1978): 411-445.

Castles, S.W. and Wustenberg, W. The Education of the Future. (London: Pluto, 1979)

Civil Affairs Office of the Shen-Kan-Ning Border Region Government 'Yenan University Educational Policy and Temporary Regulations (May 21, 1944)' in Revolutionary Education in China. Ed. Seybolt, P.J. pp. 376-384. (White Plains: International Arts and Sciences Press, 1973)

Coles, G.S. Adult illiteracy and learning theory: a study of cognition activity. Science and Society Vol XLVII No. 4 (1983-84): 451-482.

Cross, K.P. Adults as Learners. (San Francisco: Jossey-Bass, 1982)

Da Rocha Reufels, C. Mobral: Literacy for Brazil. Adult Education and Development 20 (1983): 77-84.

Dale, R. E202 Schooling and Society. Unit 31. Block VI. Alternatives? (Milton Keynes: Open University Press, 1977)

Davis, R. 'Education for awareness: a talk with Paulo Freire', in Literacy and Revolution: the Pedagogy of Paulo Freire. Ed. R. Mackie, pp. 57-69. (London: Pluto, 1980)

De Kadt, E. Catholic Radicals in Brazil. (London: Oxford University Press, 1970)

De Leon, S. Radical approach to literacy. New York Times May 1 (1977):36.

Delker, P.V. Governmental roles in lifelong learning. Journal of Research and Development in Education 7(4) (1974): 24-33.

Elias, J.L. and Merriam, S. Philosophical Foundations of Adult Education. (New York: Kneger, 1980)

Elshtain, J.B. 'The social relations of the classroom: a moral and political perspective', in Studies in Socialist Pedagogy. Eds. Norton, T.M. and Ollman, B. pp. 291-313. (London: Monthly Review Press, 1978)

Engels, F. 1844. 'The condition of England', in Marx, K. and Engels, F. Collected Works. Volume 3. (London: Lawrence and Wishart, 1975)

Engels, F. 1876. 'The part played by labour in the transition from ape to man', in Marx, K. and Engels, F. Selected Works. Volume 2. (London: Lawrence and Wishart, 1950)

Engels, F. 1878-1882. Dialectics of Nature. (Moscow: Progress Publishers, 1976)

Engels, F. 1888a. 'Preface to the English Edition 1888 [of the Manifesto of the Communist Party]', in Marx, K. and Engels, F. Selected Works. Volume 1. (London: Lawrence and Wishart, 1950)

Engels, F. 1888b. 'Ludwig Feuerbach and the end of classical German philosophy' in Marx, K. and Engels, F. Selected Works. Volume 2. (London: Lawrence and Wishart, 1950)

Engels, F. 1890. 'Engels to J Bloch', in Marx, K. and Engels, F. Selected Works. Volume 2. (London:

Lawrence and Wishart, 1950)

Engels, F. 1892 'Socialism: Utopian and Scientific', in Marx, K. and Engels, F. Selected Works Volume 2. (London: Lawrence and Wishart, 1950)

Engels, F. 1893. 'Engels to F. Mehring', in Marx, K. and Engels, F. Selected Works. Volume 2. (London: Lawrence and Wishart, 1950)

Entwhistle, H. Antonio Gramsci. Conservative Schooling for Radical Politics. (London: Routledge and Kegan Paul, 1979)

Esland, G. E202 Schooling and Society. Block IV. Processes of Selection. (Milton Keynes: Open University Press, 1977)

Femia, J.V. Gramsci's Political Thought. (Oxford: Clarendon Press, 1981)

Filson, G. and Green, G. Towards a Political Economy of Adult Education in the Third World. (Toronto: International Council for Adult Education, 1980)

Freire, P. Cultural Action for Freedom. (Harmondsworth: Penguin, 1972)

Freire, P. Pedagogy of the Oppressed (Harmondsworth: Penguin, 1972)

Freire, P. 'A few notions about the word 'conscientisation'', in Schooling and Capitalism. Eds. Dale, R., Esland, G. and Macdonald, M. pp. 224-227. (London: Routledge and Kegan Paul, 1976)

Freire, P. 'Are literacy programmes neutral?' in A Turning Point for Literacy. Ed. Bataille, L. pp. 195-200. (Oxford: Pergamon, 1976)

Freire, P. Education: The Practice of Freedom. (London: Writers and Readers Publishing Co-operative, 1976)

Freire, P. Pedagogy in Process. (London: Writers and Readers Publishing Co-operative, 1978)

Freire, P. The people speak their word: learning to read and write in Sao Tome and Principe. Harvard Educational Review Vol. 51, No. 1 (1981): 27-30.

Freire, P. The Politics of Education. (London: Macmillan, 1985)

Frith, S. and Corrigan, P. 'The politics of education', in Society, State and Schooling. Eds., Young, M. and Whitty, G., pp. 253-268. (Ringmer: Falmer Press, 1977)

Further Education Curriculum Review and Development Unit. How Do I Learn? (London: Further Education Curriculum Review and Development Unit, 1981)

Gagne, R.M. The Conditions of Learning. (London: Holt, Rinehart and Winston, 1970)

Gandy, D.R. Marx and History. (Austin: University of Texas Press, 1979)

Gelpi, E. A Future for Lifelong Education. Volume 2. (Manchester: University of Manchester, Department of Adult and Higher Education, 1979)

Geras, N. Marx and Human Nature. (London: New Left Books, 1983)

Gintis, H. 'Towards the political economy of education: a radical critique of Ivan Illich's Deschooling Society' in Schooling and Capitalism. Eds. Dale, R., Esland, G. and Macdonald, M., pp. 8-20. (London: Routledge and Kegan Paul, 1976)

Giroux, H.A. Ideology, Culture and the Process of Schooling. (Sussex: Falmer Press, 1981)

Giroux, H.A. Theories of reproduction and resistance in the new sociology of education - a critical analysis. Harvard Educational Review Vol. 53, No. 3 (1983): 257-293.

Glaser, R. Ed. Instructional Psychology. Volume 1. (Hillsdale: Lawrence Erlbaum, 1978)

Glaser, R., Pellegrino, J.W. and Lesgold, A.M. 'Some directions for a cognitive psychology of instruction', in Cognitive Psychology and Instruction. Eds., Lesgold, A.M. et al. pp. 495-517. (New York: Plenum Press, 1978)

Goody, J. The Domestication of the Savage Mind. (Cambridge: Cambridge University Press, 1977)

248

Gorz, A. 'Technical intelligence and the capitalist division of labour', in <u>Society, State and Schooling</u>. Eds. Young, M. and Whitty, G. pp. 131-150 (Lewes: The Falmer Press, 1977)

Grabowski, S.M. Ed. <u>Paulo Freire: A Revolutionary Dilemma for the Adult Educator</u> (Syracuse: Eric Clearing House on Adult Education, 1972)

Gramsci, A. <u>Prison Notebooks</u>. Eds. Hoare, Q. and Smith, G.N. (London: Lawrence and Wishart, 1971)

Gramsci, A. <u>Selections from Political Writings (1910 - 1920)</u>. Ed. Hoare, Q. (London: Lawrence and Wishart, 1977)

Griffin, C. <u>Curriculum Theory in Adult and Lifelong Education</u>. (London: Croom Helm, 1983)

Gutierrez, G. <u>A Theology of Liberation</u>. (London: SCM Press, 1974)

Hall, B.L. Continuity in adult education and political struggle. <u>Convergence</u> Vol. XI, No. 1 (1978): 8-15.

Harasim, L. 'Literacy and National Reconstruction in Guinea-Bissau: A critique of the Freirean Literacy Campaign.' Unpublished PhD thesis. Ontario Institute for Studies in Education, 1983

Harold, B. 'Beyond student-centred teaching', in <u>Studies in Socialist Pedagogy</u>. Eds. Norton, T.M. and Ollman, B. pp. 314-334 (London: Monthly Review Press, 1978)

Harris, D. and Holmes, J. 'Open-ness and control in higher education', in <u>Schooling and Capitalism</u>. Eds. Dale, R., Esland, G. and Macdonald, M. pp. 78-87. (London: Routledge and Kegan Paul, 1976)

Heather, N. <u>Radical Perspectives in Psychology</u>. (London: Methuen, 1976)

Hextall, I. 'Marking work', in <u>Explorations in the Politics of School Knowledge</u>. Eds. Whitty, G. and Young, M. pp. 65-74. (Nafferton: Nafferton Books, 1976)

Hoare, Q. and Smith, G.N. Eds. <u>Selections from the</u>

Prison Notebooks of Antonio Gramsci. (London: Lawrence and Wishart, 1971)

Hoffman, J. Marxism and the Theory of Praxis. (London: Lawrence and Wishart, 1975)

Holland, J.G. 'Are behavioral principles for revolutionaries?' in Behavior Modification. Applications to Education. Eds. Keller, F.S. and Ribes-Inesta, E. pp. 195-208. (New York: Academic Press, 1974)

Houle, C.O. The Design of Education. (San Francisco: Jossey Bass, 1974)

IDAC. Guinea-Bissau '79. Learning by Living and Doing. (Geneva: IDAC, 1979)

Illich, I. Deschooling Society. (Harmondsworth: Penguin, 1973)

Illich, I. and Verne, E. Imprisoned in the Global Classroom. (London: Writers and Readers Publishing Co-operative, 1976)

Institute of Adult Education Adult Education Handbook. (Dar Es Salaam: Tanzania Publishing House, 1973)

Johnson, R. 'Notes on the Schooling of the English Working Class 1780-1850', in Schooling and Capitalism. Eds. Dale, R., Esland, G. and Macdonald, M. pp. 44-54. (London: Routledge and Kegan Paul, 1976)

Kahn, J.S. and Llobera, J.R. The Anthropology of Pre-Capitalist Societies. (London: Macmillan, 1981)

Kamin, L. The Science and Politics of I.Q. (London: Wiley, 1975)

Kaye, A. and Rumble, G. Distance Teaching for Higher and Adult Education. (London: Croom Helm, 1981)

Keddie, N. 'Adult education: an ideology of individualism', in Adult Education for a Change. Ed. Thompson, J.L. pp. 45-64. (London: Hutchinson, 1980)

Kee, A. A Reader in Political Theology. (London: SCM Press, 1974)

Keller, F.S. and Sherman J.G. The Keller Plan Handbook: Essays on a Personalised System of Instruction. (Menlo Park: Benjamin, 1974)

Kidd, J.R. How Adults Learn. (New York: Association Press, 1973)

Kidd, R. Popular theatre and popular struggle in Kenya: the story of the Kamirithu Community Education and Cultural Centre. Theatrework Vol. 2, No. 6 (1982): 47-61.

Kidd, R. and Kumar, K. Co-opting Freire. A critical analysis of pseudo-Freirean adult education. Economic and Political Weekly Vol. XVI, Nos. 1 and 2, January 3-10 (1981):27-36.

Kitching, G. Rethinking Socialism. (London: Methuen, 1983)

Knowles, M. The Modern Practice of Adult Education. (Chicago: Association Press, 1970)

Knox, A.B. Adult Development and Learning. (London: Jossey Bass, 1977)

Koch, S. 'Psychology and emerging conceptions of knowledge as unitary', in Behaviorism and Phenomenology. Ed. Wann, T.W. pp. 1-41. (Chicago: Chicago University Press, 1964)

Koffka, K. The Growth of Mind. (London: Kegan Paul, Trench, Trubner, 1928)

Lane, D. The Socialist Industrial State. (London: Allen and Unwin, 1976)

Leach, T. Paulo Freire: dialogue, politics and relevance. International Journal of Lifelong Education Vol. 1, No. 3 (1982): 185-201.

Lenin, V.I. 1899. 'Our programme', in Lenin V.I. Collected Works. Volume 4. (Moscow: Progress Publishers, 1964)

Lenin, V.I. 1908. Materialism and Emipirio-Criticism. (Peking: Foreign Languages Press, 1976)

Lenin, V.I. 1914-15. 'Philosophical notebooks', in Lenin V.I. Collected Works. Volume 38. (Moscow:

Progress Publishers, 1972)

Lenin, V.I. 1916. 'Imperialism, the highest stage of capitalism', in Lenin V.I. Collected Works. Volume 22. (Moscow: Progress Publishers, 1964)

Lenin, V.I. 1917a. 'Letters on tactics', in Lenin, V.I. Collected Works. Volume 24. (Moscow: Progress Publishers, 1964)

Lenin, V.I. 1917b. 'The state and revolution', in Lenin V.I. Collected Works. Volume 25. (Moscow: Progress Publishers, 1964)

Lenin, V.I. 1921. 'The New Economic Policy and the tasks of the Political Education Departments', in Lenin V.I. Collected Works. Volume 33. (Moscow: Progress Publishers, 1964)

Leontiev, A.N. 'The nature and formation of human psychic properties', in Psychology in the Soviet Union. Ed., Simon, B. pp. 226-232. (London: Routledge and Kegan Paul, 1957)

Leontiev, A.N. and Rozanava, T.V. 'The formation of associative connections: an experimental investigation', in Psychology in the Soviet Union. Ed. Simon, B. pp. 165-182. (London: Routledge and Kegan Paul, 1957)

Levine, N. The Tragic Deception. (Oxford: Clio Books, 1975)

Lindsay, M. 'The educational system: early communist origins, 1939-1946', in Education and Communism in China. Ed. Fraser, S.E. pp. 27-48. (London: Pall Mall, 1971)

Littler, C.R. The Development of the Labour Process in Capitalist Societies. (London: Heinemann, 1982)

Lovell, R.B. Adult Learning. (London: Croom Helm, 1980)

Lovett, T., Clarke, C. and Kilmurray, A. Adult Education and Community Action (London: Croom Helm, 1983)

Lukacs, G. History and Class Consciousness. (London: Merlin Press, 1971)

Luria, A.R. Cognitive Development. Its Cultural and Social Foundations. (Cambridge: Harvard University Press, 1976)

Luria, A.R. The Making of Mind. (Cambridge: Harvard University Press, 1979)

Luria, A.R. Language and Cognition. (New York: Wiley, 1981)

Macleish, J. Soviet Psychology. (London: Methuen, 1975)

Mackie, R. 'Contributions to the thought of Paulo Freire', in Literacy and Revolution: The Pedagogy of Paulo Freire. Ed. Mackie, R. (London: Pluto, 1980)

Mackie, R. Ed. Literacy and Revolution: The Pedagogy of Paulo Freire. (London: Pluto, 1980)

Mager, R.F. Preparing Instructional Objectives. (Belmont: Pitman, 1975)

Mahai, B.A.P. Health and nutrition education through radio study group campaigns: the Tanzanian experiences. Adult education and Development. 19 (1982): 133-140.

Mao, T. 1937a. 'On practice', in Mao, T. Selected Readings. (Peking: Foreign Languages Press, 1971)

Mao, T. 1937b. 'On contradication', in Mao, T. Selected Readings. (Peking: Foreign Languages Press, 1971)

Mao, T. 1943. 'Some questions concerning methods of leadership', in Mao, T. Selected Readings. (Peking: Foreign Languages Press, 1971)

Mao, T. 1963. 'Where do correct ideas come from?' in Mao T. Selected Readings. (Peking: Foreign Languages Press, 1971)

Mao, T. 1971 Selected Readings. (Peking: Foreign Languages Press, 1971)

Marx, K. 1843. Critique of Hegel's 'Philosophy of Right'. Ed. O'Malley, J. (Cambridge: Cambridge University Press, 1970)

Marx, K. 1844. Economic and Philosophic Manuscripts of 1844. (Moscow: Progress Publishers, 1977)

Marx, K. 1845. 'Theses on Feuerbach', in Marx, K. and Engels, F. The German Ideology. Ed. Arthur, C.J. (London: Lawrence and Wishart, 1970)

Marx, K. 1847. The Poverty of Philosophy. (Moscow: Progress Publishers, 1975)

Marx, K. 1852. 'The Eighteenth Brumaire of Louis Bonaparte', in Marx, K. and Engels, F. Selected Works. Volume 1. (London: Lawrence and Wishart, 1950)

Marx, K. 1857-58. Grundrisse. (Harmondsworth: Penguin, 1973)

Marx, K. 1859. 'Preface to a Contribution to the Critique of Political Economy', in Marx, K. and Engels, F. Selected Works. Volume 1. (London: Lawrence and Wishart, 1950)

Marx, K. 1867. Capital. Volume 1. (Harmondsworth: Penguin, 1976)

Marx, K. 1872. 'Speech on the Hague Congress', in Marx, K. The First International and After. Ed. Fernbach, D. (Harmondsworth: Penguin, 1974)

Marx, K. 1875. 'Critique of the Gotha Programme', in Marx, K. and Engels, F. Selected Works. Volume 2. (London: Lawrence and Wishart, 1950)

Marx, K. and Engels, F. 1844. The Holy Family (London: Lawrence and Wishart, 1976)

Marx, K. and Engels, F. 1846. The German Ideology. Ed. Arthur, C.J. (London: Lawrence and Wishart, 1970)

Marx, K. and Engels, F. 1848. 'Manifesto of the Communist Party', in Marx, K. and Engels, F. Selected Works. Volume 1. (London: Lawrence and Wishart, 1950)

Marx, K. and Engels, F. 1850. 'Address of the Central Committee to the Communist League', in Marx, K. and Engels, F. Selected Works. Volume 1. (London: Lawrence and Wishart, 1950)

Marx, K. and Engels, F. 1879. 'Circular Letter' in Marx, K. and Engels, F. Selected Works. Volume 2. (London: Lawrence and Wishart, 1950)

Maslow, A. The Farther Reaches of Human Nature. (New York: The Viking Press, 1971)

Mayer, R.E. The Promise of Cognitive Psychology. (San Francisco: Freeman, 1981)

McLellan, D. The Young Hegelians and Karl Marx. (London: Macmillan, 1969)

McLellan, D. Marx Before Marxism. (London: Macmillan, 1980)

Melo, A. Portugal's experience of reform through popular initiative. Convergence Vol. XI, No. 1 (1978): 28-40.

Melo, A. Adult Education in Portugal. (Prague: European Centre for Leisure and Education, 1983)

Melo, A. and Benavente, A. Experiments in Popular Education in Portugal 1974-76. (Paris: UNESCO, 1978)

Mepham, J. The theory of ideology in Capital. Radical Philosophy 2 (1972): 12-19.

Miliband, R. Marxism and Politics. (Oxford: Oxford University Press, 1977)

Mobilisation Society of Wuhan. 'Educational method at K'angta', in Revolutionary Education in China. Ed. Seybolt, P.J. pp. 333-348. (White Plains: International Arts and Sciences Press, 1973)

Moumouni, A. Education in Africa. (London: Andre Deutsch, 1968)

Myrdal, J. Report from a Chinese Village. (London: Pan Books, 1975)

Ngugi wa Mirii. 'On literacy content', in Participatory Research. Eds. Kassam, Y. and

Mustafa, K. pp. 230-250. (New Delhi: Society for Participatory Research in Asia, 1982)

Ngugi wa Thiongo. Detained. (London: Heinemann, 1981)

Ngugi wa Thiongo. Barrel of a Pen. (London: New Beacon Books, 1983)

Norman, E. Totalitarianism in the making. Times Educational Supplement 24.11.78:2.

Norton, T.M. and Ollman, B. Studies in Socialist Pedagogy. (London: Monthly Review Press, 1978)

Ollman, B. Alienation. (Cambridge: Cambridge University Press, 1971)

O'Malley, J. Ed. Marx, K. Critique of 'Hegel's Philosophy of Right'. (Cambridge: Cambridge University Press, 1970)

Osborn, M., Charnley, A. and Withnall, A. The Psychology of Adult Learning and Development. (Leicester: National Institute for Adult Education, 1982)

Oxenham, J. Literacy. (London: Routledge and Kegan Paul, 1980)

Pierce, R. Contemporary French Political Thought. (London: Oxford University Press, 1966)

Price, R.F. Marx and Education in Russia and China. (London: Croom Helm, 1977)

Price, R.F. Education in Modern China. (London: Routledge and Kegan Paul, 1979)

Reed, D. Education for Building a People's Movement. (Boston: South End Press, 1981)

Retamal G. Paulo Freire, Christian Ideology and Adult Education in Latin America. (Hull: Department of Adult Education, University of Hull, 1981)

Riegel, K.F. Foundations of Dialectical Psychology. (New York: Academic Press, 1979)

Rogers, C.R. 'Toward a science of the person', in

Behaviorism and Phenomenology. Ed. Wann, T.W. pp. 109-133. (Chicago: Chicago University Press, 1964)

Rogers, C.R. Freedom to Learn. (Columbus: Nerrill, 1969)

Rogers, C.R. Encounter Groups (Harmondsworth: Penguin, 1973)

Rogers, C.R. and Skinner B.F. Some issues concerning the control of human behavior. Science. 124 (1956): 1057-1066.

Rogers, J. Adults Learning. (Milton Keynes: Open University Press, 1977)

Rose, H. and Rose, S. The Political Economy of Science. (New York: Holmes and Meier, 1976)

Ruben, D-H. Marxism and Materialism. (Sussex: Harvester Press, 1977)

Sarup, M. Marxism and Education. (London: Routledge and Kegan Paul, 1978)

Searle, C. Words Unchained. (London: Zed, 1984)

Seddon, D. Relations of Production. (London: Cass, 1978)

Selden, M. The Yenan Way in Revolutionary China. (Cambridge: Cambridge University Press, 1971)

Seve, L. Man in Marxist Theory and the Psychology of Personality. (Sussex: Harvester Press, 1978)

Seybolt, P.J. 1971. The Yenan revolution in mass education. China Quarterly No. 48 (1971): 641-699.

Seybolt, P.J. Ed. Revolutionary Education in China. (White Plains: International Arts and Sciences Press, 1973)

Shapin, S. and Barnes, B. 'Science, nature and control in interpreting Mechanics Institutes', in Schooling and Capitalism. Eds. Dale, R., Esland, G. and Macdonald, M. pp. 44-65. (London: Routledge and Kegan Paul, 1976)

Sharp, R. Knowledge, Ideology and the Politics of

Schooling. (London: Routledge and Kegan Paul, 1980)
Shaw, R. Attacking the liberal tradition. Times Higher Educational Supplement. 1980

Shor, I. Critical Teaching and Everyday Life. (Boston: South End Press, 1980)

Simon, B. Ed. Psychology in the Soviet Union. (London: Routledge and Kegan Paul, 1957)

Simon, B. Intelligence, Psychology and Education. (London: Lawrence and Wishart, 1978)

Simon, B. and Simon, J. Eds. Educational Psychology in the USSR. (London: Routledge and Kegan Paul, 1963)

Sketchley, P. and Lappe, F.M. Casting New Molds. (San Francisco: Institute for Food and Development Policy, 1980)

Skinner, B.F. Walden Two. (New York: Macmillan, 1948)

Skinner, B.F. The science of learning and the art of teaching. Harvard Educational Review 24 (1954): 88-97.

Smith, W.A. The Meaning of Conscientizacao - The Goal of Paulo Freire's Pedagogy. (Amherst: University of Massachusetts, 1976)

Squires, G. Cognitive Styles and Adult Learning. (Nottingham: Department of Adult Education, University of Nottingham, 1981)

Squires, G.T.C. Learning to Learn. (Hull: Department of Adult Education, University of Hull, 1982)

Sticht, T.G. 'Cognitive research applied to literacy training', in Cognitive Psychology and Instruction. Eds. Lesgold, A.M. et al, pp. 475-491. (New York: Plenum Press, 1978)

Stoer, S. 'Democracy and socialism in education in Portugal', in Schooling and the National Interest. Volume 1. Eds. Dale, R, et al. pp. 335-350. (Sussex: Falmer Press, 1981)

Stoer, S. 'The April Revolution and the Contribution

of Education to Changing "Portuguese Realities".'
Unpublished PhD Thesis. Open University, 1983.

Thomas, D. 'Psychology and Adult Education', in
An Introduction to the Study of Adult Education.
Eds. Brown, L. and Okedara, J.T. pp. 92-113 (Ibadan:
University Press, 1981)

Thompson, E.P. Time, work-discipline and industrial
capitalism. Past and Present Vol. 38 (1967): 56-97.

Thompson, J.L. Adult Education for a Change.
(London: Hutchinson, 1980)

Thompson, J.L. Learning Liberation. (London: Croom
Helm, 1983)

Thompson, P. The Nature of Work. (London: Pluto,
1983)

Thorndike, E.L. et al. Adult Learning. (New York:
Macmillan, 1928)

Timpanaro, S. On Materialism. (London: New Left
Books, 1975)

Torres, C.A. From the 'Pedagogy of the Oppressed' to
'A Luta Continua'. An essay on the political
pedagogy of Paulo Freire. Education with Production
Vol. 1 No. 2 (1982): 79-96.

Vygotsky, L.S. Thought and Language. (New York:
Wiley, 1962)

Vygotsky, L.S. Mind in Society. (Cambridge: Harvard
University Press, 1978)

Walker, D.A. Understanding Pictures. (Amherst:
University of Massachusetts, 1979)

Walker, J. 'The end of dialogue: Paulo Freire on
politics and education', in Literacy and
Revolution: The Pedagogy of Paulo Freire. Ed.
Mackie, R. pp. 120-150.(London: Pluto Press, 1980)

Wann, R.W. Ed. Behaviorism and Phenomenology.
(Chicago: Chicago University Press, 1964)

Watson, J.B. Behaviourism. (London: Kegan Paul,
Tranch and Trubner, 1925)

Weis, L. Education and the reproduction of inequality - the case of Ghana, Comparative Education Review Vol. 23, No. 1 (1979): 41-51.

Weiss, D.D. 1977. The philosophy of Engels vindicated. Monthly Review Vol. 28, No 8 (1977): 15-30.

Westoby, A. 'Education, inequality and the question of a communist "new class"' in Education and the State. Volume 1. Eds. Dale, R. et al., pp. 351-371. (Lewes: Falmer Press, 1981)

White, G. 'Revolutionary socialist development in the Third World: an overview', in Revolutionary Socialist Development in the Third World. Eds. White, G. Murrary, R. and White, C. pp. 1-34. (Sussex: Wheatsheaf Books, 1983)

Whitty, G. and Young, M. Eds. Explorations in the Politics of School Knowledge. (Nafferton: Nafferton Books, 1976)

Whyte, M.K. Educational reform: China in the 1970s and Russia in the 1920s. Comparative Education Review Vol. 8, No. 1 (1974): 112-128.

Williams, G.A. The concept of 'egemonia' in the thought of Antonio Gramsci: some notes on interpretation. Journal of the History of Ideas (1960): 586-99.

Williams, G.A. Proletarian Order. (London: Pluto, 1975)

Williams, R. Marxism and Literature. (Oxford: Oxford University Press, 1977)

Willis, P. Learning to Labour. (Aldershot: Gower, 1977)

Wood, S. The Degradation of Work. (London: Hutchinson, 1982)

Yarnitt, M. '150 Hours: Italy's experiment in mass working-class adult education', in Adult Education for a Change. Ed. Thompson, J.L. pp. 192-218. (London: Hutchinson, 1980)

Yarnitt, M. 'Second Chance to Learn, Liverpool: class and adult education', in Adult Education for a Change. Ed. Thompson, J.L. pp. 174-191. (London: Hutchinson, 1980)

Young, M. and Whitty, G. Eds. Society, State and Schooling. (Ringmer: Falmer Press, 1977)

AUTHOR INDEX

ADULT EDUCATION & SOCIALIST PEDAGOGY

## ADULT EDUCATION & SOCIALIST PEDAGOGY

269

policy in Ecuador 188
research on counter-
insurgency 122-3
USAID 188
utopianism 121-2, 184-5
vanguardism 34-5
'war of movement' 74-5
Wayne State University
'weekend college' ex-
periment 102
women
co-operative of, in
Kenya 229
studies of, in Central
Asia 84-6
work 102n17
see also feminism
work see labour
Workers' Educational
Association 39
workers' movements 71-2,
218-23, 226-7, 230
see also revolution
(theory of)
working class 22-3, 33-
7, 71-2, 106
defined 16
World Education, Inc.
188-9
Yugoslavia 32